DATE DUE

MAR — — 2006	arrival	Date

DEMCO 38-296

—— CHICANAS AND CHICANOS IN SCHOOL ——

Book Eleven
Louann Atkins Temple Women
& Culture Series
Books about women and families, and their
changing role in society

CHICANAS AND CHICANOS IN SCHOOL

Racial Profiling, Identity Battles, and Empowerment

MARCOS PIZARRO

UNIVERSITY OF TEXAS PRESS
AUSTIN

The Louann Atkins Temple Women
& Culture Series is supported by Allison, Doug, Taylor, and Andy Bacon;
Margaret, Lawrence, Will, John, and Annie Temple; Larry Temple;
the Temple-Inland Foundation;
and the National Endowment for the Humanities.

Portions of Chapter 1 previously appeared
in Marcos Pizarro, Power, borders, and identity formation:
Understanding the world of Chicana/o students,
Perspectives in Mexican American Studies 6 (1997): 142–167.

Portions of Chapter 3 previously appeared in Marcos Pizarro, Racial
formation and Chicana/o identity in the twenty-first century: Lessons from
the *rasquache*. In P. Wong, ed., *Race, Ethnicity, and Nationality in the
United States: Toward the Twenty-first Century,* 191–214
(Boulder, CO: Westview Press, 1999).

Library of Congress Cataloging-in-Publication Data

Pizarro, Marcos, 1967—
    Chicanas and Chicanos in school : racial profiling, identity battles, and
    empowerment / Marcos Pizarro.—1st ed.
        p.   cm.—(The Louann Atkins Temple women & culture series ; bk. 11)
    Includes bibliographical references (p.   ) and index.
    ISBN 0-292-70636-7 (alk. paper)—ISBN 0-292-70665-0 (pbk. : alk. paper)
    1. Mexican American youth—Education—Social aspects—California—Los
    Angeles—Case studies.   2. Mexican American youth—Education—Social
    aspects—Washington (State)—Case studies.   3. Mexican Americans—
    Ethnic identity—California—Los Angeles—Case studies.   4.   Mexican
    Americans—Ethnic identity—Washington (State)—Case studies.
    5. Discrimination in education—California—Los Angeles—Case studies.
    6. Discrimination in education—Washington (State)—Case studies.
    I. Title.   II. Series.
    LC2688.L7P59 2005
    373.1829′6872′073—dc22

                                                                    2004020252

This work is dedicated to raza youth,
who live these stories every day.
They are warriors.

CONTENTS

PREFACE
ix

ACKNOWLEDGMENTS
xiii

INTRODUCTION
*Rethinking Research
in Chicana/o Communities*
I

PART ONE
INSIGHTS FROM LOS ANGELES CHICANA/O YOUTH
39

ONE
IDENTITY FORMATION IN LOS ANGELES
41

TWO
IDENTITY AND SCHOOL PERFORMANCE IN LOS ANGELES
58

THREE
LESSONS FROM LOS ANGELES STUDENTS FOR
SCHOOL SUCCESS
101

PART TWO
INSIGHTS FROM ACOMA CHICANA/O YOUTH
113

FOUR

IDENTITY FORMATION IN ACOMA
115

FIVE

IDENTITY AND SCHOOL PERFORMANCE IN ACOMA
158

SIX

LESSONS FROM ACOMA STUDENTS FOR SCHOOL SUCCESS
201

TIME-OUT

ERNESTO SANCHEZ'S AUTOBIOGRAPHICAL ANALYSIS OF IDENTITY AND SCHOOL IN ACOMA
227

PART THREE

UNDERSTANDING AND TRANSFORMING THE SCHOOL LIVES OF CHICANA/O YOUTH
237

SEVEN

RACIAL PROFILING, IDENTITY, AND SCHOOL ACHIEVEMENT: LESSONS FROM POWER CONFLICTS IN DIVERSE CONTEXTS
239

EIGHT

CHICANA/O STUDENT EDUCATIONAL EMPOWERMENT
251

EPILOGUE
267

NOTES
271

BIBLIOGRAPHY
277

INDEX
283

PREFACE

This book has been a life's work. The most conscious sense I have of its beginning is when I taught elementary school in inner-city Los Angeles. Teaching in a working-class community that was almost all Latina/o, mainly Mexican, I saw things I had always known but never wanted to witness in such vivid detail. In the three years I worked there, I faced the constant and systematic denial of educational opportunity to all but a select few students. I was enraged and determined to use my academic work to address the needs of Chicana/o students.

During that time, as a doctoral student, I began research that would help me understand how certain Chicana/o students survive and even thrive in the midst of the educational injustice I had witnessed. I was particularly interested in how issues of race themselves affect Chicana/o students' success and failure. This work led me, several years later, to embark on a massive research agenda. I wanted to deconstruct Chicana/o students' social identities. That is, I wanted to understand how Chicana/o youth understand themselves within their social worlds. In addition, I wanted to determine how, if at all, these students' social identities were related to their school lives.

My interests were shared by many others I had met in a number of different arenas of my experience. In every Chicana/o community in which I have spent any time, the same concerns hang thick in the air. Although different communities and individuals emphasize specific issues such as crime, underemployment, or gangs, two interconnected factors shape these concerns: poverty and education. The roles of poverty and education in shaping Chicana/o community life are grounded in a legacy of oppression that is far removed from the twenty-first century and yet ever present in the daily lives of millions of Chicanas/os. Parents, community members, and students themselves do not sit idly and watch these problems wreak havoc. In barrios across the United States, members of these communities dedicate their lives to addressing those concerns. They link their concerns to larger issues of political, economic, and social inequality and injustice.

In striving to address these injustices, there is always a large group that focuses on education and schooling. Education is seen as the means by which families can climb out of the poverty that has often plagued them for generations. The concerns of Chicana/o communities about the schooling of their children are many. In the end, parents want their children to have committed teachers who have the resources to provide students with the skills to obtain good jobs. Parents are frightened by the possibility that their children will suffer and struggle to survive as they themselves have. The questions that have been asked in these communities for generations are these: Why are so many Chicana/o students failing in the schools? Why are so many schools failing Chicana/o students? And what can be done about this failure?

Over the years, both Chicana/o communities and researchers have found a number of answers to the first question regarding failure. Even at the turn of the new century, however, I heard a leading researcher on Latina/o schooling explain that although we have a great deal of data and we can attempt to link poverty, segregation, and other factors to Latina/o school failure, the data do not tell us why this failure has happened and why it continues to happen. This book will provide answers to that question in very concrete terms. In so doing, the book will help us understand the second question—why schools fail so many Chicanas/os.

Unfortunately, the final question regarding what can be done has been even more difficult to answer. It is that question that drives my work. I want to be able to help Chicana/o communities (and those who want to work with these communities) do something about Chicana/o school failure. I have been frustrated at the consistent inability of the schools to improve Chicana/o school performance. I have been equally frustrated with the research community. While we have made significant progress in understanding what is happening in our schools, researchers have made little progress in coming up with ways to address the problems we have seen. We talk about the need for changes in the system but do not address the structural forces that make such changes almost impossible. We do not discuss or develop ways to short-circuit those forces. For this reason, in my research, I have taken a different direction. I have asked Chicana/o students who are in the schools to give us ideas. In particular, I have asked them to help us understand what their experiences are like in the schools. The students and I talked a lot about who they are in the schools and what this means to them in terms of their school performance. I talked with students who are struggling, with some who dropped out of school, and also with those who are extremely successful. I talked with students in a large urban area and in a small rural town. I talked with high school students, community college students, and university students. I talked with people who call themselves Chicana, Mexican, and Hispanic. I talked with young men and women. I talked with cholos, gays, aspiring lawyers, farmworkers, upper-middle-class youth, ROTC students, mothers, immigrants, and students whose families have been in the United States for generations. My hope is that the readers can begin to understand, respect, and care about all of these different students because they each have important stories to tell and insights from which we can learn.

The stories the students share about what it means to be a Chicana/o in school are truly revealing. Most importantly, the stories they tell as individuals and as a group provide us with the building blocks for interventions that can help Chicanas/os in different contexts to educationally empower themselves. This book is a tour of my path in getting to these solutions, with each chapter taking a slightly different approach. Some readers may not want to follow the tour in order, and others may want to concentrate on certain parts of the journey. Chapter 8, the final chapter, provides guidelines for developing interventions with Chicana/o students. It is intended to assist parents, community members, teachers, school administrators, students themselves, and anyone else who wants to develop programs or interventions to help Chicana/o students educationally empower themselves.

My hope is that readers will take the lessons from the book and apply them to their own communities. I have discussed the research described in this book with students across the Southwest, and each time I do, I am struck by the similarity between the stories I share and the experiences that audience members feel compelled to describe. The issues addressed in this book affect Chicana/o youth in communities across the country. It is my hope that the insights readers obtain from this work will allow them to conduct analyses of their own communities that will lead to the creation of formal and informal programs to address specific issues in those communities. If enough communities can engage in the strategies and actions developed in Chapter 8 and can begin to share this information with still other communities, we will have a foundation upon which to build our efforts to address our shared concerns and to empower our communities.

A FINAL NOTE TO THE READER

In sharing this work in the last few years, I have come to a realization. An important part of the work we have to do in addressing the needs of Chicana/o youth is simply to affirm the validity of their own voices. Unfortunately, this is often hard for many to do. As a result, I have begun to perform the stories shared by the students in this book, and I have asked students and workshop participants to do the same. When we truly become the student who shares her story, our ability to understand her world is enhanced dramatically. Even an extreme act like head-butting a teacher makes "sense" despite how irrational it always appears at first glance. You the readers are encouraged to become the students as you read the book. That makes it much easier to begin to understand and work with Chicana/o youth and to confront the issues they face in their school lives. So try your best to walk in the shoes they put on every morning and wear up and down the halls of schools from East L.A. to eastern Washington State.

ACKNOWLEDGMENTS

This work belongs to so many people. It belongs first and foremost to the Chicana/o students. Hundreds of students agreed to work with me on this project, and hundreds more provided inspiration for the work to move forward. These students include the many kids I went to school with who were smarter than me but never found their way out, the brilliant young *raza* at Oak Street Elementary School when I taught there, the *gente* who came to all those talks where I shared the work and who explained what worked and asked the questions that allowed me to clarify those ideas that were unclear, the *mechistas* at Washington State University who fought hard to create change for their little brothers and sisters and who always inspired me, and the students in my classes and in *MAESTR@S* who have always made it clear that this work needs to continue.

I want to thank several editors and colleagues who helped me with different concepts, approaches, and insights that have become essential to this book. Laurence Parker and Sofia Villenas helped me develop the methodological approaches that underlie my work (Pizarro 1998). Brian McNeill and Liz Vera helped me solidify my analysis of the previous work on Chicana/o identity, which allowed me to push this work in new directions (Pizarro and Vera 2001). Tom Gelsinon and the folks at *Perspectives in Mexican American Studies* helped me develop the analysis that has evolved into Chapter 1 (Pizarro 1997). Paul Wong created a space for me to do the innovative work that evolved into Chapter 3 (Pizarro 1999).

I am grateful for the financial support received for conducting the research that led to this book. The Institute of American Cultures and the UCLA Chicano Studies Research Center provided me postdoctoral support for the year in which I began work on Chicana/o research methods (see the introduction) and then conducted the Los Angeles Project. The Spencer Foundation funded the Washington study. In addition Paul Wong, formerly the chair of the Department of Comparative Cultures at Washington State University, was a constant source of support and pushed me to seek the Spencer funding. While I was at WSU, the

Meyer Fund of the College of Liberal Arts also provided support for the project. After the research was complete, the Ford Foundation provided me with a postdoctoral fellowship that allowed me the time to work with the interviews carefully. Eugene Garcia, then the dean of the College of Education at the University of California, Berkeley, was a great mentor for that year and really helped me move the work forward.

I also received some important support along the way. I am indebted to Luci Loera, who was invaluable as she helped me conduct and make sense of interviews and provided feedback to various drafts of the work. She worked tirelessly because it mattered, and she made this book possible. Other friends and colleagues also read the work and provided essential feedback, particularly Amy Best and Jose Gonzalez. Finally, Theresa May and the staff at the University of Texas Press have been tremendous. Without their support, patience, and guidance, this never would have been possible. In particular, I want to express my gratitude to Rosemary Wetherold, whose careful editing made this a much better read.

The personal support I received along this journey was much more important to its completion than any of the professional. My family— Leonard, Helena, and Charlie—in no uncertain terms made me what I am today. They lived justice in a loving and powerful way that forced me to always strive to be the change I sought.

My *suegros* were also a great moral support and grounding for me in those times when I was away from my own family. In addition, my *suegra* always made sure my translations were tight and showed me how to be in the world when I would forget.

My *camaradas* in *MAESTR@S* have been my strength. Raquel, Margaret, Julia, Prishni and Serg, Rafa, Danielle, Mario, and all the others who have joined us push me, inspire me, and make me work harder to live up to their examples.

Most important of all is my partner, Esther. She has grounded me in ways that no one else can. She pushes me farther than anyone ever has. She is my greatest teacher and the passion in my life. She is all that I aspire to be.

Finally, everything has made much more sense through the lessons of our daughters, Xóchitl and Citlali. They have made me whole and have helped me understand this work much more fully. They are the warriors I want to be.

I extend my deepest thanks to all of these people. This work is theirs. The mistakes and shortcomings are mine.

—— CHICANAS AND CHICANOS IN SCHOOL ——

INTRODUCTION

Rethinking Research
in Chicana/o Communities

Chicana/o students live much of their lives in great jeopardy. Of all the data that point out the severity of this situation, perhaps the most alarming is that as recently as 1998 more than one of every three Chicana/o and Latina/o youth were being raised in poverty (U.S. Census Bureau 1998).[1] The limited opportunities that define a life of poverty translate into numerous negative outcomes that reveal the dangers of life as a young Chicana/o today: high rates of teen pregnancy, gang involvement, drug abuse, and incarceration. The cyclical nature of the inequality that has defined much of the Chicana/o experience over the past 150 years is perhaps best understood by considering the school outcomes of Chicana/o youth during this time. Chicanas/os face the highest dropout rates of any major ethnic group in the United States—as many as half of a given cohort of Chicana/o students does not complete high school—and their relative educational outcomes have been stable or have worsened over time (National Center for Education Statistics 1999, 2001). Correspondingly, Chicanas/os have faced little progress in the job market, particularly with regard to measures such as relative incomes and unemployment (Lopez, Ramirez, and Rochin 1999; National Center for Education Statistics 2001; Reddy 1995; U.S. Census Bureau 2000).

This stark reality comes as no surprise to most, for the media teaches the U.S. citizenry that these are expected outcomes for Chicanas/os. The average U.S. resident comes to learn early in life that a Chicana/o identity is associated with these low educational and life outcomes. The weight of the social forces behind these popular understandings is often so great that Chicanas/os themselves not only believe them but also shape their lives around these low expectations. Chicana/o identity is far more complex than this, however. In fact, many Chicanas/os are successful in school and in life and develop a sense of identity that challenges the commonly understood notions of what it means to be a Chicana/o in the United States today. This book attempts to explain the various Chicana/o identities that exist today and the forces and patterns that lead to their development. By understanding these trends, I argue, not only can we see some of the critical forces that lead to Chicana/o failure, but we can also learn strategies for addressing this failure from those who are successful.

Very little research has been done in this area. Although interest in the importance of identity in the Chicana/o experience is increasing, the complexity of identity has limited much of this work to quantitative studies, which, though informative, cannot delve deeply into the intricacies of students' experiences. The present book represents perhaps the only research being conducted to qualitatively understand Chicana/o identity in educational contexts, its evolution, and the ways in which interventions can be developed to assist at-risk Chicana/o youth. Still, as this chapter will reveal, a large body of work informs my research. This chapter explains the need for this book and also provides an explanation of how the research was conducted.

LABELS AND DEFINITIONS

I have made a conscious and careful decision to use the word "Chicana/o" to refer to the groups of young men and women of Mexican descent who participated in the projects described in this book. Labels have been a source of great debate both within the larger Latina/o community and among researchers who work with different groups of peoples of Latin American descent. Some researchers have selected the label they use to refer to participants, whereas others have tried to use the label with which participants are most comfortable. There is simply no way to choose a label that is accurate or acceptable to everyone. Beyond the multiple labels that are used not only within the community but even among individuals, multiple meanings are attached to each of these labels. Conversely, some individuals attach almost the same meaning to different labels.

Many of the students I worked with used the term "Chicana/o." Others were unclear of its meaning, and still others would not use this label for themselves. Some students had always used the Chicana/o label, others picked it up in college, and some were in the middle of a long process of adopting the term. I chose to use this term in this project because, regardless of the label chosen by individuals, as a whole the participants revealed that they are political subjects in their schools and communities. Most described contexts in which they were targets at racial, ethnic, class, gender, sexual orientation, or other levels. Even more powerful, together these students painted a portrait that all but demands a political response from their communities. The forces that bear on their lives are the same ones that led youth in the 1960s to adopt the "Chicano" label. "Chicana/o," therefore, is used in this text out of respect for the tremendous struggle that these students fight on a daily basis. Yet I also want the reader to understand that these Chicanas/os include "Mexicans," "Latinos," "Hispanics," and "Americans." This is all part of the Chicana/o experience.

At times, I make reference to the actual labels that individuals used. More often, I explain the unique characteristics of individuals that make them distinct from their peers. At a technical level, in this text "Chicana/o" refers to females and males of Mexican descent living in and socialized in the United States. Traditionally, researchers use this term only for those born in the United States, but the nuances involved in making this distinction are so complex that it is more useful to discuss them in the research itself rather than to simply eliminate Mexican-born students. Simply put, the distinctions between "Mexicanas/os" (traditionally meaning foreign born) and "Chicanas/os" (traditionally meaning U.S. born) are easily blurred. For example, some of the first-generation immigrants in this study came to the United States at such a young age that they have no memories of Mexico, and some Chicanas/os were born in the United States a short time after their families immigrated. Furthermore, the experiences of many of the Mexicanas/os reflect a marginalization whereby they become something that is neither American nor Mexican within a few short years. Adding a 1.5-generation subgroup (that is, students who moved to the United States during early childhood) does not add significant clarity. In fact, many of the first-generation participants themselves believe that they have been socialized as Chicanas/os, whereas other U.S.-born participants identify only as Mexicanas/os. Further complicating these classifications is that some students are first or second generation on one side of their family and third or fourth generation on the other. For these students, the degree to which they are connected to their culture is often influenced by the importance of their connection to different family members, their closeness to these family members, and the amount of influence these family members have over the larger family dynamic. Because of these complexities, I include all Mexican-descent participants in this analysis of Chicana/o students' experiences, regardless of their immigration status, for this reflects the reality of the Chicana/o experience today. What is far more important than ethnic labels, however, is the life experiences of the students. This book attempts to portray those experiences as vividly as possible. Regardless of the reader's feelings about different labels, understanding these experiences should be the motivation for reading this book.

Whenever "Chicana" is used in this book, it refers to females only, and "Chicano" is used to refer to males only. Gender dynamics are a significant component of the students' lives and of this book. I have worked to stay conscious of my limitations as a male in fully understanding these dynamics. I attempted to confront these limitations by constantly raising gender issues with the students and by relying on the insights of Chicana researchers and colleagues who helped with this project. These complexities are explored throughout the work, and my own limitations in this regard should be considered throughout the book.

Beyond these issues, clear definitions of the terms employed in the analyses are required. "Chicana/o identity," in this work, refers to the social identity that Chicanas/os establish for themselves. This social identity is simply how given individuals define themselves in their own social world—specifically, with regard to social groups in which individuals place themselves (and with which they interact), along with the conscious significance they attach to these groups and interactions. Chicana/o identity, therefore, theoretically encompasses the identities of all Chicanas/os, including those who define themselves as upper-middle-class or as lesbian, for example, as well as those who do not consciously ethnically identify. The term also includes Chicanas/os who define themselves as Catholic, Mexicano, and working-class simultaneously, as another example. This investigation thus considers the self-perceptions of all types and categories of Chicanas/os so as to understand the full complexity of Chicana/o identity formations.

Finally, a careful explanation of the use of the terms "race" and "ethnicity" is needed. Ethnicity is understood as the unique cultural characteristics of groups of people that make them distinct from other groups with different cultural characteristics. Chicanas/os are typically defined as an ethnic group because in terms of language, religion, and other cultural practices, they clearly constitute a unique group of people. Ethnicity often becomes an important means of categorizing specific groups because structural forces such as segregation, as well as internal factors

4

such as the need for community, lead these groups to create and live in distinct communities. Racially, Chicanas/os are legally defined as white and are therefore not considered a racial minority. Despite this legal definition, in daily life in the United States, Chicanas/os are not seen as white. In fact, since the earliest interactions between Mexicans and white "Americans," Mexicans have been seen as *racially* inferior. Furthermore, since 1848, when the first Chicanas/os were *created* through the Treaty of Guadalupe Hidalgo, countless Chicanas/os have been the victims of multiple forms of discrimination based solely on their physical or racial features. Even in the current era, the racialization of Chicanas/os defines life for many. California's Proposition 187 of 1994 provides just one example. This legislation was designed to deny undocumented immigrants access to health care and other social services that were seen as a drain on the economy. Many whites, however, used the passage of this legislation as validation of their right to limit the freedom of brown-skinned individuals. During the days following the passage of the proposition, numerous stories appeared that documented cases of brown-skinned U.S. citizens who were denied access to schools, public transportation, and even their own bank accounts. The only means by which these Chicanas/os were targeted was their physical appearance. This reality suggests the need to consider the role of both race and ethnicity in shaping the experiences of Chicanas/os in and out of school today. Other researchers have addressed these issues both directly and indirectly in their work. Gitlin (1994, 169), for example, uses the term "racialized minority" to characterize the process whereby culturally distinct groups are categorized via phenotypical attributes that are supposedly linked to human qualities such as morality, intelligence, and personality. Omi and Winant (1994) provide a detailed analysis of these processes as they outline racial formation theory. Because of the complex interaction between race and ethnicity among Chicanas/os, discussions of race and ethnicity throughout this book are complicated by emphasizing their connections.

A NOTE ON APPROACH

This book and the research from which it emerged are grounded in a radical Chicana/o Studies. Chicana/o Studies emerged in the late 1960s as a challenge to the academic establishment in the United States. Its goals were many and included (1) rewriting the history of Mexican-descent people in the United States through the experiences of those very people; (2) revealing the way in which racism and colonialism defined the Chicana/o experience through formal systems such as politics, economics, and education, as evidenced in generations of biased academic analyses of the Chicanas/os by Anglo intellectuals; and (3) empowering Chicana/o students with a critical analysis that would help them use their education to address the needs of their communities. Over the past thirty years, researchers in Chicana/o Studies have effectively developed a body of work that challenges the traditional belief that the lack of Chicana/o mobility in the United States is the product of intellectual, cultural, and socioeconomic deficits. Chicana/o Studies research has shown the perseverance and the important contributions of Chicanas/os in U.S. society.

At the same time, much of this work has been attacked by those in the academic mainstream who have critiqued it as biased, activist in nature, and nonacademic or anti-intellectual. Recent work by Chicana/o scholars and critical race theorists, however, has built on the analyses begun by Octavio Romano and others in the late 1960s, which explained that, in fact, all academic work is fundamentally biased. This bias is deemed unavoidable simply because the individuals who develop, conduct, and write about research are influenced at each stage by their own understandings and interpretations of the issues under study, which are shaped, for example, by their own cultural lenses. Interestingly, however, Chicana/o Studies is among the few areas of academic research that are critiqued for bias simply because the work makes its biases clear to readers.

As the preface and initial paragraphs of this chapter emphasize, this book is grounded in a conscious agenda that strives to achieve Chicana/o educational empowerment. As Acuña (1998) powerfully argues, "sometimes there is no other side."[2] If we are to understand the world of Chicana/o students, we have to ask the students themselves. In order for them to feel comfortable and to be forthcoming, we have to let them know that we are asking them about their experiences because we want to help them and others achieve success. This commitment to helping students demands extreme rigor in conducting the research. Helping students requires understanding their world in all its complexity, regardless of how difficult that may be and how much work it might take. In fact, one could argue that this commitment demands a form of motivational validity in research in which the strength of the motivation to do the research well exceeds that of researchers who are motivated to do their work by their careers or funding. Although there are other approaches and stories to be told, this book strives to tell the story of the students. For this reason, I put the analysis in the hands of the students as much as possible, to be sure that readers have a chance to look deeply into their world from as many different approaches as they shared. This makes some chapters long (Chapters 2, 4, and 5), but that depth is essential to the work. This book therefore engages in theory building from the students themselves because it is necessary and almost never done. Because of this approach, the conventional academic contextualization (comparing findings to previous research and theory) that typically accompanies research in the United States is abandoned throughout most of the text, although a backdrop of previous research is provided in this chapter. Later in this chapter the strength of this approach is discussed in more detail. A look at the directions in which past research is leading us will show why a new approach is needed.[3]

PAST RESEARCH ON CHICANA/O IDENTITY

During the late 1960s and early 1970s the Chicana/o community, like many other communities of color in the United States during that time, went through a significant transformation with regard to social identity. Abandoning the assimilationist goals of earlier generations, Chicana/o communities (led by students) began a process of redefinition. They developed a new, radicalized identity that stood for community empowerment through affirmation rather than through the adoption of majority traits (García 1997).

By the late 1970s the significance of ethnic identity to the Chicana/o community and the Chicana/o experience became a focal point of study for Chicana/o researchers. These researchers realized that ethnic identity was a critical filter through which Chicanas/os understood their experiences and lives and that it might also shape their behaviors in important ways.

The National Chicano Survey was the first major study that specifically addressed the issue of Chicana/o ethnic identity, although earlier research had considered issues of assimilation and acculturation as they related to Mexican-descent individuals in the United States (see Lai and Sodowsky 1996a for several examples). Abandoning past approaches that emphasized the difficulties Mexican Americans had in adopting U.S. social and cultural practices, the National Chicano Survey attempted to understand how Chicanas/os defined their own identities. The early work with these data revealed what would become a fundamental limitation facing almost all future research on Chicana/o ethnic identity: it is extremely difficult to study ethnic or social identity in ways that allow us to understand these constructs as they are experienced in the real world. Although the research with the National Chicano Survey suggested some intriguing relationships between different Chicana/o characteristics, ethnic identity was understood by way of the labels respondents chose to identify themselves. As many of the researchers themselves pointed out (see Arce 1981), this methodology limited their ability to understand identity, because labels are unreliable determinants of how individuals understand their social identities. For example, two people can have very different definitions of "Chicano," while two others could have very similar definitions for "Chicano" and "Hispanic," and still others might not make any significant distinctions among several ethnic labels (see Sanchez-Jankowski 1999 for one description of the different meanings attached to labels). Still, this preliminary research was important because it suggested how fundamental ethnic identity was to the experiences of Chicanas/os and the many aspects of their lives to which identity might be related.

Later, researchers became interested in how ethnic identity evolved among children. Knight et al. (1993) provided perhaps the most complex model of the process of Chicana/o ethnic identity development. Their socialization model of ethnic identity proposed that both enculturation and acculturation work together to shape the ethnic identity and ethnic behaviors of children. Enculturation is the process whereby Chicanas/os learn Mexican and Chicana/o cultural practices, and acculturation is the process whereby they learn mainstream cultural practices. Ethnic behaviors are defined as specific actions that are typical within Chicana/o communities, such as Spanish language use.

In this model, the social ecology of the family (e.g., generation of migration, acculturation, ethnic identity of parents, language, cultural knowledge, family structure) interacts with the ecology of the community in which they live, and these ecologies work together to influence children's socialization. Family members teach ethnic content, for example, and nonfamily communicate views about ethnicity and ethnic group membership. These factors, the authors suggested, shape the child's ethnic identity, which in turn shapes ethnic behaviors. In addition, the authors explained that cognitive development is an overarching process that moderates the influence of various socialization agents, as well as the extent to which such influences shape ethnic behaviors. This model provides some important insights into the ways in which identity may evolve for Chicana/o youth, but as the authors pointed out, most of the model had not been empirically tested (and that is still the case). Furthermore, the research did not increase our understanding of the meaning of social identity in the lives of Chicanas/os.

Phinney (1993) attempted to address these issues through her research with racial and ethnic minority adolescents (including Chicanas/os), when she asked them to discuss the degree to which they had dealt with and resolved ethnic identity issues. The early identity research led to the development of the Multigroup Ethnic Identity Measure (MEIM), in which Phinney (1992) posited three components of ethnic identity: affirmation and belonging (the sense of group membership and attitudes toward the group, including attachment and pride); ethnic identity achievement (the extent to which a person has achieved a secure and confident sense of his or her ethnicity, including knowledge and understanding of the ethnic group); and ethnic behaviors (activities associated with group membership, such as customs, traditions, and social interactions).

Phinney (1993) noted that the first stage of ethnic identity development is unexamined ethnic identity, in which adolescents have given no thought to issues of ethnic identity (whether they are steeped in their own culture or trying to adopt mainstream culture). This unexamined stage continues until an identity crisis occurs, whereby the next stage, ethnic identity search/moratorium, begins. No pivotal event is required to initiate this shift, but the search process is necessary for reaching an achieved identity, the third and final stage. At this stage, individuals are confident and comfortable with their ethnicity, as well as their place in the society at large. An achieved identity status is proposed to be the most adaptive identity status, a proposal supported by research suggesting that adolescents with achieved identities have high self-esteem, strong ego identity, and healthy family and peer relationships (Phinney 1989).

Phinney's work (1993) is important because it considers how ethnic identity may evolve. At the same time, the work is limited by its effort to place individuals into categories that betray the complexity of identity as it exists in the real world, where, as just one alternative example, Chicanas/os may have engaged in a careful assessment of their identities and decided to seek assimilation. In addition, a conversation with almost any Chicana/o will reveal multiple and ongoing shifts in identity far beyond adolescence. Despite Phinney's innovations, the complex process of identity development is still not well understood in her work.

Ethier and Deaux (1994) avoided emphasizing categories in their research with college students. Their work is significant because it looked at three points in time over students' first year in an Ivy League college. Among their central findings was that participants went through a process of "remooring," whereby they replaced the ethnic identity supports they had before college with new ones in the college context. The authors found that the degree of "Hispanic group involvement" before coming to college determined the degree of this involvement at college. Students who made efforts to be involved in their ethnic community at college showed an increase in ethnic identification, whereas those who did not showed a decrease. Ethier and Deaux also had the important insight that these differing degrees of involvement do not necessarily indicate differing degrees of ethnic salience but rather may reflect different responses to the salience. For example, they found that students who felt threatened about their ethnic identity experienced losses in self-esteem. Ethier and Deaux also found that ethnic identification decreased in students who had negative feelings about their ethnic group, whereas it increased in students who had positive feelings about their group.

Earlier work by Deaux (1993) is helpful in analyzing this research, for she suggested the need to consider how ethnic identity interacts with other aspects of social identity and how this larger social identity shapes individuals' lives and behaviors in important ways. Her critique brings us full circle as we return to the difficulties of translating the complex process of identity development into simple terms that can be easily researched. For example, almost all of the work that has considered any aspect of Chicana/o social identity has focused exclusively on ethnic identity. This work has been insightful, as Ethier and Deaux (1994) suggest, but ethnic identity interacts with racial identity (through experiences with discrimination, for example), as well as a number of other arenas of social identity that might be important to individuals.

This limitation also applies to work that focuses on interventions intended to help Chicanas/os in their identity development, such as research in counseling. For example, Casas and Pytluk (1995) noted that the vast majority of counseling research dealing with Chicana/o ethnic identity has focused on the level of acculturation rather than the process of its development. Lai and Sodowsky (1996a, 1996b) provided a bibliography of much of this research, all of which focused on acculturation and, in particular, issues like language usage and preferences as reflected in the common use or adaptation of the Acculturation Rating Scale for Mexican Americans (Cuéllar, Harris, and Jasso 1980). This work on acculturation has not considered the complexities of Chicana/o identity that other researchers have suggested are so essential (e.g., Phinney, Bernal and Knight, Hurtado, among others). It has also been unable to provide understanding of the processes of Chicana/o identity formation and the way in which counselors can aid in those processes (see

Atkinson, Morten, and Sue 1998 for further discussion of the limits of such research). Although researchers have attempted to analyze the link between acculturation and ethnic identity, a close review of their work reveals that the measures of ethnic identity and acculturation overlap significantly (see Cuéllar et al. 1997 for a comparison of students' scores on the Acculturation Rating Scale II and the MEIM).[4]

Over the course of the last two decades, the research on Chicana/o ethnic identity has evolved tremendously. Perhaps the most important aspect of this body of work has been the new directions it has suggested for research. First, a more uniform and conceptually complex definition/understanding of Chicana/o ethnic identity, grounded in efforts to understand the process of Chicana/o identity development, is needed. The wide range of conceptualizations of Chicana/o ethnic identity makes it difficult to see how different analyses contribute to our understanding of ethnic identity as it is experienced by Chicanas/os in the real world. Similarly, the complex nature of ethnic identity makes it difficult to understand how specific analyses of individual relationships (such as those between acculturation and ethnic consciousness) relate to the daily processes of ethnic identity development. For example, the identity struggles that Chicana/o youth face are often related to their experiences not only as members of an ethnic minority group but also as members of a racialized group. Furthermore, a number of other aspects of Chicana/o life overlap their ethnic and racial identities, including gender, class, sexuality, family, and, of course, education. Arce (1981, 182) put it this way:

> Virtually all studies of Chicano identity have been too exclusively focused on the ethnic aspects, without adequately examining an individual's private definition and categorization of his or her total social identity. If such a distinction were adopted, it would be possible to assess the importance of ethnic identity in the broader framework of a multidimensional social identity. For Chicanos, ethnic identity is not simple or unidimensional. It potentially operates on multiple levels (on a private to public continuum), each of which has several components that may be ethnic in general character.

As Arce noted more than twenty years ago, there has been little effort to distinguish between and understand the relationship of racial and ethnic identity in Chicanas/os. The significance of the forces shaping racial identity and their role in determining ethnic identity have not been considered. Because many of the psychological issues facing contemporary

Chicanas/os may be connected to racial oppression in the United States, understanding ethnic identity necessarily involves clarification of the role that race plays in the daily lives of Chicanas/os. As Pardo (1998) has suggested, identity is situational and is influenced by a number of forces that simultaneously intersect and shape the larger social identities of Chicanas/os.

Another need that has been identified is to use qualitative research methods to capture the complexity of the aforementioned types of information. At a conceptual and practical level, designing research projects that can deconstruct multiple aspects of Chicana/o ethnic identity and the identity formation process in general is an enormous task. However, some qualitative investigations have begun to consider these complexities.

Olsen (1997) investigated identity issues among students in a California school district and exposed a racial hierarchy regarding who can and cannot be successful and who can have access to the school capital that will lead to later life successes. Her analysis included observations, participation in classes, and interviews with students, teachers, and administrators. Through this in-depth analysis, she uncovered illuminating aspects of the complex reality of students. Olsen found that the racial hierarchy was subtly maintained in the school, given that teachers and administrators alike were among the first to espouse ideals of diversity and equality. The dominant belief among these school staff was that the school operated as a meritocracy, and few saw the subtle ways in which the staff constricted the opportunity of Latina/o students to access resources necessary for the demonstration of merit (through tracking and discipline, for example). Olsen's research suggested the need for qualitative studies that work with Chicanas/os to critically evaluate the complex forces that shape their experiences and identities.

In addition, Chicana feminist writers (most notably Anzaldúa 1987, Castillo 1994, and Moraga 1983), have constructed complicated frameworks that explain the need to understand the interaction of gender, sexuality, ethnicity, and race in shaping the identities of Chicanas. These writers have pushed the discourse on identity forward by suggesting that ethnic/racial, gender, sexual, and class identities are neither static nor firm; rather, they are continuously intersecting and evolving as a function of various social forces. Thus qualitative research needs to investigate and develop an understanding of identity as Chicanas/os themselves experience it. Rather than forcing individuals' lives into specific categories, researchers need to engage in the development of grounded theory through extended interviews and oral histories with Chicanas/os in different contexts, of varying age groups, and across diverse life experiences.

At a more basic level, researchers also need to reexamine the epistemological foundations of our approaches. For the most part, identity research is grounded in a shared academic epistemology or worldview, although multiple epistemologies exist in the different communities in which this work is conducted. Chicanas/os do not produce and pass on knowledge in the ways that other communities do (see Pizarro 1998 for a more in-depth description of Chicana/o epistemology). When the dominant epistemological framework or system of knowledge is applied to the study of a group that operates under a different way of thinking, researchers force themselves to employ tools that cannot begin to comprehend the issues and processes involved in what is being studied. By acknowledging the validity and uniqueness of Chicana/o epistemology and of the worldviews that shape a distinct knowledge system among Chicanas/os, researchers can begin to construct frameworks for understanding and intervening in the social identity formation of Chicanas/os that are based in the complexities of Chicana/o life.

In summary, the research into Chicana/o ethnic identity has been groundbreaking and important, but it has been limited in its focus and ability to explain identity as it is actually lived. This limitation is the product of both the quantitative emphasis of past research and the lack of a Chicana/o perspective in designing the research. Some of these critiques are applicable to research on Chicanas/os as a whole, but given the focus of this book on the educational implications of identity, we must also evaluate the research on Chicanas/os and education.

PAST RESEARCH ON CHICANA/O EDUCATIONAL OUTCOMES

Demographic research over the past thirty years shows that Chicanas/os and Latinas/os have the highest dropout rates of any major ethnic or racial group in the United States (California Postsecondary Education Commission 1994; Carter and Segura 1979; Duran 1983; Gey et al. 1992; LAUSD 1985; National Center for Education Statistics 2001; Rumberger and Rodríguez 2002; Schick and Schick 1991; U.S. Census Bureau 2000; U.S. Commission on Civil Rights 1971; Valencia 1991). In 1972, 34.3 percent of "Hispanics" aged 16–24 had officially dropped out of high school. By 1998 this rate had decreased only to 29.5 percent.[5] Today the national dropout rate for Chicanas/os approaches 50 percent, and in some urban areas, such as parts of Los Angeles, the dropout rate is as high as 70 percent (Bennett 1988; Chapa and Valencia 1993; LAUSD 1985; National Commission on Secondary Education for Hispanics 1984; Rumberger and Rodríguez 2002; Schick and Schick 1991).[6] Sixty-one percent of Chicana/o adults over age 24 in California in 1992 had not completed high school (Gey et al. 1992, 33). Even more shocking is that in 1990 Latinas/os were 62 percent of the dropout population aged 16–19 in California, but they comprised only 35 percent of all members of that age group in the state (California Postsecondary Education Commission 1994, 65). Most important of all, the educational outcomes (especially graduation rates) of Chicana/o students have improved little, if at all, over the last fifty years (Carter and Segura 1979; Chapa and Valencia 1993; National Center for Education Statistics 1989), while the significant disparity between Chicana/o and white students' educational outcomes has not narrowed (National Center for Education Statistics 1999, 2001; Rumberger and Rodríguez 2002; U.S. Census Bureau 2000; Valencia 1991). In fact, the dropout rate for whites has decreased faster than that for Latinas/os since 1980, resulting in a larger gap in high school completion in 2000 than in 1980 (National Center for Education Statistics 2001).

The significance of these figures becomes even more apparent when we consider the growth of the Chicana/o student population. In California the Chicana/o population is increasing rapidly, and the number of counties, districts, and schools in which Chicanas/os are the majority is steadily rising. Furthermore, projections suggest that by 2005 Chicanas/os and Latinas/os will form the majority of students enrolled in kindergarten through twelfth grade in California. The complex role of language and immigration status must be analyzed in the context of such trends. Clearly, addressing Chicana/o school failure has become a matter of urgency both for the Chicana/o population and for the larger society.[7] Since the 1970s, this urgency has spawned increasingly innovative analyses of the influences on Chicana/o school outcomes. These analyses have moved beyond deficit models, providing a deeper contextualization of the Chicana/o school experience. As continuing school failure has shown, however, these analyses have been unable to provide strategies for making realistic changes for a large percentage of Chicana/o youth. We are still faced with a critical question: Why have researchers and schools been unable to significantly address the school failure of Chicana/o students?

By briefly considering the history of Chicana/o schooling in the United States as our starting point, we can begin to answer this question. Interestingly, although some powerful historical analyses of the Chicana/o educational experience have been made, for the most part this history is not integrated into our contemporary analyses. While not surprising, it may be detrimental that researchers interested in the history of Chicana/o schooling and those interested in the modern context tend to live in two different worlds.

From the earliest interaction between the United States and Mexico, the Mexican was viewed as inferior on multiple levels: socially, politically, culturally, economically, religiously, and intellectually (Acuña 1988; De León 1983; Menchaca and Valencia 1990). These perceptions of Mexican inferiority were shaped by a combination of ignorance, fear, and greed that were framed within the larger political ideologies of the United States during the eighteenth and nineteenth centuries. In short, the United States rationalized its policies of expansion and exploitation by propagating notions of Mexican inferiority. In so doing, the United States founded its interaction with Mexicans on these ideas such that both individuals and institutions that interacted with the Mexican did so on these premises. By the time that public schooling in the Southwest became fairly common practice in the latter part of the nineteenth century, Mexicans were already both informally and formally excluded from attending public schools on the grounds of their assumed intellectual and cultural inferiority.

As child labor fell out of favor and the mainstream within the United States saw the necessity of "Americanizing" the Mexican, increasing numbers of Mexicans began attending school. During the early twentieth century, "Americans" were concerned that the Mexicans were not properly prepared for their economic and social roles in this country. Although Mexicans were still characterized as inferior, schooling was deemed an important tool in their integration into society and their preparation for their eventual contributions through manual labor. Thus, by the time the Chicana/o child began entering American schools with regularity and in significant numbers, their school participation was fundamentally different from that of "American" children. Chicana/o children were prepared for manual labor and subservience both by the nature and the content of their schooling, which was inferior and segregated (G. Gonzalez 1990; San Miguel 1987).

The ideologies explaining the Chicana/o students' needs in school have evolved over time from intellectual inferiority to cultural inferiority and finally to being limited by their own socioeconomic status and the corresponding attitudes prevalent within a "culture of poverty." Chicanas/os for the most part were relegated to segregated and inferior schooling for the duration of the twentieth century. In fact, studies at the end of the twentieth century found that Chicanas/os had become the most segregated of any ethnic group in U.S. schools, attending underfunded and poorly staffed schools (Applebome 1997).

Throughout this history, Chicanas/os have challenged the notions of inferiority with which they have been confronted, but each time their arguments have built momentum and gained attention, they have been redirected in ways that only change the labels with which their "inferiority" is explained. The reality is that researchers, schools, and politicians too often fail to acknowledge the history upon which the schooling experiences of Chicanas/os today have been built. This immobility has tremendously limited efforts to address Chicana/o school failure. Historical analyses have shown that racist ideologies have been at the foundation of Chicana/o schooling and continue to play a critical role through their more subtle, contemporary manifestations. Still, many people fail to integrate this history into our understandings of contemporary society. Others do not address the reality that the forces presently at work in maintaining Chicana/o school failure also prevent systemic changes that would improve Chicana/o school outcomes.

Today the typical explanation for Chicana/o school failure is that Chicana/o youth and their families lack preparation and interest in school. Quite often, teachers and administrators say that their efforts to educate Chicanas/os are severely limited because the students and their families are uninterested in educational success and have no experience with this success (for various examples of these attitudes, see Olsen 1997, Romo and Falbo 1996, and Valdés 1998). Some school staff believe that the culture of these families works against efforts to educate Chicana/o youth and that the school thus faces a steepening uphill battle to educate these students and prepare them for the world of work. Without question, school personnel have important insights to share on educating Chicana/o youth. At the same time, they also learn to think in specific, often pessimistic ways about what is possible and why within the school. As research in the 1970s suggested, teachers are quite capable of influencing and producing the student outcomes that they expect, despite equal measures of hard work and concern for their students (see Solórzano and Solórzano 1995 for a discussion of the applications of this work to Chicanas/os). As one teacher stated, "It's scary to realize the terrible power that teachers have to create in students a certainty that they belong at the bottom" (Olsen 1997, 83). This is not to say that Chicana/o school failure is simply a function of teacher expectations, but rather that teacher expectations and their role are just one indicator of the social complexity at work in the schooling process, a complexity that belies oversimplified explanations that focus on families and parents alone. The successes of Chicana/o youth who have the same socioeconomic status, parental interest, teachers, and even ability as do their failing peers suggest that we need to look more carefully at these contexts in order to develop strategies for success (Arellano and Padilla 1996). As one of the students I interviewed put it in our discussions about Chicana/o school failure,

> It's a real easy answer for a real complex question. I mean you could say, "Oh, just get 'em to try." But to get 'em to try, you gotta really understand why they're not trying—what's going on in their lives, their own personal life—to see what is stopping 'em, what's hindering 'em. What are their thoughts? What are their mentalities? Are they being raised like this? Are they trained to think that they're not good enough? Or what is it?

Whereas the 1970s and 1980s were dominated by research that attempted to expose the educational injustice Chicanas/os were experiencing in the schools (Carter and Segura 1979; San Miguel 1987; U.S. Commission on Civil Rights 1971), the 1990s began with efforts to understand the complexities of Chicana/o school performance with an eye toward attainable improvements. Early in the 1990s, Richard Valencia (1991) compiled what remains the most comprehensive contemporary analysis of Chicana/o schooling (a revised version was published in 2002). Exposing the historical, demographic, linguistic, cultural, familial, testing, and institutional forces influencing Chicana/o school failure, the contributors to *Chicano School Failure and Success* left the reader pessimistically wondering what could realistically be done to improve the situation. Like many to follow him, Valencia did not provide much hope in the conclusions he drew, although they did expose the elements of Chicana/o schooling that must change. He called for making large-scale efforts to embrace integration; unifying the work of practitioners, researchers, and policy makers to provide evidence of the strength of bilingual education and a justification for its further development; changing the popular perceptions of Chicana/o parents and fully involving them in their children's schooling; overhauling testing and assessment in schools; and, finally, instituting democratic governance and curriculum development that include Chicana/o participation, along with a shift from the institutional perception of Chicana/o youth to one that is hopeful and positive. The work done by Valencia and others was crucial in deconstructing the educational experience of Chicanas/os, although the macroemphasis of the conclusions also left the reader with doubts as to the possibility of implementing the major changes that Valencia revealed as necessary.

More recently, Romo and Falbo (1996) engaged in a similar effort to decipher the complexity of Chicana/o schooling by engaging in a comprehensive study with a more focused analysis. By interviewing a large group of Chicana/o students and categorizing their experiences, the authors provided a different angle on Chicana/o schooling. With fairly detailed descriptions and analyses of the experiences and feelings of Chicana/o students, their parents, and their schools, Romo and Falbo helped us understand Chicana/o issues of tracking, gangs, pregnancy, immigration, dropping out and opting for the GED equivalency diploma, cultural barriers to parental involvement, and struggles with inappropriate or unfairly applied policy and bureaucratic practice. Again, the reader is left wondering how so many and such complicated problems can be realistically addressed. Even the authors seemed to struggle with this issue. They provided a list of tactics parents could employ, but they relied heavily on a number of major institutional shifts that would have to occur. While their recommendations are interesting and important—involving administrators in instruction, increasing teacher interactions across grades, rethinking testing, mobilizing support for students at risk, reorganizing learning from individual- to group-based interactions, respecting parents, rewarding hard work rather than ability, and giving a diploma value by linking it directly to opportunities after graduation—these changes are also so sweeping that they make us wonder what it would take to implement them in the face of traditions that have generated Chicana/o school failure for generations.

These few examples demonstrate the difficulty of addressing Chicana/o school failure. This review is not intended in any way to minimize the importance and necessity of previous research. At the same time, the struggle these authors had in developing recommendations that would readily make inroads for overcoming Chicana/o school failure suggest the need for new approaches. Other researchers help put these difficulties into perspective, for they see the significant role that historically ingrained ideologies continue to play in school and the impediments to systemic change.

Solórzano and Solórzano (1995), for example, provided a comprehensive critique of the forces limiting Chicana/o educational opportunities at elementary, secondary, and even postsecondary levels. While discussing some important strategies for addressing these problems through research on Effective Schools and Accelerated Schools programs, they also raised concerns. The authors suggested that even the popular acceptance of the Effective Schools program, which they showed to have strong possibilities for improving Chicana/o schooling, has had almost no impact on Chicana/o youth. Stanton-Salazar (1997, 2001) sheds light on this finding through a complex study that integrates the roles of social networks and social capital in the lives of minority school youth. Beginning with an analysis of the role of networks, Stanton-Salazar noted that "decades of educational research strongly suggest that urban/metropolitan, working-class schools have historically not been strategically oriented toward development of students' social support networks" (1997, 5). By revealing the significance of access to and facility with dominant discourses in school, Stanton-Salazar then described how minority youth are denied access to the basic tools (social capital) necessary for school and life success. He argued that what minority students bring into the school is deemed inappropriate for eventual success, and thus the decision is made not to invest the time in the development of critical network-building tools and social capital among these youth. Stanton-Salazar exposed the daunting reality that not only the school but society itself is structured in ways that hinder both minority school success and the possibility for influencing changes that will address these problems. Fortunately, Stanton-Salazar provided a possible means for Chicana/o school success—he described the minority child with a bicultural socialization that allows for the development of both the skills for gaining access to the dominant discourse and the social capital that are prerequisites for educational success. The complexity and potential problematic of his analysis, however, lies in his belief that the bicultural student cannot maintain school success "without consistent access to institutional support," a requirement that seems difficult to attain, given the counterforces that he already exposed. Nevertheless, Stanton-Salazar provided a turn in the research on Chicana/o schooling by suggesting a means by which dramatic changes in school performance might be possible.

Vigil (1997) provided a similar hopefulness in his analyses of Chicana/o school performance in 1974 and 1988 Los Angeles, which suggested that certain forces, such as identity, role models, and family environment and support, can be controlled by families and can also help Chicana/o students pursue school success. In work with a group of Chicana/o students at an elite university, Arellano and Padilla (1996) made important progress toward this end by considering the external and internal forces that allow certain Chicana/o students to achieve success through their own "academic invulnerability." This research builds on earlier analyses of successful Chicana/o students (Gándara 1995) and is essential to the present project because, although it did not include intervention strategies, it provides perhaps the best framework to date for seeing the importance of factors like school climate, teacher-student interactions, students' school beliefs, and mentors, and it also demonstrates that some Chicana/o students are able to deal with both positive and negative varieties of these influences in ways that lead to their success.

In recent years the school needs of Chicana/o and Latina/o youth have been increasingly emphasized. Much of this work provides helpful insights to those who know little about the experiences and resources of Latina/o youth, but much of it also ignores the complex realities uncovered by some of the authors mentioned above (Koss-Chioino and Vargas 1999). Many studies provide recipes for successful schools in Latina/o communities that are intriguing but require an institutional commitment that few Chicana/o schools and districts exhibit (M. Gonzalez, Huerta-Macias, and Tinajero 1998; P. Reyes, Scribner, and Scribner 1999; Slavin and Calderon 2001). Still others consider the unique needs of non-English-speaking Latinas/os and shed light on their academic lives and curricular and pedagogical needs, but because of this focus many of these works do not unpack the complex racial-political forces involved in shaping their identities (Brice 2002; M. Reyes and Halcon 2001; Valdés 2001). Some researchers have analyzed identity in the school context, but they created identity categories for students that focus primarily on the degree of academic investment they manifest, thus ignoring some of the critical forces that define that investment (Flores-Gonzalez 2002; Rymes 2001). Still others, as discussed earlier, continue to suggest the need for dramatic changes in the system at large (Garcia 2001; Stanton-Salazar 2001).

Overall, the research that has looked at Chicanas/os and the schools has carefully examined various components of the Chicana/o school experience. All of these works make important contributions to the field of Chicana/o education. At the same time, they also leave many wondering how to make changes that can help students today. So much of this research points to the need for dramatic systemic change in U.S. schooling, but this call has been made for generations with little response. Readers find little guidance for realistically pursuing the success of Chicanas/os in the schools today. Other works provide models and ideas for helping Latina/o students, but these studies are almost always based on the assumption that there is institutional and systemic interest in making change when in fact the majority of Chicana/o youth attend schools in districts that have little interest in moving in the suggested directions. Much of the research has not effectively and fully engaged Chicana/o students themselves. The dramatic conditions facing Chicanas/os in the schools all but demand that we consider their own analyses of their school lives so that we might help them immediately rather than emphasizing idealistic but unrealistic solutions.

Perhaps the most important study of the experiences of Chicana/o school youth is Valenzuela's *Subtractive Schooling* (1999). Valenzuela looks at the world of school through the eyes of Chicana/o youth and exposes a process by which schooling "divests [Chicana/o] youth of important social and cultural resources leaving them progressively vulnerable to academic failure" (1999, 3). She uncovers the daily realities that shape so many of the issues that other researchers have touched on. Valenzuela cuts right to the heart of the racialization process that is central to the schooling of so many Chicana/o youth and that often shapes the failure of these students. Her work also uncovers the potential power of resources within Chicana/o families, although she herself does not provide a detailed analysis of how to tap into these resources.

THE NEED FOR ANALYZING IDENTITY AND SCHOOLING

My personal experiences in school as both a teacher and a student have helped me consider a different approach to understanding and improving Chicana/o student outcomes. When I was a sixth-grade teacher, I taught the most advanced reading group in our elementary school. During reading class, the students changed classrooms because many of them were below their grade level in language skills. This situation had arisen at least partially because about 90 percent of the students were Latina/o, and a great majority of them had Spanish as their first and/or dominant language. Although I taught this class more than ten years ago, I still think about several students often. One of them, "Luis," has influenced my work a great deal. Luis, a fifth grader who was placed in my top reading group, was one of the few students who were reading above grade level. He was usually somewhat shy in class but also had a good sense of humor and was, to me, a nice student to have in class. About the time he started fifth grade, Luis began emulating the appearance of the gangbangers in the community. He had no "positive" role models in his world, and gangbangers represented the only powerful figures he could actually touch and feel. Furthermore, as the oldest child in his family, he had no one but these gang members to protect him from his harsh surroundings. His interest in gang life was expected. Never-theless, his evolving persona as a gangbanger wannabe had serious im-plications for him at school. The schools in this inner-city Los Angeles district developed strict dress codes in their efforts to limit gang activity, and Luis became a target for school personnel. With the goal of strin-gently enforcing the dress code, one of the school administrators made Luis public enemy number one. This administrator would go out every morning before school and look for Luis to try and nail him on a dress code violation. Luis would spend the first few hours of most school days getting busted, going home, and changing clothes. He was made to feel marginal and soon became marginal in the school. The last time I saw him, Luis was on the streets and was no longer just a wannabe.

While some people may view Luis's story as an extreme or rare ex-ample, it is not an isolated case. Throughout my teaching experience, I was constantly made aware that the students I taught were not expected to be successful in school or life. Some of the messages were subtle, while others were more blatant. Teachers and administrators had developed a system whereby intelligent Latina/o youth were targeted for disciplinary measures and prevented from learning opportunities precisely because racially based characteristics were used to identify "problem students" and "troublemakers." Furthermore, Luis's story illuminated a critical point to me: the identity of Chicana/o students is often a central force that shapes their school experiences and performance. In every school in which I have taught, researched, or been a student, I have known stu-dents who have been labeled in some negative fashion that resulted in a pattern of treatment distinct from that of the "successful students." The point of including Luis's story is not to suggest that all Chicana/o stu-dents are the victims of vicious attacks by school personnel (surely, Luis was complicit in his situation), but rather to suggest that identity is a crit-ical factor involved in the way in which school staff interact with stu-dents and vice versa. While most of us have probably seen students who have been negatively labeled and also know that this labeling almost au-tomatically defines their school persona and outcomes, no one has effec-tively explained what determines the nature of identity development and how it is linked to outcomes for Chicana/o students. Okagaki, Frensch, and Dodson (1996), however, provided a preliminary analysis, suggest-ing that Chicana/o children's feelings about school can be related to their ethnic identity as early as the fourth and fifth grades. Other research has suggested relationships between identity and school performance, but it has been based on a reductive analysis that ignores the complexity of the forces that shape both identity and school performance.[8] Finally, a number of researchers who have conducted preliminary analyses of the relationship between identity and school performance (particularly among college students) have laid an important foundation while also demanding the need for in-depth, qualitative analyses that will allow us to complicate identity beyond ethnic labels and practices (Bernal, Saenz, and Knight 1991; A. Hurtado, Gonzalez, and Vega 1994; S. Hurtado 1994; Velez, Longoria, and Torres 1997).

That some researchers have exposed the need for qualitative analyses is related to the second realization that came from my experiences as a teacher. The complexities of the forces at work in the development of Chicana/o identity and Chicana/o school outcomes (as well as their relationship) are so significant that making advances in this area requires building on the few works that have carefully considered these relationships by performing in-depth, innovative analyses of the experiences of Chicana/o youth (e.g., Franquiz 2001; Olsen 1997). By relying on Chicana/o students' own analyses of the relationship between their identity and school performance in my qualitative analysis, I attempt to address their continued failure and to suggest ways in which students and parents can develop empowering identities that facilitate school success.

TOWARD A CHICANA/O METHODOLOGY

In trying to become "objective," western Culture made "objects" of things and people when it distanced itself from them, thereby losing "touch" with them. This dichotomy is the root of all violence. (Anzaldúa, 1987, 37)

Today Chicana/o communities face many of the same social problems that they faced a generation or more ago, despite the increasing attention that researchers give these problems. Research on and in Chicana/o communities has a long history of reifying the oppression and justifying the unequal outcomes of Chicanas/os. For years, researchers have gone into Chicana/o communities, extracted the information they were seeking, and used that information to explain the condition of Chicanas/os, most often blaming them for this condition and unintentionally or intentionally ignoring a host of systemic influences. Although Chicana/o intellectuals have critiqued this tradition for years, it still exists in new forms today.

Academic research has been built on certain ground rules that reinforce the status quo. For example, objectivity has long been considered an essential component of any research project. The idea behind objectivity is that researchers should not allow any biases to influence their work. The reality, of course, is that even taking on a specific research project reflects one's interests and biases. Furthermore, "objectivity" in this context does not mean lack of bias; rather, it means that the researcher's biases are unclear to the reader and/or are not made explicit. Almost all researchers, for example, share the bias that they are able to understand the world and its complexities better than their research subjects. The dramatic mistakes that researchers have made in their work in Chicana/o communities over the years have made it clear that this is not the case. "Objectivity" in research therefore means not that the researcher is unbiased but rather that the researcher shares the biases of those who have shaped the trajectory of accepted academic research.

With regard to Chicana/o Studies research and other arenas of innovative academic work, even those scholars who have sought a more innovative and just form of research have remained significantly influenced by the conventional research paradigm. As Gitlin argued, despite the shift begun in recent theoretical discussions of innovative research, "these changes in educational research methods have done little to alter the alienating relationship between the researcher and the researched" (1990, 443). Gitlin added that "educational research is still a process that for the most part silences those studied, ignores their personal knowledge, and strengthens the assumption that researchers are the producers of knowledge" (1990, 444).

I contend that one of the reasons that research with Chicanas/os has not led to more dramatic changes in Chicana/o educational outcomes is that the research itself is not grounded in principles of social justice, although it seeks this justice. Even work within the innovative field of Chicana/o Studies has rarely produced research that is participatory *and* transformative. Instead, Chicanas/os have seen little substantive change in their condition in the United States despite years of scientifically acceptable research and numerous corresponding policies and policy changes in schools.

The primary obstacle for researchers studying the world of Chicana/o youth is that even as we increasingly incorporate the participation of these youth, most of us have not expressed concern that our methods be as true to notions of social justice as we are asking schools and institutions to be. We have not given much thought to the way in which the dominant paradigm not only ignores but also works against social justice through our own methods. My primary concern is that research on and in Chicana/o communities almost always shapes and controls the input of those communities in damaging ways. By defining the focus of the research, the questions that are asked, the answers that are considered appropriate, and, most detrimental of all, the meaning of the answers, we dramatically limit our ability to understand the experiences of Chicanas/os as they themselves do.

The research discussed in this book strives to address these issues. It is an initial attempt to employ social justice research, which I define as research that is engaged in trying to understand Chicana/o experiences in conjunction with communities, under the direction of those communities, and *with a recognition of the unique knowledge systems and knowledge bases in those communities.* This research process strives for social justice as both process and product and shares the same objectives of community-based activism. By seeking to participate in the creation of new knowledge and "truth" that attacks convention, Chicana/o social justice research helps activist efforts by confronting the intellectual rationales and arguments that support, for example, an anti-Chicana/o hysteria. Finally, Chicana/o social justice research assists community efforts at empowerment by providing opportunities for community-based Chicanas/os to participate in intellectual exploration that can support those efforts.

As was discussed above, this work has been described as nonacademic and anti-intellectual, but it is neither. Instead, it strives to be more truthful in its pursuit of knowledge through academic inquiry. Rather than ignoring the biases implicit in all research, this research exposes them as a means of helping participants and readers understand the role of politics and of position in daily life and in academic work.[9]

It is not my intent to suggest that Chicana/o social justice research is the only method of educational research worth pursuing; much of the research on the state of education for Chicanas/os has been insightful. Nor is it my belief that we can ever fully address the complex problematics of social research (e.g., the role of power). Even more important, I am not suggesting that research is itself empowering or that it can necessarily be made integral in efforts at social change. Chicana/o researchers (and others pursuing social justice) must, however, confront our complicity in the continued school failure of Chicanas/os. We must seek "the truth" as Chicanas/os experience it, and we must attempt to disrupt academic conventions that reinforce racism. Although the research discussed in this book does not attain all of the goals of social justice research, the discussion of this approach to research is critical to understanding the methodological underpinnings of the work.

THE PROJECTS

I began my research into Chicana/o identity and its link to school performance through a research project in East Los Angeles. The following
year I conducted a mirror project in rural Acoma, Washington.[10] The
stark contrast between the two research sites is important because it allows us to consider the role of context in shaping identity and school
outcomes. Furthermore, as a quickly growing rural area, Acoma provides a preview of issues that are now facing communities across the
United States with newly emerging Mexican enclaves.

In both projects, Chicana/o students at a major university, a community college, and a high school completed surveys and participated in interviews. Through open-ended and a few closed-ended questions, the
students discussed their school experiences and the major influences on
their school performance. The projects relied almost exclusively on students' own responses. Although the reliability of such data has been debated, the projects intended simply to understand Chicana/o student
performance as the students themselves interpreted it. Thus the data col-
lection techniques were appropriate, although the conclusions should be
understood within this context (see Valdés 1998 for a similar rationale
for focusing on students' perceptions).

In both projects, the students and I attempted to develop a schema to
explain how Chicana/o students understood themselves in their social
worlds, as well as the meaning this had for them. We began this work
with an exploratory survey distributed to Chicana/o students attending
a university, a community college, and a high school in each area. The
survey was designed to get a sense of how students talked about the arenas of social life that were important to them. Before distributing the
survey, I already knew that the core of the research would be done
through interviews with students (research I had conducted earlier had
suggested that traditional survey methods were ineffective in understanding the full complexities of Chicana/o students' identities). The
heart of the survey, therefore, was a series of open-ended questions intended only to provide an opportunity for students to reveal the arenas
of their social worlds that were of greatest importance to them and how
these arenas might interact with and shape their identities. Because the
complexity of Chicana/o identity made it difficult to understand these issues with closed-ended questions, students were asked to identify the aspects of their social worlds that were significant to them and why. Students were provided with the opportunity to select from a list of possible
arenas of social life that might be significant and to add to that list when

necessary. Given the extensive writing involved in responding to the survey, I expected that the number of students who responded would be small, but I also knew that their responses would provide detailed information equivalent to that generated in interviews I had conducted in earlier projects, and that this detail would allow me to conduct more complex and rich interviews afterward.

The surveys were not identical in the two studies, because the findings from the first project led me to seek new information in the second. In the first project, students were asked to discuss the importance of issues that were related to different aspects of social identity. They were also asked to discuss aspects of their social lives that were important or with which they struggled, since previous research indicated that identity is most often formed around those aspects of social life that are most conflict-laden. In addition, students were asked to simply describe their social identities.

In the second project, the survey was intended to consider every possible social grouping that might be significant to the identity development of Chicana/o students. Students were asked to choose from a list of these arenas of social life. The list was limited to the following categories for the survey: class, community, culture, family, gender, job/employment/financial difficulties, race/ethnicity, religion/spirituality, school, and sexuality/sexual orientation. Although some of these categories overlap, my previous research had revealed that students interpreted some of these things differently and that they focused on aspects of certain categories that distinguish them from other similar categories. As mentioned, the survey also allowed students to add their own categories, and eventually the list of categories was expanded to include disability/ability/physicality/appearance, friendship groups (cliques, organizations, gangs, etc.), immigration status/generation, interethnic interaction, language, and skin color (all of which were addressed through follow-up interviews). Students also discussed the issues that were important to them. Finally, they were asked to discuss school, the influences on their school performance, and any connections between their school experiences and their identities. The students were also asked to simply describe their social identities.

While the findings from the surveys were important and interesting, they were intended to provide insight into the directions that should be pursued in follow-up interviews with students. I wanted to know all of the potential arenas of identity formation that mattered to students. I also wanted to know if students understood themselves in terms of social identities or if this concept seemed foreign to them. In fact, the survey was quite useful and showed both the importance of social identity to

Chicana/o students and the appropriateness of the different potential identity arenas that were listed for the students. With an expanded list, I conducted interviews with students so that we could talk through the significance and process of identity formation face-to-face. The surveys helped us see what was important to students and even some of the reasons for its importance, but much more depth was still needed.

The interviews were open-ended and intended to allow students to create their own framework for explaining themselves. Each interview lasted from one hour to an hour and a half. Students in Los Angeles were asked to discuss identity issues that mattered to them and the influences that made these issues important. In addition, the participants were asked to discuss their schooling, the influences on their schooling, and the links among all of the issues discussed in the interview (identity and its influences, and school and its influences). In addition, I described patterns and issues that had come out of the surveys and asked the students to discuss and explain them. In this part of the interview, some students would tell me why something was happening, whereas others would challenge the finding itself. These initial interviews were followed by a second interview that asked students to discuss the influence of specific identity issues on their lives. The students also discussed their identity formation through open-ended questions that allowed them to cover any issue. Finally, they were asked to discuss issues from their first interviews, as well as findings from the first interviews as whole.

In the first interviews in Acoma, students were asked to discuss school and their educational influences, building on the responses they provided in the surveys. They were again asked which of the issues from the list of potential arenas of identity formation were important to them. More specifically, the interview asked students how these issues were linked to their sense of who they are (identity). Furthermore, the interview asked students why these issues were important and how that importance had evolved over time (considering conflicts and struggles students might have faced when appropriate). To provide the participants with different opportunities to describe themselves in all their complexity, the interview also included discussions of the links and intersections of different aspects of identity, as well as open-ended questions that asked the students to describe themselves in their social worlds. Finally, they were asked to discuss the links between identity and education.

With the student introspections developed through both surveys and interviews in Acoma, we had a great deal of data that unpacked the role of identity in Chicana/o students' lives. Still, I wanted to delve deeper and to have students rethink their self-analyses. In second interviews that we conducted with some of the students, we focused on rethinking the most important parts of identity and why they were so important to students. We also reconsidered the links among different facets of identity and the influences that shaped identity formations. Throughout the second interview, I challenged the students' responses from the first interviews and asked them to consider alternative explanations, so that they could think more critically about the answers they were providing (and to consider the answers of other students when appropriate). This additional information allowed us to look carefully at the forces that shaped students' lives, and it added some texture to our understanding of all the interviews. The second interviews in both projects engaged the students as co-researchers, involving them in directly answering the research questions for the project rather than simple interview questions.

RESEARCHING IDENTITY

In these projects, the specific means of making identity something that could be researched departed from those employed in quantitative analyses, which define the terms that determine the nature of an individual's ethnic identity. Instead, the students were asked about the social issues that were important to them, in order to discover the role of different arenas of identity within their overall social identities, and, more importantly, they were asked to explain who they are in their own minds and which identities were most pertinent in their lives. The rationale for this approach was the need to understand how Chicanas/os define their own identities and why they develop these particular identities, so as to avoid defining students' identities through measures that are unable to grasp the value, meaning, and influences behind an individual's response to specific statements related to identity.

In fact, students themselves determined how social identity could be researched by collectively framing this identity as the aspects of their social lives that dominated their own understandings of who they are in their social worlds. Through the aspects of identity that they emphasized, their return to these themes throughout the interviews, and the emotions they attached to these identities in our conversations, the students demonstrated that although social identity cannot be entirely understood via quantifiable data, this is the only way to understand their identities in all of their complexity.

This process of making identity a construct that we could research excludes the possibility of and the role of at least two facets of social identity: unconscious identities and suppressed identities. Unconscious identities are those aspects of social identity that influence students' larger social identities but are not consciously experienced. One example is the way in which gender often unconsciously shapes the identity of many young men. Suppressed identities are those that an individual has chosen to push out of his or her public social identity for any number of reasons. Some students, for example, may try to blend in with their white peers and not identify as Chicana/o. In the end, the students selectively re-created their lives throughout these projects. They did not provide an objective or even a complete history. The goal of this book, however, is to understand identity as students themselves understand it, so as to help them negotiate identity conflicts that they face. Accomplishing this goal requires a focus on students' conscious identities. For this reason, the emphasis on students' definitions and reconstructions of identity is appropriate for the project. The role of unconscious and suppressed identities is discussed in depth in Part 3 of this book.

All of the interviews were taped, transcribed, and coded around the themes students covered. In conducting the analyses for this book, I focused on how each student described her or his own identity and the forces that influenced this identity formation. I created a framework that described each student's analysis and then developed a larger framework that not only included each of the students' analyses at a given site but also looked at every student from the point of view of every other student, in order to understand the relationships among their analyses and how a particular student helps us better understand all of his or her peers. Finally, I pulled out excerpts from interviews that served as models of students' experiences and analyses.[11]

EAST LOS ANGELES

Students volunteered to participate in the study after I made presentations explaining the project in their classes during the winter of 1996. The total sample surveyed included 158 Mexican-descent students (37 from a four-year university, 37 from a community college, 32 high school seniors, and 52 high school freshmen).

The four-year university is a major research institution, and at the time of the study 13.01 percent of its student population was Chicana/o, and 58.8 percent was white. At the university, I recruited participants through the Chicana/o Studies classes being offered, attending all of the larger classes in Chicana/o Studies (ten in all), and I also sought participants in three non–Chicana/o Studies classes that had significant numbers of Chicana/o students. These classes were an education course and a sociology course, both of which dealt with minority issues, and a Spanish class for native speakers. The Chicana/o Studies classes were about 90 percent Chicana/o, while the non–Chicana/o Studies courses averaged about 30 percent Chicana/o. Later discussions with participants indicated that the students in Chicana/o Studies courses included Chicana/o Studies majors, students interested in Chicana/o issues, as well as students who were uninterested in Chicana/o Studies but needed to fulfill a diversity requirement. The participants in non–Chicana/o Studies classes similarly indicated diverse reasons for enrolling in these classes.

The community college is at the edge of a large Chicana/o barrio, and at the time of the study 59.6 percent of the student population was Chicana/o (another 16 percent were non–Chicana/o Latinas/os), and 3 percent were white. At the community college, I recruited students through six Chicana/o Studies classes and three non–Chicana/o Studies history classes. Chicana/o Studies classes were about 99 percent Latina/o, and history classes were about 95 percent Latina/o. Discussions with participants indicated that the students also had a wide variety of interests and reasons for being in the classes from which they were recruited. Few students in Chicana/o Studies courses, however, had an interest in pursuing the subject as a major field of study, and most were interested in training for specific careers in business.

The high school is in the middle of a Chicana/o barrio (the same one served by the community college), and at the time of the study 99.1 percent of the student population was "Hispanic." At the high school, I recruited ninth and twelfth graders through mandatory English classes (five classes for each grade level). The response rates of these two groups were affected by the teacher's decision to give freshmen class time and credit for completing the survey, whereas none of the seniors were formally given class time to participate in the survey, and only two of the senior classes were offered any type of credit.

After completing the surveys, students volunteered to participate in the interviews. Four individuals from each site were randomly selected from subgroups of the sample. A male student and a female student who were recruited through Chicana/o Studies classes, as well as a male and a female who were recruited through non–Chicana/o Studies classes, were selected from the college and university samples, respectively (one additional university student was also interviewed, because this was the only graduate student who had participated in the project). At the high school, a male and a female were selected from the ninth grade and from the twelfth grade. Six of these students—a male and a female at each site—were selected for second interviews. The interview sample was crucial because the interview data were exceptionally detailed and rich and are the heart of the project.

In terms of general demographics, it seems that the East Los Angeles sample is fairly representative of the larger Chicana/o population, given that most of the students are working-class[12] (75 percent are working-class, and 16 percent are middle-class; the remaining participants were unable to provide this information) with limited education (63 percent of fathers and 66 percent of mothers did not attain the equivalent of a high school education, and 18 percent and 19 percent, respectively, went only as far as a high school diploma). Additionally, the participants are mostly second-generation (63 percent), with a significant first-generation immigrant population (24 percent) and a smaller third-generation group (13 percent). Gender distribution in the sample reflected that in the classes sampled the number of females tended to be slightly higher in these classes, and 60 percent of the participants were female.

ACOMA, WASHINGTON

Acoma is in the midst of rapid demographic transformation, as this working-class Mexicana/o community has grown dramatically in recent years. Acoma is a small rural town in the heart of a large agricultural region that provides a great deal of wealth to the farm owners in the area. Despite the wealth that agriculture brings to the region, 21 percent of the population was living in poverty during the time of this study, and although an ethnic breakdown of the figure was not available, it is popularly understood that Mexicanas/os make up the vast majority of those in poverty.

The most recent census figures reported that Acoma had a population of 65,000, of which 78 percent were classified as white, and 16 percent Hispanic. The shift in the demographic makeup of the area can be seen when we look at the schools and find that, at that same time, 67 percent of the students were white and 26 percent were Hispanic. In the specific schools I worked in, during the time of the study 3 percent of the university students were Latina/o and 87 percent were white (with small percentages of African Americans, Asian Americans, and Native Americans). Although the vast majority of the Latina/o students attending the university are Chicanas/os from the Acoma Valley, it is important to note that their experience at the university is quite different from their lives at home. The university is in a small town where most residents are either students or employees of the university. This town is almost entirely populated by whites and has none of the ethnic-specific amenities found in the Chicana/o communities from which the students come. The community college and the high school are near each other, and both are near large Chicana/o communities. At the community college, 73 percent of the students were white and 19 percent were Latina/o (with small percentages of African Americans, Asian Americans, and Native Americans). The high school had the greatest racial balance: 51 percent of the students were white, and 40 percent were Latina/o (again with small percentages of African Americans, Asian Americans, and Native Americans).

As mentioned above, while the two projects had similarities, I never attempted to replicate the first study in Acoma. I chose to make changes in the research design to allow me to obtain information that might not have been accessed in the previous study. In Acoma, instead of recruiting students from classes, I obtained addresses from each of the schools and recruited students through the mail. I mailed surveys to a random sample of students at each site in 1997, and the total sample of survey respondents was 24 university students, 24 high school students, and 17 community college students.

All of the students who expressed interest in being interviewed were contacted for interviews. Because of the inability of some students to make interviews, additional students were selected for interviews at the high school and the community college. These additional students had interacted with my contacts (both of whom were counselors) at these sites. Four males and 4 females were interviewed at each site (with an extra female at the high school and 3 extra females at the university). After the interviews were transcribed and analyzed, all available students were included in second interviews (2 males and a female at the high school, 2 females and a male at the community college, and 2 males and 3 females at the university).

The Acoma sample exhibited an obvious diversity among the students. Sixty percent were females, a figure that seems to reflect the higher attrition rates of males. At least 40 percent of the students had been born in Mexico (most of these were in the high school and the community college, and most had migrated to the United States at a very young age).[13] At least 52 percent of the students had been born in the United States, 32 percent reported that one parent had been born there, and 20 percent reported that a grandparent had been born there. Only 13 percent of students reported that their mothers had completed high school, and 17 percent reported that their fathers had diplomas. The economic impact of these educational outcomes is reflected in the students' socioeconomic status: only 11 percent of the students stated that their families were middle-class or higher (based on the employment of their parents). Although a number of students did not provide information on their parents' employment, these students tended to be the children of immigrants who had received little education. The students' responses as well as the demographics of the communities suggest that the vast majority of the students come from working-class families. Some groups of students were very similar at some of the sites, such as the four students at the community college who belonged to MEChA (Movimiento Estudiantil Chicano de Aztlán, or Chicano Student Movement of Aztlán), but they show some significant differences among themselves. Other students— and the emphasis I put on their counterstories—help us understand the diversity I have been discussing.

LIMITATIONS

Without question, the greatest limitation of both projects is the difficulty of addressing the tremendous diversity of the Chicana/o population. While the popular media, politicians, and even some researchers tend to describe Chicanas/os (and Latinas/os for that matter) as a homogenous body, there is as much diversity within this population as there is outside it. Chicanas/os vary greatly with regard to a number of variables: generation, language ability, socioeconomic status, religious beliefs, cultural practices, family dynamics, skin color, and a long list of other important characteristics. Although the samples include a broad spectrum of students across each of these variables, and the differences between Acoma and East Los Angeles add to this diversity, some pockets of the Chicana/o community may not be represented in these students' experiences.

This study is also limited in that it considered only the perspective of students. This limitation was important to the study, however, because the work attempts to understand the relationship between identity and school performance, with the goal of applying the lessons of successful students to the experiences of the struggling students. More important is that the project included only Chicana/o students who selected themselves for participation in the study. The concern here is that this factor might make it much less likely that the project would include students who were struggling, the logic being that struggling students would feel more marginal and thus would be less likely to volunteer to talk about their experiences. Interestingly, my research has found that this was not the case, for a broad range of students participated (with regard to their school performance). In fact, some failing students have said they were interested in the project because they were concerned about the problems that Chicana/o students face. This finding, then, presents another possible limitation: that the study would attract students who had a certain concern or commitment to helping Chicana/o students. Without question, that occurred. The issue that I have struggled with is determining to what degree this is truly a limitation. The students who express this interest in helping other Chicana/o students come from a wide range of experiences and have a number of perspectives on what it will take for students to succeed (from putting the responsibility on students themselves to blaming families and blaming schools). And a wide range of types of students participated in the study: from recent immigrants to students whose families had been in the United States for three or more generations; from students who struggled in English to students who did not know any Spanish; from students whose parents never attended school to those whose parents had advanced degrees; from students who return during breaks at school to help their families work in the fields to students whose parents are professionals; from Catholics to Baptists; from students who are thriving in school to those who rarely even attend; from those who see themselves as revolutionary activists to ROTC students; and from those who believe deeply in the importance of Chicana/o Studies classes to those who think they are a waste of time. These are only some of the most obvious differences in the students. The students who are discussed in this book were selected for no other reason than that they represented the diversity of the Chicana/o experience. The excerpts that are used from our conversations were chosen because, as the students explained, they reflected the most important experiences, concerns, and beliefs of the students. Perhaps more important than any other factor that may have influenced the sample was the sociopolitical climate in California, which at the time of the study was charged with an anti-Mexican sentiment that dominated much of daily life (see Lechuga 1997 for one example).

Of significant importance to researchers are the limits of self-report data. The focus of this project, however, is on how Chicana/o students understand themselves and how we can understand their experiences and identity formation. A number of potential avenues are available for attempting to acquire this information, but none is more effective than engaging the students themselves in the analysis. My work in the schools has shown me that school staff are typically unable to understand the complexity of Chicana/o students and their experiences. Furthermore, in my work with students, I ask that they frame their responses within their experiences and that they provide examples whenever possible. I also challenge them to consider alternate views as conveyed by other students, teachers, and parents. In all this work, the students have shown their intelligence and commitment to providing "truthful" answers, and their intellectual abilities in many ways leave arguments against self-report data smacking of condescension. There is not a more effective way to understand the lives and identities of Chicana/o students than to ask them to discuss these things.

In the end, as is always the case, the findings of this research project are specific to the sites and individuals discussed herein. Still, the students make a strong argument for applying this work to other contexts, as we will see.

Finally, several years have passed since the first interviews were conducted. It is important to note the changes in the social and educational landscape since the work was conducted, as well as new insights on the work overall. In California, Washington State, and the United States, much has changed since I last spoke with the students in this study. The U.S. school system now operates under the No Child Left Behind Act. Latinas/os are now the largest "minority" in the United States, and along with that shift has come increasing attention from politicians. There have been Latin Explosions in which the country has fallen in love with certain Latina/o cultural icons. At the same time, there is little effective representation of Latina/o issues by either of the major political parties, and Latina/o portrayals by the media have increased slightly but are still very few and most often caricatures. Racial profiling by law enforcement personnel continues, and the reality is that many Latinas/os are being left behind by the No Child Left Behind Act. Racial segregation in schools is greater now than it ever has been. The gaps between Latina/o and white students in terms of access to resources and school outcomes have remained the same and in many cases have widened. Finally, the racialization and profiling of Chicanas/os in schools are as common as ever. In short, our context is always shifting, and the manifestations of racialization are always shifting as well, but the power of racial hegemony as a defining force in the United States and its schools has remained unchanged. Beyond the statistics, my own work in today's schools, including talking with youth and coordinating workshops for teachers and youth workers, has made this clear.

PREVIEW

The remainder of the book is divided into three parts. The first describes the East Los Angeles project. The second considers the Acoma project. The final part brings both sets of analyses into an overall framework and focuses on developing strategies for addressing the needs of Chicana/o students. Although my interests in looking at East Los Angeles and Acoma are similar, as I have explained, the projects are not identical and the analyses are quite different. The differences reflect the evolution of my own thinking, as the analysis of Acoma shows increasing levels of complexity based on the work done in Los Angeles. The Los Angeles chapters are used to develop a framework, while the Acoma chapters are intended to flesh out that framework through extended analyses of students' multiple experiences. Furthermore, because of the lack of previous research with rural Chicana/o youth, more depth and detail are included in the Acoma chapters as the models developed in the section on Los Angeles are applied to the context of Washington. The final chapters consider all of these issues in detail as they look at an overarching model and proposals for interventions. In addition, throughout the book each chapter is slightly different in approach because I have attempted to tell the students' stories in multiple ways.

Chapter 1 provides a framework for explaining the evolution of identity, based on excerpts from individuals rather than case studies. The students' analyses of identity in Los Angeles fit tightly together and tell a single compelling story through the similarities and differences they described. This is the only chapter in which the preliminary survey data are used, for they help us begin to understand the students' beliefs. Chapter 2 is a series of case studies that analyze the influences on students' school lives. I found that a detailed analysis of individual experiences at each site was powerful and would help readers understand individuals and their complexities better. As in Chapter 1, the case studies are used as examples for constructing a framework that addresses the experiences of the entire group. Thus these two chapters provide an initial overall framework for understanding the forces that shape both identity and schooling for Chicana/o students and in particular for considering the detailed analyses of the experiences of the students in Acoma. Chapter 3 builds on this framework by focusing on one individual who was exceptionally introspective and insightful and who modeled a path for change that was applicable to the experiences of others.

Part 2 looks at identity, schooling, and lessons for empowerment in a much different way, by analyzing in detail the multiple arenas that influence students' lives in Acoma. Chapter 4 looks at each site and each issue that students raised to carefully depict the intricate connections among the different forces that shape students' lives and to also suggest the possible evolution of their analyses and thinking. Similarly, Chapter 5 examines the several themes that are common across the sites and compares them with the framework from Chapter 2. Chapters 4 and 5 are based on extensive excerpts from students' analyses, for several reasons. As the students themselves explain, they have an almost desperate need to have their voices heard. In addition, it is necessary for all of us to hear the multiple voices and experiences of students outside of case studies and for parents to be able to understand in vivid detail how their children's lives are influenced. Furthermore, so little research is available on the experiences of rural Chicana/o youth that it is critical to understand their lives in as much depth as possible. These two chapters form a natural transition into the more complex analyses that are the heart of Chapter 6. That chapter focuses on a few of the women at the community college because they describe very similar experiences in facing some of the most psychologically damaging struggles that were reported in either project. Their experiences are compared with those of two male students (one at the high school and one at the university). Together, these students point to one path for resistance that is empowering and is reflected in the interviews with many of their peers. This chapter is particularly important because it highlights the dramatic conflicts that many Chicana/o youth will face in the many emerging Mexican communities in rural areas across the United States. Part 2 ends with "Time-out," a powerful first-person narrative from a student who carefully breaks down the development of his identity and its connection to his school performance.

The two chapters in Part 3 analyze the lessons of the first two parts of the book. Chapter 7 provides a framework for understanding both the school lives and the identity development of Chicana/o students, and Chapter 8 provides a model for addressing the needs of these students.

PART ONE

INSIGHTS FROM LOS ANGELES CHICANA/O YOUTH

ONE

IDENTITY FORMATION
IN LOS ANGELES

I felt overwhelmed the first time I walked into Harding High School in East Los Angeles. It was exactly the type of place I wanted my work to eventually affect. The school sits in the heart of a Chicana/o barrio. The student body is huge, and almost every student is Chicana/o. The walls of the school are covered with murals, many of which are student creations and most of which have indigenous and Chicana/o themes.

Harding is also an important historical site, since it was at the heart of significant protest and uprising by Chicana/o students in the late 1960s. At that time the students had risen to attack what they felt was an inferior education. They identified themselves as the victims of a lack of commitment by the school district to address their needs. When I walked those halls for the first time, I wondered how much things had changed in the last thirty years. After entering the classrooms and spending some time in a number of different classes, I wondered what those students who walked out in protest would say about what was happening in Harding today. In one class I visited, the teacher barely interacted with the students at all. He had a system in which the students knew their assignments and worked on them in class, while he worked on a crossword puzzle. He was a small Anglo teacher, and I got a strong sense that he felt intimidated by his students and uncomfortable in the school. His behavior and his body language suggested that he did not want to be there. In another class, I spoke with a teacher who made it clear that she was dedicated to addressing the needs of her students. When I sat in on her classes, however, I found that she had little control over what happened and the students mainly did whatever they wanted. One student later confided in me that students had even smoked weed in her classes. Although this may seem impossible, the look on that student's face and what I witnessed myself led me to believe that it surely could have happened. In other classes, I found teachers who demanded that their students engage in learning and who worked hard to educate them. I remember one who had students building bridges and testing them for their strength. The students in that class were very focused and excited about the project.

Harding seemed full of contradictions. It had received national recognition for the efforts of one teacher to accelerate the learning of students. It had been at the heart of the Chicana/o movement to achieve educational empowerment in the 1960s. And it was one of the first high schools to offer courses focused on the Chicana/o experience. At the same time, it seemed that the vast majority of students in 1996 were unaffected by these aspects of Harding and remained "at risk." Many of the students felt, for example, that the racial tension created by Proposition 187 was mirrored in their own interactions with teachers.

I experienced similar feelings when I returned to the local community college campus. It had been a stronghold for Chicana/o student organizing in the 1980s, and as a college student, I had been there more than once to attend Chicana/o student events. When I entered the classrooms for the first time as a researcher, I was overwhelmed by the commitment of the students. Most worked full-time, many had gone on to get GEDs after dropping out of high school, and a great number were raising families. They were fighting to get an education that would help them improve the lot of their own children. I was also shocked by much of what I saw in the classrooms, however. While the students were often very committed to their schooling, many of their professors lacked that same dedication. I sat in on some classes in which it was clear that the students were not going to be prepared for university-level work even though this was the reason that they were attending the college. As at Harding, however, there were also teachers who were pushing their students to engage in a learning process that would not only prepare them for university work but also show them how to combine their personal lives and their schooling in empowering ways. Still, I was concerned. Many of the students said that they would pursue graduate and professional degrees, but most were unaware of how hard it would be for them to overcome the educational deficits they were developing while at this college.

The university was a different story. It is a top-notch school in an upscale area of Los Angeles. The vast majority of the students are white and Asian American, while Latinas/os made up a much smaller percentage of the student body and community than was the case at the community college and Harding. The students were fairly well engaged in their classes, and the professors were typically quite committed to their students and enthusiastic about their teaching. What is striking, of course, is the dramatic differences between schooling and life at the university and schooling and life in the community college and Harding. I wondered how the students at the university felt about this situation, given that many had come from East Los Angeles and other similar neighborhoods. I recalled my own struggles dealing with a similar culture clash during my time as a college student. The university students, however, had a fairly well-developed Chicana/o infrastructure that they could rely on. The university offered a lot of hope, although the relatively low number of Chicanas/os enrolled there cast a shadow of concern over that hope.

These observations, as helpful as they may be for the reader, were all firmly grounded in my own perspectives, biases, and understanding of school and its meaning. I had not gone to these schools to develop observational or even ethnographic insights. I was there to learn from the insights and analyses of the students themselves. I wanted to know what they knew and what any of that had to do with their identities and their school performance. This chapter considers what the students said about their own identities. It begins with a brief look at a number of issues raised in preliminary surveys. It then focuses on what students said in interviews and ends with a framework for understanding Chicana/o identity formation that is grounded in all of the students' experiences. Thus, although the early sections provide information on the responses of many students to specific issues, these findings are not intended to speak to the entire sample, whereas the conclusions are informed by the whole sample.

LOS ANGELES CHICANA/O STUDENTS' IDENTITY FORMATIONS

In the preliminary surveys, the Los Angeles students demonstrated that their identities were largely shaped by the unique contexts in which they lived. Two important facets of Chicana/o students' social identities that almost immediately emerged for many were school-based identities and familial-based identities. These were key aspects of how the students see themselves in their social world, although they were not the most central aspects. That is, for most students the familial identity was a grounding force in their lives, and they found solace and release in their familial roles, while school was seen as important because it was a potential means toward change and improving their condition in life. However, students did not view these two identities as critical to themselves, because of other social issues with which they were often confronted. The most common way Chicana/o students defined themselves in their social world was through other arenas of identity, and it was the identities that emerged in these other areas that both shaped school identities and were guided by familial identities. What follows is a brief glimpse at each of the areas of potential identity formation considered by Chicana/o students, which is succeeded by an in-depth model explaining the forces that led them to place importance on some areas of identity over others.[1]

Religious/Spiritual Identities

Despite the importance that conventional research places on religion in Mexicana/o and Chicana/o populations, the students themselves did not emphasize religion or religious issues in their lives. Many students practice religion regularly, but few saw it as a central component of their identities (only half of the university students, 26 percent of the college students, and 6 percent of both high school freshmen and seniors discussed the importance of a religious issue in any way). Rather, religion is viewed as an assumed part of who they are, and it is given little thought or emphasis in daily life beyond its ritual, often unconscious aspects. Interestingly, the most common discussions about religion in the surveys (reflected most often in university students' responses) emphasized that students were questioning their religion (usually Catholicism) and had problems with the teachings and/or practices of the church. Some students had stopped practicing their religion altogether, while others had looked to their indigenous roots for a new spiritual grounding. Regardless, in almost every case, religion was not a core facet of how students defined themselves or of the identities they had developed over the course of their lives.

Community Identities

Community played a similar role to that of religion/spirituality in identity formation, but community was given slightly greater significance. Although many students (about 30 percent at each site) felt that the issues

44

of their communities were important to them (particularly those related to gang violence and drug dealing), these issues were not central to the students' identity formations nor were they major influences on the students' social worlds. Students were concerned about younger siblings and their safety but also felt that they could do little about these concerns beyond simply keeping themselves and their families safe. Other students had strong bonds to their communities and took pride in them, but for the most part these feelings were secondary to other aspects of their identities. The few students whose communities played a fundamental role in the formation of their identities were those with strong affiliations to gangs. Gang affiliations are typically based on physical location, and thus their local community was critical to their social identities as gang members. Still, for the vast majority of the students, community itself was not central to their social identities.

Sexuality-Based Identities

Sexuality is another of the less significant realms of identity formation for the majority of Chicana/o students. Most students did not give any thought to the role of sexuality in their daily experiences, and this assumed aspect of their lives played no role in their identity formations. A small number of students (5 percent and 8 percent in the community college and the university, respectively), however, placed a great deal of significance on the role of sexuality in their identity formations. The Chicanas/os who discussed the centrality of sexuality in their identities were all gay and lesbian students, and they explained that this was the core, and often the only pertinent aspect, of their social identities. For them, who they were was defined almost entirely by their sexuality and, for many, by the covert and overt discrimination they experienced from both Chicanas/os and mainstream society, a factor that heavily determined their experiences as gays and lesbians.

Gender Identities

Like sexuality, gender often played an assumed or even an unconscious role in the identity formations of Chicanas/os, although it was of much greater significance in the overall identity formations of the students than the above-mentioned identity categories (27 percent of high school freshmen, 44 percent of high school seniors, 62 percent of community college students, and 75 percent of university students referred to the importance of gender issues to them). Both males and females cited gender as an important issue. Although a smaller number of males mentioned gender issues, those who did so reported that they are burdened with more severe stereotypes as minority males (by store owners and the police, for example) and with greater expectations about providing for their families. Males did not deem these as central arenas of their identities but rather considered them simply as issues they had faced. Like the males, the Chicanas often linked the salience of gender in their identity formations to their experiences as racial/ethnic minorities. A number of the Chicanas more deeply emphasized the role of gender and gender biases within the Chicana/o community. Interestingly, however, their experiences were deemed to be normal aspects of the Chicana experience and were even regarded as unchangeable by many, a perception that echoed other students' discussions of gang violence. These Chicanas said they observed and even experienced gender bias, but it was not a central emphasis in their lives or a key facet of their identity. This lack of emphasis was due to a perception of gender bias as unchangeable, which seemed to underlie their feelings, and to the view, held by many of them, that gender bias was entrenched in racial issues that were more central to their identity formations at that point in their lives.

Class Identities

Class was one of the least significant aspects of identity for Chicana/o students. The students (three-fourths of whom were working-class) acknowledged that class issues, like community issues, were a reality in their experiences, but these issues were never central to how they defined themselves nor to the issues they felt were most pertinent in their lives. Thus the students mentioned economic hardships faced by their families, but each of the class-based issues they raised was seen as the product of specific circumstances that they and their families would change through continued effort. Most of the students who focused on class issues in any significant way, however, did so by integrating issues of race into these discussions. That is, they discussed the class position and economic hardships faced by Chicanas/os as a function of their race. In these cases, the economic issues discussed were important to the students and part of how they defined themselves, but it was the racial aspect of their identity that they emphasized. The class identities of 8 percent of community college students and 14 percent of university students, however, had more developed class identities, grounded in an awareness of economic inequality in society.

Racial/Ethnic Identities

Racial and ethnic identities were the core of the students' identities (the distinctions between ethnic and racial identities are covered in the next section, "Racialization, Intersection, and Identity"). When students discussed the issues that are important to them, roughly 70 percent referred to racism. When they talked about the most severe difficulties they had faced, 12 percent of freshmen, 35 percent of seniors, 49 percent of community college students, and 73 percent of university students referred to race issues. Even when they merely explained who they were in their own minds, race and ethnicity were most often at the center of their discussions. Students talked primarily about the significance of racial discrimination and differential treatment on the basis of race. These issues and experiences were not only important to them but also central to how they defined themselves. This centrality became clear when students were asked simply what they are—17 percent of freshmen, 31 percent of seniors, 36 percent of community college students, and 54 percent of university students answered with a racial or ethnic descriptor. The significance of these figures is even greater when we consider the number of students who did not provide responses indicative of social identities but rather focused on personal characteristics (65 percent of freshmen, 31 percent of seniors, 27 percent of community college students, and 14 percent of university students). It is also important to note the students' self-chosen ethnic labels. The most striking findings with regard to these labels are that many students used multiple labels throughout their discussions; suggesting that even individuals exhibit a significant degree of variation in the use of labels. Most important, of course, is that their social identities were most frequently grounded in their racial/ethnic experiences and identities.

Summary

In short, Chicana/o students revealed critical patterns both in the arenas of identity formation that were important to their social sense of self and in the intersections of these different areas. Although the students had all been touched in some way by each of the areas of identity formation addressed here, many of these identity-related issues were not crucial to how they viewed themselves in their social world.[2] Each of these issues and areas of identity formation is therefore a part of their lives, but most are not critical to students' social identities, and some are important only as they are interpreted through the lens of another facet of identity.

Overall, the survey data suggest that racial/ethnic identity is the pivotal arena of Chicana/o students' social identities.

RACIALIZATION, INTERSECTION, AND IDENTITY

The reality of Chicana/o students' identity formations is far more complex than the preceding brief explanations portray. Many of the students, for example, blended their discussions of the different aspects of their social identities. Chicana students, for example, discussed gender issues when asked about racial/ethnic issues and vice versa. To a lesser extent, Chicanas/os integrated their discussions of their racial and class-based experiences and identities. It is in the interview data that the nuances of identity, its formation, and its most significant influences were revealed.

First, the interviews, like the surveys, showed that race is by far the most dominant facet of students' identities. Nine of the 13 students interviewed brought up race as a central part of their development. Two students provided examples of this when they were asked to specify which of a number of issues was important to who they were:

> [Race is] really the basis of who I am. Like, I mean class will always change. You can get poor. . . . You can always change everything, to a certain degree, but your ethnicity is who you really are. It's not something that's instilled in you. . . . You're basically born into it.

> I have to say race, ethnicity, and culture. And the reason why my race is very important to me [is because it's] my roots, where I come from. . . . With culture, it all stems from heritage for me. Things that my ancestors went through. . . . I believe that my culture is being targeted in [an] immigrant-bashing type of way.

Although the students interpreted race/ethnicity in many different ways, it was clearly the dominant theme in their discussions and usually with reference to the sociopolitical position of Chicanas/os (grounded in the larger context of racial discrimination). As one student explained, race/ethnicity is something that most Chicanas/os can neither avoid nor change.

In addition, 5 of the 13 students interviewed felt that their socioeconomic status was a key part of their development and who they were

(4 of them felt that it was central), but 3 of these students viewed class as part of their ethnic or racial experience. One student provided a good example as she described experiences and issues that dealt with class, but she also integrated race issues into the discussion:

> [Class] was the big problem for me as I was growing up. Because I've always been discriminated [against]. We grew up in a upper-middle-class environment, and we were the only minorities, my sister and I, growing up, with most of the student population [in] elementary school being Anglo. . . . And growing up, I always felt like an outcast. They would say racial remarks like "wetback," and [another Chicana's] name was Rosa, so they used to call her "Rosarita Beans." Things like that, so class was a big problem for me because even when I went to my girlfriends' house, they lived in these big houses up in the hills, where[as] we lived in a small little underdeveloped, I guess, impoverished house where my mom kind of always made us feel embarrassed for living there. She never liked us bringing friends over. . . . So class in that sense, that was a big problem for me growing up.

Another student described in more detail how Chicanas/os link race and class:

> I mean race, race was important. Races fighting against other races and being put down. . . . And the different levels of society. You've got your upper class, middle class, and lower class. Most of the lower class is two races, Mexican and black. Middle class, you've got your Orientals, some whites, some Mexicans and stuff. . . . And your upper class: all the white-collar society. All your executives [are] mostly Anglo. . . . When I started working, I was working in a bank and I'd see the separation. I'd see supervisors—the majority of supervisors were all white. You know they were the decision makers. They handled your money, they handled your paycheck. . . . It was hard for someone of a different race to climb that ladder. You saw more white people getting promoted, more white people getting the job spots and all that. That's when I started seeing that this ain't right.

As these examples show, while students brought up other realms of potential identity formation that were involved in their development, many of these realms were embedded within the construct of (if not confused with) race itself in their discussions. Class, for example, was most often deemed, either consciously or subconsciously, as something that is a part of or defined by being Chicana/o, as seen in the two excerpts above.

Later, when asked whether the different realms of identity were linked in their lives, students explained how race encompassed many of the different realms of identity formation. One student gave his view of how the different facets of identity are linked when he was asked if the issues he had been discussing were connected or distinct:

> I'd say distinct in their definition but connected in their function. . . . Well, I can give you a definition of each one of these issues, like what it means to me, like separately. But if I discuss gender, sexuality is going to come up, class is going to come up, spirituality and religion is going to come up, community is going to come up, race and ethnicity is going to come up. I can't talk about one without the other. They're all connected in the way they operate, in the way they affect me.

In fact, 7 students felt as if all of the different realms of identity formation were related and mentioned this idea within their discussion of specific issues. Specifically, race was seen by many as encompassing class, religion, family, community, and gender. Similarly, when students were asked about the importance and impact of particular aspects of their racial/ethnic experience, they also lumped these aspects into their larger racial experience, so that issues like language background, immigrant status, and skin color were not central to identity formation beyond their use by non-Chicanas/os as criteria for determining the students' racial status and were all therefore related to racial discrimination.

Two students did a good job of describing what they and their peers meant when they linked the different realms of identity. As one student said, the family incorporates a number of different areas of students' identity development. She referred specifically to religion, sexuality, gender, and class within the cultural aspects of family life and identity formation. Another student was more specific as he explained that there are different categories within the linkages of these different identity themes. He linked gender, race, and sexuality as related identity themes in their connections to discrimination, and he then linked community, class, religion, and race (again) as a more general area of identity development.

> They're all connected. . . . I think I would view, like, community, class, race, and religious spirituality more in one sense. Gender, sexuality, and then race would be kind of more in terms of discrimination that's going on out there. . . . I would say, like, gender, sexuality, and race in terms of discrimination; others . . . community, class, race, and spirituality are more separate.

This student cut to the heart of the distinctions within students' identity development, suggesting that their racial/ethnic experiences can be perceived in two ways: as political in response to discrimination (racial identity) and as cultural (ethnic identity), although he does not emphasize the latter aspect.[3] The political facet of this identity is linked to discrimination and therefore to gender and sexuality (depending on the individual), whereas the cultural aspects are linked to family, community, class, and religion. Still, no black-and-white categorization of these different areas is possible, for specific experiences shape individuals in different ways. Class, for example, was typically incorporated within students' interpretations of their experiences as Chicanas/os, but for many it was linked more to the cultural aspects of these experiences than to political, discrimination-based aspects, simply because most students did not have a class consciousness. One student, however, clearly interpreted class as a political issue, and his configuration of identity linkages reflected that understanding. Similarly, gender can be seen both as cultural and as political, depending on the individual. In fact, only a few students felt that gender and gender discrimination were crucial issues they *had* to deal with, whereas most saw gender and differential treatment of males and females as being embedded in local, familial histories and not addressable. This is not to suggest that gender is never a crucial arena of identity formation for Chicanas/os. Rather, gender most often becomes central in Chicanas' identities when power is asserted across gender lines in ways that parallel or exceed the exertion of racial power. It is critical to acknowledge that the unique gender dynamics within the Chicana/o community (e.g., the often-discussed role of machismo) are not central to how most students define themselves, because other facets of identity formation are more dominant in their eyes.

The most important finding overall, then, is that two distinct realms of identity formation exist within the Chicana/o student population: the political and the cultural. Not all students have both, however. Furthermore, as students describe themselves and their identities, they reveal that, in their eyes, their ethnic-cultural identity is that part of their experience as Chicanas/os that is local and embedded in the lives of all Chicanas/os, and so it is an assumed facet of identity. Therefore it is the racial-political identity that is the most dominant in the self-perceptions of Chicanas/os. Their sense of social self evolves from experiences with, and observations of, discrimination in their communities and schools. It is also reinforced through the life experiences of their families and their own experiences with racial confrontation.

POWER AND IDENTITY FORMATION

Despite the prevalence of a central racial identity among Chicana/o students, the social identities of some of these students are not grounded in their race or ethnicity. It is in looking at these students—comparing the whole of their experiences with those of the others—that we can begin to understand the forces at work in Chicana/o identity formation. First, by returning to the students whose social identities were most firmly grounded in race, we can understand the means by which their identities are shaped.

As might be expected, those students with strong racial identities are deeply influenced by their social contexts. The two primary means of influence are interracial interactions (in interracial contexts or in all-Chicana/o contexts with authority figures of a different race) and parental influence. All of the Chicana/o students who had developed a strong racial identity had experienced interactions with members of another race during which it was made obvious that they were in a position of inferior status and power. Additionally, some of these students had a parent who had helped them negotiate these experiences and reinforced the importance of race through positive messages. The role of context in identity formation therefore is based primarily on the particular context to which a Chicana/o student is exposed. Background characteristics like immigrant status and socioeconomic status influenced identity formation, but mainly as they affected the individual's interracial interactions and the importance that parents placed on factors such as education and race, for example.

In a number of instances, students talked specifically about the racial confrontations that had been critical to their process of identity formation. Ernesto (who is integral to the next two chapters) discussed the significance of race in both elementary and junior high school:

> We had a substitute one day [in sixth grade], and everybody, the whole class, was messing around, it was a ruckus. And the teacher came up to me and she said, "If you don't like it, you can go back where you came from." And then she told that to my friend, and we were the only two Mexicans in the class and I think there was one black guy. . . . And so that was the theme of the day, like every time everybody else messed up, it was "Shut up, shut up!" but when we messed up, it was "Go back to Mexico!" And so we already knew by sixth grade, I guess we were already socialized like not to make a big deal out of it. . . . And in junior high it was more evident. You know, like if you ditched, they had to call the cops.

But if a white kid ditched, they would just send X teacher to go get him. So that was different. I was constantly suspended, expelled.

Susana (who is also featured in Chapter 2) related a somewhat less direct, racialized incident whose connotations, however, were quite clear to her:

I was still worried about whether or not I was going to [get into the university]. I mean, I graduated with like a three-nine [3.9 GPA]. But I was still really worried . . . probably because I had a counselor, who I despised, in high school. I told her I wanted to go to [the university], and she saw my grades and she said, "You know, I don't think you're going to get into [the university]," and she said, "But you might, because you are a minority, so you might get in." And I thought, I know it plays a big part, but it still really upset me that she said that. . . . I had good grades and she was just like, "I don't know if you'll get in, but you might because you're Mexican."

Some students also described the importance of the messages conveyed by family members to their dealing with these issues and their identity formation itself. For example, Liz (a high school student who shares more in Chapter 2) provided the following explanation when she was asked where her pride, which she had mentioned earlier, came from:

My uncle, because he was like another father. He was the kind that'd listen to you, and like you could say whatever you wanted to him and he would help you out, just tell you, "You're Mexican and you have to be proud of it 'cause that's who you are." My grandpa too, he sat me and my *nina* down to talk about where we come from so that later on it won't be a question to us.

Finally, other students related stories of powerful racial confrontations outside of school that were critical to their evolving views of themselves. Diego (a high school student who also appears in Chapter 2) talked about incidents he and his father had experienced:

A lot of the cops, they treat me bad. . . . Me and my friend, we were in my car and they stopped us. I turned off the car and he told me to turn down the radio, and I turned it down, and for no reason he took out a gun and put it on my head. And both of 'em [the police officers] were white. And my friend had a beanie with the Mexican eagle on the front. [The cop] took off his beanie; he threw it on the floor and stepped on it. And he pulled me out of the car and then he put my hands on my back. He took out that little black [rubber stick]. . . . And he smacked me in the head with it, and he told me that we were in [a white neighborhood] and . . . what were we doing over there, that we belong in [the barrio], that over here that it's pure white people . . . and that us wetbacks should go back over there. . . . But there's nothing I could do about it. It's just hate—that's why. . . . My dad too, they treat him bad. Because they arrested my dad because supposedly he was hitting my mom, but it was just a neighbor calling because they were arguing. And they were two white cops too, and they tied my dad from the hands and feet and they dragged him all the way to the cop car.

These descriptions provide clear evidence of the types of racial confrontations and issues that lead to strong racial identities among Chicana/o students, while they also help us better understand the identity formations of the other Chicana/o students.

Victor, a university student who did not have a racialized identity, had a sense of social self that was firmly grounded in his sexuality. The importance of sexuality in his identity construction evolved from his being gay. Being gay had had a significant impact on him in that his sexual orientation was the basis of confrontations with others in various arenas of his life. It is interesting that this student also attended high school with a predominantly white student body and that both of his parents had strong Chicana/o identities, as embodied through their beliefs and jobs (both of these factors contribute to strong ethnic identity formation in other Chicana/o students). As Victor explained, however, an overriding factor in his experience was that he shared the socioeconomic background of the upper-middle-class students in the private school he attended. This was important because he felt he had a great deal in common with his fellow classmates and that he could identify with them (which was not the case with other Chicanas/os who went to school with a majority of whites from a significantly higher class background). Furthermore, this student never encountered racial bias or discrimination from his teachers or peers, although his physical characteristics made it clear that he was Chicano. In fact, it is only with regard to his sexuality that he ever faced any form of bias or discrimination, and it is in that context that he was made aware of his lower status and lack of power as a result of being gay. Similarly, one of the other students whose social identity was not grounded in her ethnicity also lived and went to school with a majority of white students who shared her same class background. She too felt a common bond with her classmates, and the core of her identity was actually based in aspirations for upward mobility. Both of these cases suggest that when Chicana/o students attend school and reside in neighborhoods where they are one of only a few Chicanas/os (or other minorities) and where they share the class backgrounds of their peers, they might not have experiences with discrimination and bias that force them to acknowledge the lack of power they have as Chicanas/os.

Two other students grew up and attended schools in predominantly Chicana/o contexts but did not develop central racial identities. Neither of them had experienced or witnessed any form of racial discrimination. The first student reported that he had led a fairly sheltered life in which most of his time was spent in a tight circle of family members, with whom he interacts almost exclusively. The second student, although she had not faced racial discrimination, had been made aware of gender bias through observations of her family and of her mother's struggles. The issue of gender bias is clear in her world, and she has felt its constraints in her own life by the lack of power she is granted as a female.

Thus, in looking at the lives of all 13 of these Chicana/o students, who represent a variety of different experiences in and out of school, we can see that power is central to their identity formations. The students' encounters with power were clearest in those arenas of their social world in which they had little or no power. This does not mean that other influences were nonexistent, but simply that they were less important facets of the students' identities. In fact, virtually all arenas of potential identity formation affected most of the students. That some students are considered the norm in a specific social realm (e.g., with regard to gender or sexuality) often makes these arenas unconscious aspects of who students are. These are not fundamental means by which they identify themselves, simply because it is around social difference that these individuals define who they are and are outwardly defined by others, particularly when this difference is coupled with some form of subjugation.

Ernesto provided a good example of the role of power in defining his experience as a member of a racial minority:

> When I went to high school, like that's where everybody goes, the *raza*, the black, brown, everybody. So then I started seeing my Chicano friends and started hanging out with them, and that was probably one of the first times I really thought about race because I noticed the difference. Because when I hung out with white dudes, like X white boy was "big nose," you know, you joke around. This white boy was "big butt". . . and I was always "beaner." Like that was the joke. . . . It was, like, good-hearted, so

I thought, but then I thought about it and thought, "No, that's bullshit! That's fucking racist!" And so then I just told all my white friends, "Shine you," and started hanging with the Mexicans again. And they always said, "Oh, look. He changed. He became a gang member," you know; that's what the white dudes would say. And like, to me, I was kind of like reacting against the way they treated me. And I was hanging with the Mexicans and we were a smaller number, so, you know, you have to defend yourself some way, so we were numbers. You know, white boys got . . . the [new] Jeeps and the [new] Honda Accords and stuff and they were so cool, you know. And the only thing we had was power. We were like, you don't walk by the tree. White boys walk by the tree, you get fucked up.

This student helps us understand not only the means by which power is used to define Chicana/o social identity (externally), but also how some Chicanas/os reacted to their lack of sanctioned, institutional power by taking physical power over their immediate surroundings.[4] As one student excerpt detailed earlier, race is a facet of identity that cannot be changed. It cannot be avoided, because not only is difference obvious, but it is also reinforced through power and concretized borders that separate whites and Chicanas/os, males and females, and heterosexuals and homosexuals.

In essence, these students exposed the reality of border identities. While the physical border between the United States and Mexico marks a clear distinction between power and subordination, the Chicana/o experience is almost always blatantly stamped by symbolic borders conveying the same message. Just as Mexican residents (especially those who live near the border) are made well aware of the line in the sand that marks the fundamental distinctions in power held between the United States and Mexico, Chicanas/os are made aware of factors that distinguish them from other "Americans" of the dominant society with regard to power along race, class, gender, and other lines. The power held by whites, males, and heterosexual society demarcates difference and, in turn, defines their social selves. Just as the U.S.-Mexican border may eventually be marked by an "impenetrable" wall designed to ensure that Mexicans cannot cross that boundary, Chicanas/os are socialized to understand that they cannot cross the social borders that mark their identities in the United States.

Although most Chicanas/os develop racial identities fairly early on in their lives as a function of their exposure to racial difference, bias, and/or discrimination, their racial identities are cast and hardened through experience and an evolving familiarity with the invisible but blatant borders of power dominating their existence. This phenomenon is reflected in the more well-developed racial identities of the university students. Through their daily life in a predominantly white institution that discourages difference, these students have had greater and more intense experiences fighting to maintain a positive sense of self, given the side of the power border to which they have been relegated. The influence of these racial borders is further evidenced by the finding that, in those arenas where the borders of power are less evident or less emphasized—such as class, community, and religion—the possibility for concretized social identities grounded in these areas is minimized. Still, as some students revealed, other power borders exist—with regard to gender and sexuality, for example—that are made more obvious to certain individuals and that correspondingly become central to their identities.

CONCLUSION

The experiences of Los Angeles Chicana/o students in 1996 help us understand the complexities of Chicana/o identity and the means by which power and its borders govern the formation of their sense of who they are—their social selves. This analysis provides insights into the evolution of Chicana/o identity, as we come to understand the separation of ethnic-cultural and racial-political identity formations. As the students themselves pointed out, they were engaged in a number of different social realms that were affected by an equally diverse number of social characteristics. Although issues like class, community, religion, and culture are important parts of students' lives, their identities become crystallized in those areas of their world in which social difference is made quite apparent to them—by virtue of their lack of power along a given axis, as evidenced through interactions that are often grounded in discrimination. For the majority of Chicana/o students, their being made well aware of their lack of power as racialized people becomes critical to their understanding of their place in the world. This realization is the means by which many of these students then define their own identities.

TWO

IDENTITY AND SCHOOL
PERFORMANCE IN LOS ANGELES

More powerful than the individual stories about how identity evolved for Chicana/o students in East Los Angeles is how these experiences affected them. Conflicts related to their disempowerment shaped not only how they saw themselves but also how they understood their schooling and their educational futures. At times I was overwhelmed by the students' stories. Diego's story is just one of them:

> The dean [at the school] got me for wearing big pants, and he made, like, a comment. I go, "What are you going to send me home for?" He goes, " 'Cause of your pants." I guess he was new. And he told me to go to see my dean so he could give me a note so I could go home. And I go, "I'm not going to go home. Nah, 'cause these pants aren't big." And they *weren't* big. And he goes, "You know what? You're not in *your* house. You're in *my* house now. And you're going to do whatever I tell you." And I go, "What? Where do you come up with that? Who's talking about that?" He goes, " 'Cause you're not rolling with your homies now. You're in *my* house, and you're going to do whatever I tell you." And I got mad. I really did get mad, and I was going to fight with him. And I told him, "You think you're bad because you're in here. But outside over there, in the streets, you won't talk to me like that. And you know why. Because, like your people tell us, 'You don't belong here!' You don't belong here neither." And he goes, "Oh, you think you're a smart mouth, huh?" I go, "Well, you're the one that started telling me stuff. I was gonna go talk to the dean, and you're the one that started telling me stuff." And he told me, "Right here you're talking all back to me and all that, but I bet you when you're outside over there with your homies, you're nothing but chicken shit." And that's when I was already going to go after him, but then my

dean came. And he [asked], "What's wrong, Diego?" and I go, "Well, you heard, everybody heard, the secretaries heard, the students over there, they heard." He goes, "You know, Diego, here's a pass. Go to your class." I go, "See? All of that just for you to tell me to go to class. Why did he have to tell me all of that when my dean could have just came out and just tell me, 'Here, go to your class'?" But none of that would have happened if he would have just came out or something, but that teacher, he shouldn't have said that neither. He shouldn't have. Because I do think there's a little bit of racism in school too. I do.

I was in class a lot, when I was in tenth or eleventh grade and, like, I didn't feel like working, and the teacher, he was a white teacher too, and he told everybody to open their books and read this and this, right? So I was reading and then I didn't feel like reading no more so I put it aside and I started drawing. And I was drawing and he told me, "Diego, this is not your art class. Put it away." And I go, "All right." So then I put it away and I just stood like that and the book was just there. And then he went to the desk and he called me. And I go, "I was quiet." He called me up and he goes, "Diego, come here." And I went, and he goes, "Is there a problem, Diego?" I go, "No, there's not, sir." He goes, "Why aren't you doing your work?" I go, "'Cause I don't want to read, sir." He goes, "*What?* You don't know how to read English?" And like that, it clicked right there. That got me mad. I go, "What?" He goes, "Well, you don't know how to read English." And I go, "What do you mean by that?" He goes, "You know." And I got mad. I didn't talk back to him, and then I walked away. I got my books and everything. I was walking out of class, and he goes, "Diego, come here." And I didn't listen to him, and I just walked out. And later on after, he went to my fourth-period class, and he took me out of class and he apologized and everything. And the teacher, the one that I was in a fight with, he apologized too. Both of them apologized. But it's not like if I started anything because I don't.

I had seen the way race affected the school lives of Chicanas/os when I was a teacher, but I rarely had the chance to talk in-depth with students about these issues and to see how they made sense of them. In some ways, many of my worst fears were confirmed in these interviews. Many students described their school lives as a history of psychological attacks, and as Diego suggests, the racist underpinnings of these attacks can be overwhelming for Chicana/o teens. At the same time, these students were all surviving and provided compelling stories of determination and strength.

This chapter takes a different approach from that of Chapter 1. After an initial description of the model that emerged from Chapter 1, in-depth analyses of students' experiences expand the framework. The in-depth interviews with six students (those who were available for both preliminary and follow-up interviews) provide the most insightful information regarding the forces at work in Chicana/o educational performance. For these students, four critical areas of their experience were most central to their educational performance: the racial-political climate in which they lived and went to school; the degree of conflict they experienced from daily life in that climate; the nature and role of their identities (which were grounded in these experiences); and the degree of contextualized educational mentoring they received. At a more complex level, the power dynamics in their schools and communities were major forces that influenced each of these features of their experience (the model developed in Chapter 7 details this process). As with the frameworks developed by Alva and Padilla (1995) and Arellano and Padilla (1996), the students explained that, in their eyes, these are the central forces that shaped their school experiences, their own beliefs and understandings about schooling, and even their educational performance. As we will see, the complexity of these influences is far greater than the simple list suggests.

What is important and unique about this analysis is that it is entirely grounded in the students' own categorizations and discussions of what influenced their school lives. Most often, I simply asked them general, open-ended questions about their school lives. The fundamental difficulty in describing the nature and impact of these different influences is that they are interwoven and inseparable. In the following discussion, I will attempt to address each area separately, but the heart of the findings will be covered subsequently as we consider the intersections of these different forces and their impact on school performance for each of these individuals.

RACIAL-POLITICAL CLIMATE

The racial-political climate in which Chicana/o students live and (in particular) attend school is critical primarily as it affects the nature of the other forces underlying their school performance (degree of conflict experienced, nature and role of identity, and degree of contextualized educational mentoring). The racial-political school context defines how Chicana/o students fit or do not fit in at school. Although traditional analyses of the role of context and climate have focused on factors like available resources and gangs, of possibly even greater importance are the demographics within the school and the degree of distance between the racial and class status of the authority figures and that of the students. When Chicana/o students attend school in a context in which it is clear to them that they are distinguished from the authority figures in the school by class, race, or both, this situation can have a significant impact on the connection that they make to their schooling. Students are not blind to the subtle and sometimes overt messages that are conveyed when their home lives, culture, language, and experiences are deemed irrelevant and even detrimental to school success and success in society at large. If a Chicana/o student is made aware that she or he is racially and socioeconomically distinct (and inferior) from the authority figures (which can also include other students if the status of these students is more highly regarded), this racial-political climate can be linked to feeling a lack of ownership of the schooling process and to feeling distance between self and school. As was explained earlier, however, this type of climate does not in and of itself translate into student failure or success. Rather, it is one factor that shapes and influences the remainder of the equation.

DEGREE AND NATURE OF CONFLICT RELATED TO THE RACIAL-POLITICAL CLIMATE

The degree and nature of conflict resulting from the racial-political climate encountered by Chicana/o students are central to their school performance. Given that the encouragement and support that Chicana/o students receive tends to be limited, it is the degree of conflict they face that often becomes fundamental to their school success or failure. When Chicana/o students experience some form of racial conflict, it often initiates or solidifies their understanding of the significant limits on their opportunities for educational success. Such experiences help students explain the more subtle messages they had been receiving in school when they were, often unconsciously, learning that being Chicana/o meant that they were not expected to succeed in school. For many students, racial conflicts in the school lead them to commit their energies to other interests besides school, such as family, jobs, friends, gangs, and the like. Of course, other distractions in their immediate contexts are related to Chicana/o disinterest in school and even failure. It is important, however, to challenge the notion that these other distractions (family problems, gang involvement, and so on) are the critical factors involved in the failure of Chicana/o students. The students in this study suggest that oftentimes the racial conflicts they experience lead them to dedicate increasing attention to other issues or distractions because they have clearly received the message that they are unwelcome in the school. In fact, other students experience the same distractions away from school but ignore or escape them by immersing themselves in school, because they are able to make sense of the racial-political climate they experience and to create a positive role for themselves in the school. The importance of these conflicts then is central to the students' experiences and intricately tied to identity issues.

IDENTITY

For many Chicana/o students, not only is identity a pivotal issue in their school experience, but it is also bound to their motivations in school. As has been noted, Chicana/o students are quite often confronted with their subordinate role in school as a function of their race and class. Many students recounted experiences (typically in junior high or early in high school) when they were engaged in a racial confrontation with a teacher or administrator or sometimes with another student. These experiences were crucial in the formation of their social identity because it was made clear to them that they are "different." These experiences demanded that the students develop a strategy to deal with them. In most cases, students had to reorganize their sense of self, because who they are racially had become a critical part of who they are in the school. Many students therefore began to develop an identity that valued their ethnic background and even pushed it to the forefront of how they saw themselves, while simultaneously devaluing the need for that identity to be linked to school success, for it is often made clear to them that the two cannot be related. Olsen (1997) supports the patterns I found in working with Chicana/o students; she provided a powerful analysis of the way in which race/identity plays one of the most significant roles in the educational experiences of all youth. For many Chicana/o students in this project, in fact, the racial confrontations they experienced were the central distraction they faced, and the lack of strong support not only in their families but also blatantly from their teachers, led to dramatic disinterest in school and subsequent failure, all of which became incorporated into their identities. Other students used their identity as a tool for interpreting this racial conflict, and it became the motivation for their pursuit of school success. The difference between these two types of students is best understood through their access to mentoring.

CONTEXTUALIZED EDUCATIONAL
MENTORING

As school personnel and researchers have always emphasized, the degree of encouragement and support a student has is critical to educational performance. The experiences of the Chicana/o students in this study suggest not just the importance of this encouragement but also the need for encouragement that is grounded in the social context in which Chicana/o students live.

All of the successful Chicana/o students in the study had some form of strong encouragement for their school success. For the most part, all Chicana/o students experienced some form of parental encouragement for school success. Still, the nature of this encouragement differed greatly from student to student. Most parents provided encouragement by emphasizing the importance of school to their children's future. Their encouragement often did not go further than that (e.g., they did not monitor and facilitate completion of schoolwork, they did not become involved in the school, and they did not actively plan the student's future). Historically, schools and researchers have blamed a culture of poverty and the corresponding lack of parental interest in schooling for the failure of working-class youth, like the majority of the Chicana/o students participating in this project (Romo and Falbo 1996 and Olsen 1997 provide strong evidence of this through their interactions with school personnel). In contrast, the nature of parental encouragement for the Chicana/o participants is not directly explained by the socioeconomic status of their parents. That is, some working-class parents encouraged their children to succeed in school in very active ways. Furthermore, parental encouragement was often limited, not because of a lack of interest but because of a lack of time and understanding of or comfort in the school system. In addition, Chicana/o students received encouragement from other sources. Some students who did not receive strong parental encouragement received encouragement from siblings, teachers, or a community member. Many successful students suggested that these nonparental forms of encouragement were essential contributors to their success.

More important than simple encouragement for school success is contextualized mentoring, which bases the content and form of mentoring on the unique experiences of a specific student and which links educational goals to identity. The most successful students in this project all had a mentor who not only helped them understand how to achieve their educational goals but also helped them understand that the hostile racial-political climate they experienced—along with the resulting conflicts some had faced—could be challenged by their educational achievement. These mentors showed students why they should make this challenge, how to make it, and the benefits it offered them over other forms of resistance that lead to school failure. In essence, the mentors made sense of the confusing and psychologically painful world in which the students were living and in which their identities had developed, while focusing the students' work on the goal of obtaining school success.

INTERSECTIONS

The critical contribution of Chicana/o students' explanations of their school lives is in the complexities that they suggest underlie their school performance. Typically, schools operate under the belief that Chicana/o students in areas like East Los Angeles do poorly in school because they are not well supported in their families (as a result of minimal parental education and little familial emphasis on the importance of school). Although a general lack of support holds true for many Chicana/o students, the students reveal that other forces are also simultaneously at work in this process. In most cases, Chicana/o parents convey the importance of school to their children, but often other distractions in the home (such as familial financial needs) counterbalance this influence and force Chicana/o youth to divert their attention and energy away from school. At the same time, when the students have someone who provides them with strong encouragement for school success through active involvement in their lives, this influence can easily outweigh the distractions that they experience. Unfortunately, however, still other negative forces are at work in the lives of Chicana/o youth. The struggles that many of these youth face with regard to their race and their social identity (grounded in unsafe racial-political climates) can become the greatest distractions and obstacles in their school experiences. Oftentimes, racially based confrontations with authority figures counterbalance the active, positive encouragement that Chicana/o students might be receiving. Such confrontations push the students toward harmful, resistant stances that lead to their further marginalization in the school. Chicana/o students thus often feel forced to make their race a prominent part of their identity and are unconsciously (but often consciously) informed that this identity cannot incorporate school success. Nevertheless, the role of encouragement can come into play here as well, for those students who have someone to encourage them *and* to help them negotiate the interracial terrain of the school and life in general use these potentially damaging confrontations as additional motivation for success. This sort of guidance can lead them toward an empowering, informed resistance.

In looking at the intricacies of the lives of a number of successful and struggling Chicana/o students, we will see that their school success or failure is not understood simply as a function of their familial support for school performance or of the institutional failures of their schools. Rather, an intricate complex of factors appears to be fundamentally governed by the role of power in Chicana/o students' lives. The critical role of power in influencing the racialized "border identities" of Chicana/o students was discussed in Chapter 1. Power plays an equally critical role in the Chicana/o school experience. As the students revealed, power shapes the contexts and climates of their schools and defines the conflicts that often arise in those contexts, while simultaneously determining much of their identity formation. These influences can be counterbalanced by encouragement, particularly that which addresses the power dynamics at work. These factors all come together to define the larger context that influences school outcomes for Chicana/o youth.

The remainder of this chapter serves as a tour through the social landscape covered by six Chicana/o students living in the Los Angeles area. The individual stories of these students give concrete example to the complexities underlying their school performance. In these stories, we can see that traditional formulas of school success must be rewritten for many Chicana/o students.

ERNESTO

At the time of our last interview, Ernesto was less than a month from graduation at the university and would start a graduate program at the same university with a fellowship the following fall. Considering his success within the framework of traditional Chicana/o educational research, we might expect that he is one of the rare Chicanas/os who falls into the model of strong parental encouragement, exceptional early educational experiences, minimal distractions, and an assimilated ethnic identity. We would be wrong on all counts.

Ernesto is the son of Mexican immigrants. He grew up in a barrio on the west side of Los Angeles. His community, like his own family, was working-class Mexicana/o and Chicana/o and was confronted with the typical problems facing residents of similar barrios throughout the United States: limited opportunities, along with gangs, poverty, and drugs. As Ernesto explained, however, because of where he lived in the barrio, he was one of the few Chicanas/os to attend nearby, predominantly white elementary and middle schools. As Ernesto immediately revealed in his discussions, the interracial climate of his school had a tremendous effect on him. When asked about some of his most memorable and significant early experiences in school, he demonstrated that the subtle and blatant ways in which he was racialized in the school were what most influenced his understanding of the place for him, his family, and his community in the school. He explained that through his enrollment in English as a Second Language (ESL) classes he was classified early on as distinct from the rest of the students, while his teachers and fellow students made him very aware of his difference both racially and with regard to his educational abilities:

> I remember I went through ESL . . . till fifth grade. And I would always get all these awards, you know. They would take me to these big banquets. And it wasn't a big deal to me. Because I was like, "Man, I've been knowing English for a long time." So every year I would go to ESL and I'd be like, "All right [already], I think I'm pretty good at English" . . . because it was a stigma, you know. It's like "OK, it's time for *you people* to go to the ESL class." So that kinda affected me, but, like, it wasn't as bad for me as for others 'cause my friends spoke English whereas other people in the ESL didn't even have any friends who spoke English. So that was kinda heavy.

Although it was difficult for Ernesto to concretely understand and explain the negative impact of his ESL classification at such a young age, he knew that ESL meant that others saw him as inferior to his non-ESL peers. An experience later in elementary school, recounted in Chapter 1, gave clarity to his feelings. A substitute teacher had told him, "Go back to Mexico!" The ease with which he recalled this ten-year-old experience, along with his passion when telling the story, made it clear that this encounter played a significant role in shaping his understanding of who he was in the school.

Before Ernesto reached junior high, he had already been made aware that because of who he was—a working-class Chicana/o—he was not only different but also expendable to the school. The informal segregation he witnessed through ESL gave him a sense (unclear as it was) that he had been stuck in a restricted and stigmatized corner of the world of school. As many students revealed during this project, the linguistic rationale behind student involvement in ESL made it difficult for them to decipher the subtle messages they received about their limited value as ESL students. For Ernesto, the more obvious statements of a substitute teacher helped him understand what had been going on in his elementary schooling, as he realized that it was his race that shaped his role in the school.

Attending a junior high with the same demographic characteristics among its teachers and students only made this more clear to Ernesto. As his comments in Chapter 1 indicated, he quickly saw a system of differential treatment in junior high whereby Chicanas/os faced harsher treatment than their white peers for the same behaviors. He saw that while he was punished with suspensions for actions he engaged in, his white friends never faced the same ramifications for the same kinds of behaviors that got him in trouble. So by junior high Ernesto had not only come to realize that school personnel viewed him as less valuable or even expendable, but he also discovered that different rules applied to him that further limited his ability to survive in the school.

By the time he entered high school, Ernesto had a clear understanding that his place in the school was tenuous. His teachers, administrators, and peers viewed him as a problem both because of his racial and socioeconomic difference and because of rules and enforcement measures established by school personnel that made him an easy target. He told story after story in which the teachers made this racialization clear to him in blatant ways. His response was to take control of his educational experiences by living on the margins of school and finding power in challenging and confronting school personnel, often through his affiliation with a gang.

In short, the context of the school and the blatant differences between the power held by whites (teachers, administrators, students, and parents) and that held by working-class Chicanas/os created a climate in which comparisons were unavoidable. That the comparisons were not made only by Ernesto himself but also by all non-Chicanas/os in both their actions and their words became an unavoidable distraction that made it difficult for Ernesto to feel that school was a place where he fit in or that he could use school to his advantage. Although Ernesto's parents emphasized the importance of education by telling their children to do well, their limited experience and comfort with school meant that this was the extent of the encouragement they provided. As Ernesto explained, his parents had faith in the school staff and entrusted them to make the most educationally sound decisions for their children. Thus, the distractions of interracial difference and conflict overrode this parental influence. Ernesto provided several examples of this process.

I remember, like, this one time there was this teacher who taught architecture. . . . And everybody's [saying,] "Oh, he's the bomb. You got to take it. He's the man." And I didn't realize it, but it was like white and Chinese kids that would say that. So I took him and he was an asshole to me. And he was the one that got me expelled from school because he told me, "I'll never ever listen to you or call on you if you raise your hand." So I was, like, looking for attention, and he walked by my desk and he wouldn't call on me. I had my hand raised. So I stood up on my desk with my hand raised, and he still wouldn't answer me, so when he came back around, I jumped off and I head-butted him. And so I got kicked out of school, and my dad made a big thing of it, and then the principal started talking shit to my dad, and I cussed out the principal and I said, "Don't talk to my dad like that." Because he was being real paternalistic to my dad. And so that's, like, when I was like, "Man, fuck white people. I mean these people are just assholes."

This incident had strong racial connotations for Ernesto because of the way his teacher treated him so differently from the way he treated the white and Asian American students who liked the class so much, and because of the way the teacher treated his father (elsewhere Ernesto referred to the power and respect that white parents held in his schools). His reaction was extreme, but it was the only way Ernesto felt that he could have his own existence acknowledged in a world where he had been silenced in multiple ways. Ernesto began to demonstrate how years of this silencing and the racial conflict and violence he experienced affected his sense of who he was. In the end, he lashed out violently, but his story suggests that he had been the victim of a form of violence that was not physical but was even more powerful. He had been made invisible, and when cornered, he let the school know that he was not going to just let it happen.

Ernesto simultaneously described his evolving resistant identity as he recalled other instances of racial confrontations that he had had with teachers and a coach. During these high school years, he also became more aware of the underlying racism that had been present in his earlier school experiences with white students. In Chapter 1, Ernesto explained that in high school he realized that even his friendships with whites in earlier years had been affected by their racialization of who he was. These friends had nicknamed him "beaner" in a way that was framed as part of being buddies and teasing. By high school, he knew that he could no longer tolerate that kind of behavior. For Ernesto, his identity as a gang member and "troublemaker" (in the eyes of others) was his natural response to the violent racialization and racism he had been forced to ingest through his interactions with teachers, administrators, and even friends. In a subsequent discussion, Ernesto provided further detail of the multifaceted nature of his racialization through his response to the curriculum, when he showed how his identity itself was linked to his academic discomfort and poor performance:

> I have to admit that I always thought that I wasn't as smart as white kids, like that was just natural. Not that it was, like naturally biological or anything, but I just couldn't compete with them if I wanted to, for some reason or another. So then I was kinda like, "Well, then fuck school." . . . It was like in class they ask a question and a white kid answers it. You just see that all the time. . . . I'm sure that it was [because of] the way you were treated and stuff, but you just grow up always having this feeling. I remember a good example. I remember in eighth-grade U.S. history, we were covering the war with Mexico, and I had this total feeling—I couldn't tell you what we talked about that day. I couldn't show you the book. I couldn't say that's the story we read. But I had this horrible feeling that I was supposed to stand up and apologize. Like that's how the history was covered. I had this feeling like it's time for [me] to stand up and say, "Sorry for making you take our land and having this war with us, wasting your time with us." But that's how I felt. So I always had this feeling (maybe it was before that or maybe it started then) that this education wasn't for me, it wasn't about me. Maybe I was included in it in like certain incidents, but it wasn't for me, and that's why they got it and I didn't. And then you have like this notion of Chinos[1] just all just picking up everything, you know, "Chinos can get it 'cause they pick up everything." But after that, it was like everything wasn't for me. Like when they were talking about nouns and pronouns, that wasn't meant for [me; I was] just there to pick up what [I] could. I always had that feeling, and that's one incident where I remember, where for some reason the school just didn't feel right.

Ernesto showed the sheer force with which hidden subtexts of race and inferiority dominated the consciousness of students through the curriculum. He knew that, as a Mexican, he represented a historical problem to "America." Rationally, he said that these feelings must be the result of how Chicanas/os are treated, but at the same time, his feelings had extended beyond rationality and shaped how he saw his own academic ability. Ernesto provided a powerful explanation of the link between his racialization and his school performance in ways that are rarely made so clear in our popular educational discourse. He demonstrated that there is not a perfect formula that explains Chicana/o school performance.

Instead, his experiences suggested the intersecting importance of the racial-political climate, the conflicts that emerge from it, and identity as it is externally influenced.

Ernesto also pointed to the importance of researchers listening intently to student analyses of their school lives. The issues he addressed were almost always very subtle, and yet their impact on his life was immense. It is easy for researchers to consider that students like Ernesto might be reading too much into their experiences and that we need teacher and administrator input to acquire greater "accuracy" in understanding what is happening to these students. Ernesto, however, challenged this logic, for his story suggested that teachers and administrators do not even see the multiple ways in which they constrain opportunities for Chicana/o students and force them to ground their identities in their race in ways that cannot include the pursuit of school success. Ernesto's examples are so simple and precise and, as other Chicanas/o students revealed in the study, so common that I have included his extensive explanations as a means of exposing their validity to those who might question it. He continued,

> And then I remember this other history class the next semester. The teacher, Miss Johnson, she was like really cool, and everybody could play around except me. And I was the only Mexican in the class. And there was this guy named Abdul who was from Africa, but he was like really assimilated. . . . And there was this white kid named Jim Hernandez. I know their names because I went to [community college] with them too, and they're like clowns, just total clowns. And Jim's dad is a Inca, but his mom is white and he looks real white. His mom's Jewish, so he's got curly hair and stuff. And like they could fuck around all you could, but she just couldn't take it when I would. It was weird. 'Cause we would always have to do this thing, like you had to ask a question every time somebody gave a presentation, which was every day. And when you said it, you had to act like you were a journalist, so you had to name a magazine. So I remember like [they] would say, "Hi, I am Abdul from *Guns and Ammo,*" and the whole class would chuckle, and the teacher would chuckle. And I would say, "I am Ernesto. I'm from *Lowrider,*" right? And then [she would say] "Ah, come on, *Lowrider Magazine!*" And so it was like I couldn't fuck around like they could. And so I've always had this feeling like school wasn't for me.

In these stories, Ernesto exposed the underlying racial script that mediated his interactions with students and teachers. These included confrontations that were not blatantly racist but whose racial overtones were clear to him. Again, individually these stories are easy for teachers, administrators, and even researchers to interpret differently, yet by discussing his school life as a whole, Ernesto provided an insightful analysis that reveals the significance of his own racialization and suggests the importance of allowing students the opportunity to deconstruct their lives for others.

During his high school years, Ernesto also dealt with race and racial confrontations outside of school. He recounted experiences working in fast-food restaurants and being relegated to duties that whites did not have to do. More important to his racialized experience were an assault by the police and the role this played in his perception of police and police brutality. As he described it, this incident was in some ways a turning point for him. On the one hand, it crystallized his racial understanding of his world. On the other hand, it exposed him to community groups who assisted him and the others in his gang who were beat up by the police.

A short time later, Ernesto went to a local community college (on his father's promise to get him a car if he did). As his connection in the community became stronger and he was exposed to readings and ideas that helped him to better contextualize his racial experiences, he slowly became more interested in education. He still organized his world along the racial lines that had been so pivotal at the different stages in his life, as he hung out with other Chicanas/os and participated in Chicana/o organizations. It was a drive-by shooting that in many ways reshaped his life, however. After seeing friends shot and killed one night, he decided to focus on making change and acquiring an education as part of that process. Ernesto centered his studies on courses and issues that helped him deal with the reality of his experience, and those choices pulled him into education further. Soon after, he transferred to the four-year university, where he became a sociology major with an emphasis on Latin America.

Two critical influences that shaped Ernesto's transition from a marginal school participant to what is traditionally understood as the "successful student" were the encouragement he received and his own ethnic identity. At that stage of his life, Ernesto still interacted in school contexts in which the racial and socioeconomic lines were clearly drawn between those with power and authority (as well as those who were surefire successful students) and Chicana/o students. His own racial identity, however, shifted in that he became critically aware of the need for productive social change for the benefit of those in the barrio. Simultaneously, he found mentors in the community and in his studies who helped him to better understand the significance of this goal and the means by which he could use school as a stepping-stone toward that goal. In essence, the strong mentorship he received, which coincided with the development of a critical racial identity, helped him understand and overcome the troubling context in which he found himself and the corresponding interracial distractions he faced.

As Ernesto talked about his place in the university and his educational and career goals, it was evident that this interplay of forces had become essential. The significance of his racial identity was manifested in his academic interests, the way in which he approached his future, and the numerous potential avenues he was considering. What had previously been distractions became part of how he understood his world, and the mentorship that he received was not only a source of encouragement, providing him with confidence, but also an intrinsic component of his own racial identity, which motivated him toward his goal of transforming the context in which he had grown up through his schooling.

Ernesto painted a vivid picture of how the social identity of Chicana/o students is often defined for them. While students quickly learn that this identity is grounded in their racial difference, they also receive subtle and often overt messages that explain that their racial difference is tied to who they are as students. Oftentimes, as happened with Ernesto, racially charged interactions within the school demand that these students adopt a hostile, racial stance to ensure their psychological (and even physical) safety. Taking such a stance almost always results in school failure. Ernesto, however, overcame many of these obstacles through mentoring that showed him that his school success was needed and important and that his success was intimately tied to his racial identity, which could help him apply his education to making positive change that would address the negative forces in his early schooling.

SUSANA

Looking at a quite different university student provides us with a more complete picture of the interactions among racial-political climate, conflict, identity, and contextualized mentoring. Susana was a junior at the university when we last talked. She had been quite successful in high school and was doing well in the university. Although Susana's outcomes, like Ernesto's, were explained by looking at racial-political climate, conflict, identity, and contextualized mentoring, the influences of these forces in her life were quite distinct.

Early on in her life, Susana lived in a working-class Chicana/o community, but while she was still in elementary school, her family moved to a middle-/upper-middle-class neighborhood, and she then attended an all-girls Catholic school. Her parents were immigrants. Her father had been college-educated in Mexico, and her mother had completed the equivalent of high school in Mexico. As Susana grew up, her father was able to move his way into the middle class through his work as a sales representative. For Susana, the most critical experiences in her life were primarily those in high school. Attending an all-girls Catholic school with a strong emphasis on preparation for college was extremely important to her. She remembered fondly that she was able to focus on school because of the small class sizes, the quality of the teachers, and the supportive environment created through same-gender schooling. At the same time, the school was attended by middle- and upper-middle-class families, the majority of whom were white, while her family was coming from immigrant experiences and just pushing their way into the middle class.

Interestingly, the class and racial differences in the school had not affected her the way they had Ernesto, not because race was a nonissue in her school but because her parents had made it their responsibility to help their children deal with issues of race in their daily lives. Susana noted that students, teachers, and administrators made both subtle and blatant statements suggesting that Chicana/o students were different and not expected to succeed to the same degree as the traditional families of the school (upper-middle-class whites). She mentioned two such incidents. The first, discussed in Chapter 1, was when a counselor told her that, despite her 3.9 GPA, if she made it into her university of choice, it would be only because she was the member of a minority. As Susana discussed this incident (on more than one occasion), it became obvious that it had deeply affected her, for it had put into words and actions things she had felt within her school. Although this incident did not push her to act out or rebel, it solidified her feeling that race was a present but often invisible force at work in her school. Such incidents are often psychologically painful to successful Chicanas/os because they tell these students that, despite their successes, they are still "understood" within the school through their race. Many students then realize that they cannot escape the negative racial forces they thought school success would allow them to erase. Susana talked about the subtle racialization that had occurred in her school,

> In high school . . . people begin identifying you with certain stereotypes. [They would ask,] "Oh, you're a Mexican family. How did you get the money to come to this school?" . . . A lot of people from my high school were not astonished but just kind of surprised [by] how well a Mexican

family can do, and that's when I really began noticing that there are just definite stereotypes of certain races.

At other times, even in an environment she lauded for its support of her educational goals as a female, Susana found that teachers, counselors, and students all expected less from her and interpreted who she was in the school as a function of her race. The context and the occasional conflicts she experienced, however, do not tell the whole story.

As Susana repeatedly explained in our discussions, her parents had made it clear that cultural pride was important, through Spanish-language use and discussions of culture. They also discussed issues of race and occasional racism with her so that she understood these issues and could deal with them in a comfortable way. Thus the issues of race that came up in her school were not a distraction to Susana. For example, she remembered her parents telling her that because she was a Chicana (that is, a minority member and a female), she would have to work twice as hard in school. She mentioned this parental help several times:

> They're just really supportive, and they say, "[Racist] people like that are ignorant." [My parents'] whole thing is you get an education and do better so that they see. "Prove them wrong" basically is their motto. "Be a success, show them, and say, 'Look.'"

Although issues of class, race, and gender were all brought up in her school context, for Susana they were synthesized into her racial identity as a Chicana striving for school success. Clearly, her parents were also a strong source of encouragement for her school success. They made it known that educational success was a necessity rather than an option. Susana's parents were involved in her school and constantly monitored her academic progress, often having her do extra work beyond that assigned as homework. This strong encouragement on an academic level, in addition to the support in dealing with identity, was an essential part of Susana's success.

The significance of education in Susana's life was dominant in our conversations. Things that were distractions for other students were not so for her. In addition to using issues of race as a motivator for her success, she reported that she also dealt with other distractions by focusing on her schoolwork:

> There was a time when [my parents] were going to get separated, when I was probably about sophomore year in high school. It was really bad at

74

that time. It was hard. . . . I didn't want that, and they would fight every night and every day, and I got so sick of it. I mean, I would go up in my room and I would plug my ears with my hands. I didn't want to hear it. . . . When they would fight or something, I would be up in my room and I did-n't want to hear it, so I would do something else: I would study. So it really didn't make my grades go down. If anything, it might have helped.

In looking at Susana's life, we see that racial identity is important to her experience, and more so because the encouragement of her family for success helped her place her racial identity within the framework of her goals and school experiences. Whereas Ernesto had eventually integrated a positive sense of himself as a student into his racial identity, Susana seemed more grounded in her academic identity, which incorporated her racial/gender identity. Furthermore, it is significant that the school context was not typically a distraction to her (although in some instances it was) and that in fact it actually provided a comfortable, collegial environment in which education could really be a focus for her. It was particularly important to Susana that hers was an all-girls school, which may, at least in some ways, have superseded issues of racial difference in efforts to create the gendered bonds that Susana described with such fondness. Through Susana's experience, we see that encouragement can be critical to school success and can also be a channel through which identity becomes encapsulated within goals of school success, thus mediating the potentially negative effects of the racial script within the world of school. Additionally, we see what is already known: that positive school climates are critical to students' comfort in school and their ability to achieve school success.

SANTIAGO

Looking at the experiences of students who are struggling in school is also a critical means by which we can more clearly understand the complexity of Chicana/o students' school experiences. The community college and high school students had struggled much more than Susana and Ernesto at the time of our interviews.

The story of Santiago, a community college student, is similar to that of Ernesto, although differences point to the significance of specific influences in the lives of both students as seen through their outcomes. Santiago, the son of Mexican immigrants, grew up and went to school in a working-class Chicana/o barrio on the east side of Los Angeles.

Although he performed well during elementary school, things began to change for him on several levels upon entering junior high. Included in a desegregation program, Santiago was bused to a junior high in an upper-middle-class, predominantly white neighborhood on the west side. At that time, it became clear to him not only that he was different but also that he was not accepted in the new school context. As he explained, he was viewed as a potential troublemaker by students, teachers, and administrators, and that perception led to his marginalization in the school. Santiago in turn responded to these subtle signals by lashing out at others, fighting with both students and teachers. He described the lack of acceptance that he felt:

> In junior high you had your people that were bused from here that you can hang around and stuff, but there was a lot of racism over there. I was able to tell the different treatment we received. It was a joke, man. Like I said, junior high, that's when I started messing around, but at the same time my grades were [fine]. Academically it wasn't hard for me, wasn't a challenge for me. What I didn't like was that students and teachers treat you different. 'Cause they know you were the bused kid. You come from [the barrio]. They're always careful; they always thought you were crazy. It was just bad that I couldn't go to a school in my own neighborhood and just feel welcome.

Although Santiago was not academically marginalized at this time, the social marginalization he experienced became integrated into his social identity and later connected to his school performance. Like Ernesto's early school experiences, Santiago's made clear to him that there was a racial hierarchy in the school that everyone understood and that shaped daily interactions within the school.

Interestingly, Santiago's racialized experiences continued when he returned to his neighborhood and attended high school in an almost exclusively Chicana/o setting:

> [Teachers] would get me angered when they put me down or put people who come from [my] community down. That would upset me. I found myself getting upset when it was an instructor of Mexican descent putting down their own people. . . . In high school there was a couple of teachers I got into it [with] because of that. Some teacher's aides and stuff like that . . . they'd just say like, "All you guys do is just hang around, smoke drugs, sell drugs." We'd be like, "Nah, I mean of course it's out there man, but it's not all we do." Just because they've bettered their lives, you know, they look down

76

upon other people. Maybe they didn't struggle or go through the same things *we've* gone through. Maybe that way they live a better life than us.

As Santiago explained, the racialization of Chicana/o students also occurs in contexts that are virtually all-Chicana/o, because the popular perceptions of Chicanas/os shape school life in these contexts very similarly to the ways those perceptions are shaped in predominantly white schools. The racialization process is enforced by power structures that can include Chicanas/os as well. In fact, belonging to the established power structure and having been socialized by the schools themselves, Chicana/o teachers are often similar to their white counterparts in their beliefs about and treatment of Chicana/o students.

This type of conflict shifted the nature of Santiago's school participation. For, as Santiago expressed it, the racialization he saw in his schools went beyond social interactions to affect curriculum and teaching. Santiago exposed fundamental problems in inner-city schools. First, he considered the curriculum: "In high school and junior high, learning about the history of America and all that, [the] history of the presidents, . . . wasn't that interesting. Or maybe it was just the teachers that didn't make it interesting." He again considered the teaching itself later, saying, "I don't think [these teachers] expect *too* much from students. . . . The teachers are just getting by too." Even in an all-Chicana/o school, Santiago found that the teachers stereotyped the students and then interacted with them on the basis of these stereotypes both inside and outside the classroom. Although he said that he could always do well in school and usually got by without doing much work, he gradually lost all interest in attending high school. This process was facilitated by the distractions he faced in his home at that time, for the hands-on supervision he had been accustomed to was gone. His parents still encouraged him to be in school and do well, but their jobs made it difficult to monitor his progress, and once his sisters moved out, Santiago turned to the streets to get the attention that was no longer available in the home. Santiago became marginally involved in gangs and also sold drugs. Eventually he dropped out of high school. He described that time in his life:

> I wasn't interested. I mean, it got to a point where the classes weren't interesting anymore. It was just basically work, work, homework, homework, more work. I felt I wasn't gaining any knowledge out of it. I wasn't gaining anything I was gonna use out in the streets. That's what I thought then. But now it's a different story. Now I see the importance of high school, of an education.

In Santiago's case, we see a clear example of the significance of encouragement, because the loss of his support system left him without the resources to continue to negotiate the conflict-ridden schools in which he had been struggling. As his support system was weakened by the absence of his sisters, it became impossible for him to see a reason for continuing to make an effort in schools where he knew his race was seen as an educational handicap and where he felt that the content was irrelevant and the teachers did not care. Santiago lacked the guidance needed to make sense of his world in a way that would have allowed him to pursue school success. It is important to recognize that Santiago needed a specific form of contextualized mentorship to help him deal with these contradictions. Although his parents were an important influence on him, they could not provide that type of guidance. As he explained, his parents encouraged him to pursue his schooling primarily in informal ways, because they were an important observational influence on him through their own struggles:

> They've always wanted better for their kids, and it's always been that way with parents like that. And hearing and seeing what my parents have gone through—you know, the struggle they've gone through, coming from Mexico and getting to where we're at now—makes me want to do more for them and myself.

Teachers had also been an inspiration for Santiago, but again none served as a strong mentor, for they too tended to be observational influences. Santiago remembered:

> I took this art class on Saturdays a couple years ago, right. And [the teacher would] tell me his story, you know. He teaches right here at the school of arts on Twenty-Fifth street, and he started as a student too and developed his techniques and his art and now he's a teacher. Now that's his job: art. He does real good pieces and stuff. And that was an inspiration to see that someone from [the barrio] can get to where he's at and build up his creativity, his talents, and everything like that. Seeing people accomplish things like that is an inspiration to me. . . . I can't think of anybody in high school or anything. I mean there was teachers I *liked* but [who] weren't really a big inspiration—teachers I got along with, but no inspiration.

Despite this lack of mentorship, a combination of his strong racial identity and other sources of encouragement eventually pushed Santiago back into school (at the time of our interviews he was attending community college and working, and his involvement in selling drugs had ended). Santiago's girlfriend for several years had always been a good student. Not only had she graduated from college, but she was also a teacher. She stressed the importance of education to Santiago, and she and her family constantly pushed him to reenter school. In addition, because of his familial influences and his racialized experiences, Santiago was becoming increasingly aware of social and economic injustice that the Chicanas/os in his community faced. He realized that he wanted to help make changes in this situation. These forces led to his increased involvement in school and his gradual move toward success. The fundamental difference, however, between his experience and that of Ernesto is that his primary sources of encouragement came from peers rather than potential mentors. Whereas Ernesto had found mentors in the community and his college to guide and assist him in the process of realizing his goals, Santiago's main encouragement came from his girlfriend. Santiago's racial awareness and identity were a grounding force in his pursuit of success and change, but, unlike Ernesto, Santiago never had anyone to help him effectively channel that force toward success. As he revealed in our conversations, he was still not clear how he could be involved in the positive changes he deemed necessary, and he was unable to clearly integrate a strong academic identity into his Chicano identity that had taken shape over the years.

This is a pattern that is repeated time and again for the Chicana/o students in the project. Like Santiago, many of the students rely on observational influences, as they are inspired by the struggle and/or success of family members and others in their community. Many of these people, however, do not provide the type of mentorship that the students need to achieve their goals, because these potential mentors do not address the complex web of forces at work in Chicana/o students' lives. The local context itself also plays a critical role. For example, the community college that Santiago attended had much fewer resources than did the college Ernesto attended, and the quality of education available at the community college was far inferior to that to which Ernesto was exposed.

Overall, for Santiago the racial-political climate and the conflicts that emerged from it played a crucial role in shaping his identity as it became clear to him that, as a Chicana/o, he was not expected to succeed in school or in life. Through these experiences, he grounded his identity outside of school in his affiliations with others who had realized that school provided them no opportunities. His lack of mentorship made it easy for him to make these choices, but Santiago also had influences who continually suggested the importance of applying his awareness of the needs of the Chicana/o community to efforts to address those needs. These influences and his evolving identity led him back to school as he attempted to confront the multiple needs of the Chicana/o community through his efforts to educationally empower himself. Santiago struggled with these goals, however, for the complexities of the forces at work in his life made it difficult to see a path that would allow him to achieve these goals. At the time of the study, he did not yet have a mentor to help him find and complete that path.

JULIA

Julia was another community college student who had lacked strong encouragement and mentorship, but she tells a different story. Julia had immigrated from Mexico at the age of three, and she grew up in an integrated lower-middle-class community. In her case, the story of her identity formation is critical to understanding her goals, while the lack of encouragement/mentorship she experienced is central to her struggles in school.

Julia received little strong encouragement from her parents to succeed in school. Their approach to guiding their children was simply to support them in whatever paths they chose. In this way, they expressed their support for her educational goals but did not push her toward educational success, and none of her siblings had graduated from high school. Julia described the situation:

> In my family it was never "You better go to high school, you better go to college, and you better bring us a degree." It wasn't like that. Once again my parents just said, "Hey, if you can do it and you want to do it, then go and do it. We're right behind you." My parents couldn't say, "Try to go to college. We're right behind you financially. Don't you worry about it." My parents weren't aware of financial aid. We probably didn't let them know [that] paperwork and all that kind of stuff made a difference, but [we didn't] because we thought, "We're never gonna make it. They're not going to accept us." It was just that mentality all around: the lack of information which I now stress so much: "If you don't tell me [and] if I don't know, then how am I ever going to learn?"

Just as important, Julia said, the teachers in her schools were not interested in pushing or encouraging their students. Thus the lack of strong support at home was amplified by a similar lack at the school. Julia felt that although she had done fairly well in high school, she had had no opportunity to excel, because the teachers she had were themselves unmotivated:

> The teachers never really pushed you enough, to say, "Hey, maybe you could try a little harder in class and challenge yourself." It wasn't like that. . . . Our teachers never really pushed us. And I saw a lot of that. Ever since the last years of elementary. Now that I look back at it, [I think,] "Hey, wait a minute, you cheated me out." Because I know that if I get challenged, I can definitely do it. And I was never challenged, so that really made a big difference.

Like Santiago, Julia felt shortchanged and unchallenged, and the lack of mentorship and guidance she experienced limited her motivation to excel in school. In addition, Julia was limited by having to work, which also affected her possibilities for excelling in school. This factor came up on more than one occasion as she talked about her grades:

> I worked in high school, [at] a part-time job. Ever since then I basically always bought my own things. I never asked my parents, which brought me down from having a much better grade point average, because I was always working in the afternoons. . . . [My grades were] average, really average. I think I would be, not necessarily the excellent student, but [a good student] if my mind wasn't on other things, [like my] financial situation, and I know [my] financial situation is my worst [problem]. If I was away at college, not necessarily dealing with the problems at home [but] dealing [with] my own personal problems, I would probably be right on top of my work. I would probably be halfway done as opposed to right now, where I have no sense of direction. I think I probably would be more than halfway done.

In addition to the lack of challenge and the need to work that she faced, Julia, like many Chicana/o students, did not have an active mentor or influence to help her in school and with planning her future. The only significant educational influence on Julia was a friend.

Throughout our conversations, it became clear that Julia suffered from a lack of direction and guidance. This lack was also somewhat apparent in the story of her identity formation, perhaps the most interesting aspect of our discussions. Although Julia did not deny her ethnicity, it was not a central part of how she defined herself. Julia's main social identity was grounded in her class status:

> I feel like, "God, I don't want to be working for somebody else." That's my *biggest feeling*. And I see my family and my friends and all of us work for somebody else. And that's my biggest goal.

When asked how she felt about her life, Julia went on to explain how important finances were to her:

> I think practically in any question you will ask, it's always gonna be my financial situation. At the moment, I think that's like the *only* problem I have. . . . It's just my financial situation that always brings me down.

This theme came up time and again as Julia mentioned her financial needs and concerns throughout our discussions. She made it absolutely clear that her identity was grounded firmly not simply in her class status but also in the class status to which she aspired.

Although other students typically centered their conversations on race and racial issues, Julia continually returned to issues of class and finances. In addition, having never experienced social conflict grounded in any of her identifiable characteristics (gender, race, or even class), Julia described how much she has been influenced by the media in seeing images of economic success via material wealth:

> I want to make this really big change in my lifestyle because, growing up, I saw my aunts, uncles, cousins—they all lived in that same routine kind of lifestyle. Nobody ever had big goals to become something big, something out of the ordinary. They never had ambitions to leave the community, to want better, to think bigger, so I think TV, movies, and music have really added to my wanting to have a different lifestyle. My friend has asked me, "Do you want to be rich?" And I say, "No, I just want to be happy. I don't want to see my children have to work through high school like my parents saw me do." I want to have a different lifestyle than I've got.

Clearly, her class status and her desire for upward mobility define Julia's identity, but interestingly they were not related to race for her, for she was one of the few students in the study who did not have a strong racial identity. Part of the reason she had never developed a strong racial identity is related to the community in which she grew up, where she shared the class background of most and there were many whites. In fact, she was one of the few early Mexican families to move into the neighborhood.

I think growing up in the community I grew up in, it was never, "Oh, you're Mexican. Get out of our neighborhood." No, there was so many Anglo or white people in our community, in our neighborhoods growing up, and they never once made us feel like "You little Mexicans, get out of here." Never, never at all. So that really made a big difference. . . . And that goes anywhere I've been.

In effect, race has been something she has downplayed in her life. Julia says that this approach to her race is reflected in how some of her friends react to her:

I talked to a lot of my friends, and they say, "Oh my God, you think so *white*." And it's not that. It's just that I don't think [like] a lot of my friends think, like they're content with what is in their little circle. I don't see that happening for me. I think even though I have my culture right behind me and which I'm very aware of, I don't think that that should be the end of it. And that's the difference there. And by me thinking that I should be thinking bigger and get out of my little circle and whatnot, they think, "You think so white! My God!"

Building on this idea, Julia talked about a television show she had seen in which Spanish-speaking people were asking for federal documents to be translated from English to Spanish:

I think, "Get over it, you guys!" It *has* to be a big issue all the time. I don't know if it's wrong for me to think that way, but I just think people make it more than it should be. But then I think, "I've never been harassed. I've never had a bad experience with my nationality [that would make] me go out in public and say, 'No, this should be done.'"

Here, Julia touched upon a critical issue: when students do not encounter or witness conflict around race (or other factors), then race may not become an important part of how they see themselves. This phenomenon is even more likely when the family itself downplays the importance of race or ethnicity. As Julia explained,

Like I said, our race, our culture—[my family] didn't stress it upon us either. Never. They were never like, "This is your culture. This is how you're gonna be. This is how you have to live by." Not at all. Not at all.

Thus, Julia's identity was grounded not in her ethnicity but in her aspirations for wealth and leading a better life than those around her. She shares her aspirations with her second oldest brother:

> Our views [are] just, "No way are we going to go with just barely making it like our father did." . . . We are just determined to do it—to do it and get out and not just be making it and not just live in a bad community—because we know that by the time our children grow up, it's going to be worse. [As] opposed to my family in another community. . . . They're very content with just barely making it, with having the problems of gang violence around them constantly and even [with being] affected by it, and they don't want to get out. They're afraid. They're afraid because they don't speak English that they are just going to come across people who will just bring them back down.

In many ways, Julia expressed frustration with her family and their lack of mobility, which seems amplified by a lack of communication between her and her parents through which she could begin to understand their experiences.[2] The contradicting images between her reality and the reality she learned to aspire to through the media have created aspirations for upward mobility that are the central arena of her identity formation. Because she has never experienced any racial conflict or considered the possibility that the limitations she sees her family and friends experience may not be entirely self-imposed, she has come to identify with mainstream perspectives.

The combination of a lack of strong mentorship and guidance toward her goals, along with the discord between her reality and the reality that she had learned to pursue through the media images, put Julia in a situation where she was unclear of how to reach her goals and even how to get guidance in seeking these goals. So, although distractions were not a fundamental issue keeping her from success, the context in which she found herself had shaped her identity such that some of the contradictions of her experience were unresolved, and the dramatic lack of encouragement and role models limited her ability to plan for the goals she sought. Thus, the distractions Julia faced were not critically damaging, but, paradoxically, she had been limited by the context of having been somewhat sheltered and not having to deal with racial conflict. The result was that she did not see the limitations in her community, such as the lack of encouragement and role models. In her critique of the lack of challenge she faced in school, for example, it is intriguing that she does not connect this factor to her continued shortcomings in school.

Through this lack of active guidance in her family and in the school, she developed a sense of identity that was individual-centered in seeking economic advancement. Unfortunately, Julia has no one to help her negotiate the troubling situation in which she finds herself, which may become a fundamental problem later in life that leads to self-blame. Thus, Julia knew that her identity of aspiring for upward mobility must be connected to a strong school identity in order for her to achieve this success, but the context in which she found herself limited her ability to develop that school identity. Furthermore, her lack of mentorship prevented her from understanding some of these complexities.

DIEGO

In turning to the high school students, we are able to obtain a more complete picture of the relationships among racial-political climate, conflict, identity, contextualized mentoring, and school performance for Chicana/o students in general. Diego had immigrated to the United States at the age of three, and at the time of our interview he was in his fifth year of high school. He attended the all-Chicana/o high school in a working-class barrio on the east side of Los Angeles. Although the student population was homogeneous, Diego almost immediately made it clear that race had been a central part of his interactions within the school. Diego admittedly carried himself like stereotypical gangbangers (in terms of dress, hair, and so on), but he was vehement that he had never been involved in gangs or drugs. Yet those within the school constantly treated him as if he were an outlaw. He cited numerous incidents of confrontations both within the school and with police officers in the community. In our conversations, it was clear that these incidents were central to Diego's identity and school performance. One of the first stories he told revealed this, as he described abuse that both he and his father had received from the police (cited in Chapter 1). Diego explained that "where I live you have to be watching your back not only from gangsters and all that, but from cops too because of the way they treat you." He went on to describe another confrontation with the police that had landed him in jail:

> I was arguing with my mom. And I guess the neighbors called the cops or something and they came, and, like, usually they're white. So they came. They told me that if I thought that I was a real man, to leave the house instead of ragging with my mom. And I told them, "I'll leave." And I was getting my stuff. My mom was crying because we were arguing, right?

And then I was telling her to, like, be quiet 'cause the cops were going to make a big thing out of it. So the cop goes, "You just better shut up." And he told me a bad word. And I go, "Don't talk to me like that." I go, "I'm not talking to *you* like that. Why are you talking to *me* like that?" [He said,] "Well, just shut up and leave." And then I just stood quiet. And he goes, "What? What did you say?" And I go, "I didn't say nothing." He goes, "Come here. You're under arrest." I go, "For what?" He goes, "'Cause you talked back to me." I go, "No, I didn't." And he goes, "You're doing it right now." And I go, "Well, look what you're telling me. I'm under arrest and I didn't do nothing." And he tried to handcuff me and I didn't let myself, so we got in a fight and he called his buddy and his buddy came and he sprayed me. And they arrested me and they took me, and I served in juvenile hall for six months.

Diego made a point early in our conversations to expose the significant role that race had played in his life through continual conflicts that reflected the harsh racial-political climate in which he lived. He had been deeply affected by these experiences because of the blatant injustice he faced. What is striking about the stories Diego told is that the police made it clear that in their eyes he was guilty even though he had done nothing illegal. In turn, they pushed his buttons to create a response that would give them something to charge him with. For Diego, his choices were to simply succumb to their treatment of him as subhuman (for he was not granted basic human rights) or to challenge that treatment, which resulted in his imprisonment in the story above and might have led to his being assaulted had he done so in the example from Chapter 1. An onlooker might react by wondering why Diego did not just keep his mouth shut (just as he or she might wonder why Ernesto would head-butt his teacher). For some, it is only common sense to stay out of trouble. For Ernesto and Diego, however, their own rage and dignity would not allow them to stand for one more affront to their humanity. Although Diego ended up in jail, in his mind he at least had not stood by without challenging injustice and his own dehumanization.

These and similar incidents became a key part of how Diego saw himself outside of school, but the experiences were also mirrored within the school. Recall the stories that Diego told at the beginning of this chapter. Through these stories we can see the intersection of the forces that influence Chicana/o school performance. When interacting with authority figures, Diego faced an interracial context of conflict, and not only were these experiences a major distraction in school, but they also clearly shaped his identity. In a number of instances, school staff targeted him for verbal assault and took that assault to another level by attaching racial meaning to their attacks. Although one could argue that the racial meaning of these incidents is implied, for Diego it was quite clear. He had a strong racialized identity grounded in his ethnic pride and his awareness of the racial injustice that existed both in his school and in his community. This identity gave him strength and confidence, but it was difficult for him to connect the identity to any positive role for himself in the school. In fact, during our first conversation he was confident that there was no place for him in the school. The apologies of teachers did little to address the climate that allowed them to attack him so easily. Overall, the severity of Diego's situation is best understood by looking at the other forces that shaped his experience.

Although Diego had some encouragement from his parents, the nature of this encouragement was similar to that received by many of the other Chicana/o students discussed earlier. His parents took the time to mention the importance of school and to encourage school success, but they did not have the experience or knowledge to actively help him succeed in school. Because of the lack of strong encouragement, Diego was easily sidetracked from school success by the distractions in his life. First and foremost was his marginalization in the school through an overwhelming history of racial confrontations with school personnel. Second, his family life had been on a roller coaster since his parents had divorced. The combination of Diego's family and school lives, along with his lack of strong support, stacked the odds against his school success. These distractions pushed Diego to the point that he was committed to dropping out of high school. He believed in the importance of school, but he struggled to find a place for himself in the school, given that his interactions with teachers and administrators suggested that they had little hope for him. In fact, they discouraged his school involvement through their actions. When his family life became unstable, he had no energy left for contesting the racial hostility he experienced, and he believed his only option was to leave school. A new source of encouragement in his life, however, kept him from doing that.

To explain the significance of this encouragement, we need to understand Diego better. Diego prided himself in two things: his art and his race. For Diego the two were a syncretic and central facet of his being, through which he expressed his pain, anger, and pride:

> I feel strong for my people. Like some people, probably they don't care about it. They're just "Ah, I don't care." But I feel strong [about] where I'm coming from. I was born in Mexico, and I feel like messed up when I

see [things] in the news like "Oh, well, these Latino gangsters killed another one" and all that [or] "They're just killing themselves." I feel sad because they don't realize that they *are* killing themselves. And, like, [Governor] Pete Wilson, what he's doing to my people too. And when I see the news or when, say, the reporter's right there on the border of Tijuana and USA, like I just see all those people running from Tijuana over here, and, like, they make it seem like they're coming over here, like, to steal or something. But they're not. They just want to come over here to work. And, like, I'll feel bad because that's my people.

When I asked Diego about some of the early influences on his strong sense of pride, he then turned to his new source of encouragement:

It was probably when I started the tenth grade, and like [my art] teacher, she's really into [artwork with Mexican imagery] too. . . . And she would talk to me about it and everything, and then I started liking it. Before, I didn't even know what I meant or where I was coming from. And like ever since she started talking to me, I would read books and all that. And I will go to, like, *marchas* and all that. I started getting into it and I liked it. And then like in the news or TV or something, other people will come out talking about like Mexicans and all that. Like I don't know why I will start feeling something inside of me like hurt and anger at the same time. And that's when I realized it really did mean a lot to me. Ever since then, I started getting into it and I still am.

By affirming his racial identity and developing a strong Chicano identity, Diego was able to make sense of the racial injustice he had both seen and experienced. By developing a social critique that considered the role of racism in shaping Chicana/o outcomes, he was able to challenge the popular perception that Chicanas/os are criminals and outcasts. As mentioned, Diego exhibits his sense of pride through his artwork:

I have in my head [murals] about my heritage and all. That's what I like. I don't know if you seen that [mascot] over there with the Aztec crown and everything. That's the first one I did. That one, I liked it. I like it because it has, like, the colors and all that, the designs, all that, 'cause that's me inside. That's me. I came up with that.

Diego's artwork became a release for him, a way of expressing his social critique and dealing with the pain he felt from the racial conflicts that had been such a big part of his life. As he explained, it was both self-affirming and cathartic:

> If I can't say it, I'll draw it. That's what I do best, drawing. Like, say I have anger towards what they say in the news. Say I have anger and I can't do nothing about it; I can't go dressed all nice, go into court, and say it. I'll just draw it. Draw it and draw my anger on the paper.

Diego described his frustration and his release, and it is important to recognize that as he saw it, his artwork was his only outlet. As he mentioned earlier, about halfway through his high school career, Diego took an art class that was taught by a Chicana who emphasized Mexican imagery in the art projects of the class. This teacher connected well with Diego and became a constant source of encouragement and inspiration to him. Diego recalled:

> You could say she's like my second mom. I've known her since seventh grade. When I have problems with my mom or my dad, I will talk to her and she will tell me it's gonna be OK. When I don't want to do my work, she slaps me over the head. She makes me do my work. She pulls my ear. She's like my second mom. She helps me a lot. She's cool and I like her a lot.

This teacher faced an uphill battle in trying to keep Diego in school, however, because of the degree of marginalization he had already experienced. Although his artwork and his evolving social critique of U.S. society provided him a means of explaining his life that challenged authority figures' categorization of him as a failure, he was unable to find an alternate space in which he could pursue school success as part of that challenge. Still, as he noted, one of the only reasons he stayed in school as long as he had was because his art teacher was having him paint murals in the school. He discussed this often, as in this statement:

> I liked [school] only 'cause of that teacher. She'll help me. I would be in art class, and that was the only class I was doing real good in. . . . I'm only here because [of the] murals class, and obviously like all the murals are all over the school because like I've done those. And that's the only reason. Right now, I'm in the process of making another one. And I think that's going to be my last one. And I just want to do that one and just get out of school. If I don't graduate, [I'll] just leave school and just probably go to work or something.

At the time of our first interview, Diego informed me that he was going to drop out as soon as he finished the mural he was working on, but by the time of our last interview, he had changed his mind. Diego said that it was this teacher's guidance that helped him ignore the distractions of his experiences with the police and other teachers who labeled him and then treated him poorly based on their shallow assessments. His art teacher had gotten him involved in a program to help at-risk students accelerate their progress toward graduation. Diego explained that she showed him that it was possible for him to graduate, helped him get into the program, and kept reminding him that this process could lead to his acceptance into an art school where he could continue his work and eventually pursue art as a career. "Now that I know that I could get my diploma and go to college, that people are willing to help me," Diego said, "I wanna do it. I wanna do it."

It had been crucial for Diego to get mentorship—specifically, mentorship that was grounded in his racial experience and used his strong racialized identity as a means toward achieving his goal. Without this type of guidance, Diego would not have remained in school as long as he did, because of the nature of the school context and its resulting distractions. The mentorship he received from his art teacher began by acknowledging his racial identity and then helped him develop this identity. The mentorship then became a tool in helping him negotiate and sometimes ignore the racial confrontations that he had encountered and continued to witness. Finally, this mentorship transitioned into building on these processes and helped him translate his identity into the world of school and the pursuit of school success. By the time of our last conversation, Diego had developed a school identity that was grounded in the pursuit of success and embedded in his central racial identity. Diego's experience amplifies the critical role of mentors in helping Chicana/o students effectively pursue school success, while also further highlighting the possibility that, by assisting students in their negotiation of their own racial identities, these mentors can help them overcome the distractions embedded in their school contexts.

LIZ

Liz was a ninth grader attending the same high school as Diego. Liz was second-generation on her father's side of the family and third-generation on her mother's. Her experiences in school were quite similar to Diego's. She also had no source of encouragement for her school success. Her parents were divorced, and she had been estranged from her mother at times. Liz lived with her grandmother and, it seemed, took a great deal of responsibility for the well-being of her family.

Liz's identity was central to understanding her place in her world. She had a strong sense of racial identity grounded in her pride in both her race and her community. The community aspects of her identity were clearer than those of any of the other students interviewed, apparently because her family had been entrenched in long-standing gangs in various Los Angeles barrios. Liz herself had not been intimately involved in the gangs, but she was always surrounded by gang members and considered these groups her family. These affiliations were also central to her involvement in school. Combined with the lack of encouragement she received in and out of school, the hardships that accompanied gang associations distracted her from her studies. A critical example was the murder of her uncle and the impact it had on her in school. She told of his importance when asked what had been the biggest influence on her life:

> My uncle . . . because he taught me a lot. He taught me everything . . . how to depend on myself and not to depend on other people. 'Cause before, I used to ask help for everything when I was small. Fifth grade, that's when he died. He raised me. He was like my dad. . . . He was living with some other guy from some gang, right? And that guy had some problems with some other gang, right? So they came into the apartment, and they thought that he was my uncle. They thought that guy, they mistaked 'em, and they injected 'em. I walked in there, and I went to his apartment after school and I saw him. I didn't know what happened, and then I just be like, "Oohhh." I walked out. I locked the door, and I didn't go home that day. And I had to call my mom from a pay phone, and I told her to call the police. Everybody freaked out.

In a later interview, I asked Liz about this incident again to find out the relationship between these events and her disinterest in school. She explained why she stopped caring in school:

> Probably 'cause I didn't have nothing to look forward to, you know. It's like he would help me in whatever he could. But after, there was an empty space in me. It didn't matter no more. . . . It was boring. You would go over [the] same stuff that you would go in fourth, third grades. Like I know that stuff [already].

Like many of the other students, Liz was faced with a major distraction that led to disinterest in school, which was furthered by the fact that the school did not interest or challenge her. Later, she talked again about her decline in interest and performance: "It was boring. They don't do nothing. Sometimes the teachers are in bad moods, and they start talking stuff."

Although Liz did fine in school during her early elementary school years, after her uncle's murder she lost all interest in school. She still attended school and continued to do fairly well, but she did not care at all about her school performance. Furthermore, as she entered junior high, she experienced not simply a lack of teacher interest but also teacher animosity toward her and other Chicanas/os. This increased her lack of concern about school. At one point in our discussions Liz began talking about racial conflicts with African American girls in the school. When I asked if this type of conflict affected her in school, she began to talk about teachers:

> I didn't get along with five or six of my teachers because of [race]. I used to flaunt being Mexican around, right? Because they were from other nationalities. So they didn't really like me.

When I asked her to explain what she meant, she replied:

> They look at [Chicanas/os] and they think that right away you're going to do something bad or something, so I was like, no. . . . There was one teacher that told me something [racial], and I called him "*pinche* Paddy,"[3] and he got all pissed and he sent me to the dean and everything.

Although Liz's story was complicated and she was still trying to understand and explain the subtleties of what had happened to her, her multiple confrontations with her teachers clearly indicated that she did not feel welcome in the school.

As Liz mentioned, she had really done well only in recent courses in high school that focused on things of relevance to her, such as Mexican history. She mentioned this when she began talking about the other big influence on her life:

> My grandpa sat me down and taught me about the Mexican Revolution. He talked about a lot of things, about Pancho Villa, Zapata, [and] taught me where I was from—just brought out my heritage. That's why I'm getting a good grade in history now, because we're studying Mexico.

Liz demonstrated that she felt tension and even had conflicts resulting from the racial-political climate at her school. These experiences contributed to her identity, which was grounded in understanding her world through the gang life in her community and family. Her conflicts with teachers reaffirmed the importance of her Chicana identity and assured her that this identity was incompatible with school success. Her discussions, however, revealed that her analysis of these issues and their relationships was still developing and that she possibly could reconcile some of the contradictions in her life. For example, she had been successful when her courses focused on content that was related to what she felt was important to her life.

By the time of our last interview, Liz had improved her school attendance and performance because of a program that monitored students who were cutting classes and doing poorly in their first semester in the high school. She had not really changed her attitude toward school, however. It was clear that without direct mentorship that acknowledged her experiences and the things she deemed important, Liz might have a hard time navigating the minefields of her daily life and graduating from high school. She hinted at her needs when talking about why some students struggle so much in school:

> [They struggle] mostly because people really don't care about [them], because they just really haven't had that much attention and they need attention, and because they don't know what to do. And they have a lot of problems, family life.

The conflicts Liz encountered in and out of school all but demanded that she develop a strong race- and community-based identity. After her realization that her teachers lacked interest in her and that some were even racist, this identity became a significant part of who she was in school, even though this was in direct opposition to school success. With almost no positive connection between her identity and school and without the type of intervention that Diego had received, it seemed unlikely that Liz would succeed in school.

RETHINKING CHICANA/O SCHOOL PERFORMANCE

The insights gleaned from this small group of Chicana/o students provide a new perspective on Chicana/o school life. By listening intently to extensive explanations of what the students observed, what they were concerned about, and what affected them, we see compelling reasons to attack the problem of Chicana/o school failure. The students provide us with a sense of urgency, and they also help us see multiple avenues for making positive changes in their school lives. They convey a concrete rationale for fundamental and systemic change in schooling, as well as offering hopeful possibilities for ways in which we can make significant progress before a complete overhaul can be made. The awareness of such possibilities is one of the greatest strengths of this project, because these possibilities are ways to break through the inertia behind the educational traditions that continue to treat Chicanas/os as inferior and repeatedly allow significant Chicana/o failure.

For the entire sample of students, the school context and particularly the racial-political climate were always extremely important to their school performance. Many of the Chicana/o students told stories of what they felt were inadequate educational opportunities. Beyond the popularly discussed problems of poor resources, overcrowding, and the like, many of the students talked about teachers who seemed not to care and who did not challenge them. Repeatedly, Chicana/o students mentioned being bored and unchallenged in school. The school context can have the opposite effect, however, as in the case of Susana. Going to a private, all-girls school provided her with what she considered to be an ideal learning environment. Still, the role of context can be more complicated than the degree of challenge presented to students. Chicana/o students often focused on the racial dynamics of their schools as a major influence on their education. Through both subtle and blatant messages that school staff convey to students, Chicana/o youth quite often are made aware that they are deemed at-risk, troublemaking, inept, and/or uninterested in school merely because they are Chicana/o.

The analysis of school context leads to another issue: the conflicts that Chicana/o students faced in school. As the students explained, their confrontations with school authority figures, which were grounded in the racial-political climate, often made it hard to focus on school success or even to believe that school success was possible. At times, these distractions were as obvious as blatant discriminatory acts, but at other times they were more subtly understood through the attitudes and behaviors of teachers that suggested little interest in or hope for Chicana/o students. Distractions existed beyond the walls of the school as well. Chicana/o students also had confrontations with authority figures outside of school, such as the police, which diverted them and sometimes even led to incarceration. Furthermore, the Chicana/o students who participated in the project typically had financial situations that required them to work, which could be a major distraction in their efforts to succeed in school. Another common distraction was family problems. Many students described how issues like divorce and the problems faced by siblings demanded attention that they could otherwise have paid to school.

Interestingly, however, some students who face similar distractions respond to them differently because of the encouragement they receive. Thus, mentoring is another critical force at work in defining Chicana/o school performance. Successful Chicana/o students often have a mentor who not only encourages them to succeed but also shows them how to succeed. These mentors can be parents, teachers, community members, or any number of other contacts who care about the student and serve as a resource in the student's effort to succeed in school. Unfortunately, the students in this project rarely had such a mentor. Instead, many students relied on observational influences. That is, the great majority of Chicana/o students in this project were motivated to pursue school success by watching the struggles of their families and members of their communities. Students at the high school and community college relied almost exclusively on such influences. This pattern was reflected in their tendency to attribute their school success or, most often, their failure entirely to themselves, for they were unable to complicate this understanding with an analysis of the interaction of the social forces they discussed. Although parents were typically concerned about their children's education and told the students that they needed to do well in school, most parents did not have the time and the experience to guide their children through school. Still, some parents provided strong support and encouragement for their children's educational success, and the children of those parents tended to be successful. Most parents, however, because of their limited and often negative experiences in school, provided only a moderate level of encouragement, leaving the bulk of the support to their children's teachers and peers. In these instances, the degree of distractions a student faced often determined school performance.

Overall, it appears that most of these Chicana/o students were fairly successful through their elementary years, but once familial problems such as death and divorce occurred or became obvious (often in junior high), these distractions made it exceptionally difficult for the students involved to muster the psychological strength needed to survive the racial bias and discrimination that were becoming apparent to them (usually in junior high as well). As a result, many of these students lost interest in school and did not focus on their studies, because they were left without the directed assistance they needed to deal with the difficulties of their school experiences. The students showed that above all else Chicana/o youth need mentors to assist them as they pursue educational success. Furthermore, the study participants also revealed that it is even more helpful to have mentors who can help them deal with the school context and the distractions they face that are due to confrontations and/or subtle messages suggesting they are not valued in the school. Many Chicana/o students do not buy into the simple message "Stay in school," because they feel that they are not wanted in the school and that they do not have a real chance to use school in pursuit of their career goals (see Olsen 1997 for additional detailed examples). These students benefit from a mentor who not only provides them with support for staying in school but also couches this support in an understanding of the students' context and of the tools needed to survive in these often hostile climates. As individual students showed, through strong encouragement and mentorship, Chicana/o students can overcome distractions and obstacles as they come to see that their harmful opposition to these forces undermines their possibilities for achieving success.

The stories of the Chicana/o students in this project all point to the centrality of one other factor in their school lives: identity. Although researchers have paid little attention to Chicana/o identity and, when they have, have tended to avoid its complexity, it played a critical role in school life and performance of the students who participated in this project. Obviously, how students see themselves can affect how they do in school, but the schools typically blame the students for poor school performance. When a student, for example, creates an identity as a *chola*[4] when "everyone knows" that *cholas* do not care about or do well in school, school staff are often confident that she will not succeed in school. If the student does not apply herself and later fails in school, the staff feel that their expectations were warranted, and the student's own choices and identity are blamed for her failure. This is the traditional, one-dimensional means of explaining the link between identity and Chicana/o school failure. In fact, Chicana/o students' identities are fundamentally influenced by outside forces. As was previously suggested, when teachers and administrators attach negative labels to students, these students are forced to integrate those labels into their identity. As the majority of the students explained, the school staff with whom they interacted made it clear that Chicanas/os were not expected to succeed in school. These messages served two functions. First, they forced the Chicana/o students to deal with the importance of their racial identity in their lives, thus demanding that they incorporate a racial identity into their central identity. Second, these messages helped shape the students' racial identity by suggesting that a Chicana/o identity is incompatible with a positive school identity. In this context, the only challenge to this notion that most students can make, given that few have anyone to mentor them through this minefield, is to invoke that identity with the strength and power of resistance and protest, which, when uninformed, makes school failure almost inevitable.[5] Although not all Chicana/o students react to such messages and some students have found ways to deal with them, almost all of the students in the project conveyed a direct connection between the racial-political climate and their identities, by way of the distractions they faced around racial confrontations (see Olsen 1997 for a similar analysis of the significance of race in shaping life in a northern California school). For some, however, having a strong mentor who understood this process and intervened led to a dramatically increased ability to survive and even succeed in school. That is, when sources of encouragement built their support on the often racialized reality of the school and community experiences of Chicana/o youth, these youth were better able to contextualize their experiences and understand how school success can be an avenue toward strengthening their identities. This sort of encouragement also helped them see how to improve not only their own lot but also that of the communities they see being victimized by a systemic racialization that places Chicanas/os on the margins of the school and the larger community.

These are the general patterns that emerged from the accounts of the lives of a small but diverse group of Chicanas/os attending high school, community college, and university in the Los Angeles area. There are a great many unique experiences within these patterns, however. In fact, by looking at the various processes of identity formation and educational performance within the student population, these patterns can be more clearly fleshed out.

POWER, EMPOWERMENT, AND THE SCHOOLING OF CHICANAS/OS

The goal of this chapter was to consider the Chicana/o school experience through the eyes of the Chicana/o students themselves. From that vantage point, it is much easier to see the complexities of the processes by which Chicana/o students fail or succeed in school. There are no easy formulas that we can employ in attempting to move toward more uniform Chicana/o school success.

Nevertheless, one theme seems continually present as a critical force at work in the lives of all of the Chicana/o students of the project: power shapes and defines the experiences of Chicanas/os both in and out of the school. As we look at the four realms of experiences that are present in Chicana/o students' explanations of their educational struggles and successes, we see that power fundamentally determines each. With regard to the school context and climate, for example, the issues that Chicana/o students emphasize are all based in the power dynamics of the school. Students are critical of the power inequalities in their schools and the way in which it is made clear that not only do they lack power, but they are so disempowered that they have no voice in defining their own experiences within the school. As was discussed, Chicana/o students are often seen and treated as inferior, whether through blatantly racist confrontations or subtle differences in how teachers interact with them, subtleties that are possibly related to any number of factors. Because these power dynamics define a racial subtext that governs the school in terms of pedagogy, curriculum, school policy, and discipline, these dynamics define who Chicana/o students are within the school and shape the core identity of many of them. Frequently, a sense of desperation arises when these students experience distractions that further solidify the power dynamics they experience and make it clear that they cannot reverse those dynamics. When a Chicana student is psychologically assaulted by a teacher, for example, the effect can become such a great distraction for the student that she sees no possibility of resisting what she has learned is the inevitability of her failure. Furthermore, when a Chicano student is struggling financially and has to work part-time or even full-time, or when he is suffering because of a sibling's gang involvement, these distractions also fit into the model presented by those in power within the school, suggesting that the student is destined to the fate of his parents.

On the other hand, when students have someone who is a source of encouragement, the mentor can help them address the power inequities with which they are struggling. When the mentor, for example, rewrites the popular explanations of Chicana/o school failure and helps students understand both the inequities they are facing and how they can use that very circumstance as their inspiration for success, the result can be empowering. This power dynamic helps us understand the various possible roles of mentorship for Chicana/o students. For if a mentor simply encourages school success and says, "You can do it!" that is often not enough to assist disempowered Chicana/o students. When students are told by one individual that they can achieve their goals, and at the same time most of their daily interactions in and out of school suggest the opposite, they often feel forced to conclude that their success is unlikely. On the other hand, if they simply hear from peers or someone they look up to that the school is "messed up" without also receiving an informed critique of the power dynamics, they often believe that their only option is to lash out in rebellion in such a harmful way that they ensure their own failure.

What is critical about the possibilities that the Chicana/o students in this project have presented is that mentors can help students achieve success by offering encouragement that facilitates the development of a strong identity grounded in the students' own understanding of the racial-political climate as well as the resulting conflicts the students face. As we have seen, the power dynamics in Los Angeles schools are typically defined along racial lines to such a great extent that this is the realm in which Chicana/o students most often need significant help. This is not the only arena of power that can be critical for Chicana/o students, however. As discussed in Chapter 1, some students struggle with gender or sexuality much more than race, and this aspect of their lives becomes their core identity and the basis of their conflicts in school.[6] As Julia showed us, some students do not face confrontations that make power dynamics obvious or even an issue to them. In our discussions, Julia made it clear that race was not an issue in her life. She was even frustrated by members of her community who, as she put it, cried racism at the drop of a hat. The core of her identity was grounded in her aspirations for upward mobility. She did not describe any power confrontations that had shaped or molded her. To the contrary, because she never had experiences that made her question possible inequities in the distribution of power along racial, gender, or even class lines, she attributed her own struggles primarily to herself. Interestingly, however, she simultaneously stated that she had faced limited educational opportunities in her younger years and had never been challenged by teachers. Furthermore, the college she attended also constrained her possibilities, for the quality of education provided there was quite limited. Thus, although for Julia we might surmise that she simply needs good mentorship to guide her toward school success, it appears that without someone to also help her understand the conflicts, context, and underlying power dynamics that she faced, Julia might not be informed to the extent necessary to achieve success. In short, all the students revealed the centrality of identity and power in defining their school lives, while also providing evidence of the possibility of having mentors guide them through these experiences in empowering ways.

Having worked with a diverse Chicana/o student population that represented the many different experiences of Chicanas/os in Los Angeles –area schools, I have come to understand that Chicanas/os' lack of power has defined their school failure, while the contextualized mentoring of a select few has provided them with the skills to achieve success. We have seen that the complexity of Chicana/o schooling is such that no single solution can control for all of the forces at work in Chicana/o school failure. At the same time, although the systemic changes that researchers have continually called for are difficult to achieve in any short period of time, it seems clear that if Chicana/o students can be helped to understand the power dynamics that underlie the problems they identify in their schooling, and if this help is framed within the context of the development of a positive school identity, Chicana/o students can nurture the skills needed for optimally dealing with the forces that limit their schooling as they seek ways to overcome those forces and educationally empower themselves. It is important once again to emphasize that this mentorship and guidance need not be constructed solely around issues of race and school. In Chapter 1, I explained how Chicanas/os develop identities that are grounded in gender and sexual-preference inequities and that could just as easily fit into this model—and must fit for the students to whom it pertains. Allowing for such needs will help intervention efforts accommodate the diversity of the Chicana/o experience, given that males and females, for example, are racialized in different ways and are presented with different "accepted" responses to this racialization and to schooling in general. As the examples of Ernesto and Susana suggest, certain students may need help with grounding their racial identity or other identities within an evolving academic identity, whereas others may need help with understanding how to integrate an academic identity into their racial identities. With the possibility of a major redistribution of power within U.S. schooling so distant, Chicana/o empowerment through mentoring may be the most effective means of addressing Chicana/o school failure in a comprehensive way.

THREE

LESSONS FROM LOS ANGELES STUDENTS FOR SCHOOL SUCCESS

In our conversations the Chicana/o students at Harding, the community college, and the university focused on describing their experiences, explaining how their identities had emerged and how that process was related to school performance. Although we did not have much time during the interviews to strategize how to address the needs of Chicana/o students, the revelations of some of the students contained ideas for strategies. This chapter focuses on one student, Ernesto, who told a compelling story through which a theme of both survival and empowerment emerged. This chapter and Chapter 6 in Part 2 are not intended to cover the whole of students' experiences. Instead, this chapter looks for innovative possibilities by focusing intently on one insightful young man, and Chapter 6 focuses on five students, with the heart of the potential strategies coming from three young women. There are other stories and other strategies, but Ernesto's was the most compelling.

As mentioned earlier, it is critical that the conversations discussed in this book are set in the proper context. These interviews were conducted shortly after the Proposition 187 attack on Latinas/os in California. During this time, immigrants and Latinas/os in general were targeted as social leeches by the major political players in the state. This targeting was translating into a similar attack on multiculturalism, affirmative action, and other programs that were seen by conservatives as anti-American and antimeritocratic. The attack continues to the present day. The backlash against liberal politics and policies like affirmative action transformed the sociopolitical discourse by re-visioning the melting pot, appropriating "color-blind" imagery, and criticizing ethnic groups that avoid the meltdown. Thus the reality of the Chicana/o experience, as revealed in this study, was that the lives of these students, from an early age, were defined and categorized for them as a function of the color of their skin. The experiences of these students and the impact of those experiences on their identity formation is a powerful description of Omi and Winant's racial formation model (1994), which describes the process by which race and the racialization of people of color define life in the United States.

The severity of this situation becomes more dramatic as we look back at the history of the Chicana/o experience. Almaguer (1994) provides an in-depth analysis of the experiences of the first Chicanas/os (and of other racial groups) in California after its annexation by the United States. In his work, Almaguer exposes the significance of race and the racialization of the Chicana/o population as the key organizing principle around which the hierarchical relations of inequality in California were structured. Almaguer critiques other theoretical approaches to understanding the stratification of early Californian society as incomplete and inaccurate in that they ignored the complexity of the ideological forces at work during this period and overlooked the way in which race became a central issue in determining power and social location, regardless of class. He demonstrates that "racialization fundamentally shaped the class- and gender-specific experiences of both the white and non-white populations" (209). The same means of hierarchical stratification that Almaguer described are being invoked in the subjugation of Chicanas/os as we move into yet another century. The Chicana/o students of modern-day Los Angeles suggest that the primary changes that have occurred are reflected only in the advancement of the ideological weaponry employed to maintain the hierarchy. Rather than blatantly racist ideological positions as to the inherent or imbedded inferiority of certain races, today the hierarchy is reinforced through a racialization process that intersects with class and gender injustices to deny Chicanas/os the opportunity to demonstrate their equality. This process is achieved by limiting Chicana/o access to the resources needed to succeed in contemporary society and by boldly embedding in the popular discourse the belief that past reforms have led us to a point where effort by Chicanas/os is all that they need to succeed (as evidenced in the anti–affirmative action, color-blind ideology currently in vogue). Omi and Winant (1994) and Apple (1993) provide a detailed analysis of this process in the contemporary sociopolitical climate of the United States.

The voices of Chicanas/os, as young as fifteen years of age, exemplify that "equality of opportunity" is in many ways simply popular fiction. As the students suggest, racializing forces and their impact on Chicana/o identity formation in and out of school are a crucial part of the massive failure facing the Chicana/o community. Students are forced to deal with their placement at the low end of the school hierarchy as a function of their race. Few of these students have opportunities to understand the multitude of forces at work in this process, and thus they respond by lashing out, often resulting in their own failure and in denied access to opportunities for advancement.

RESISTANCE, *RASQUACHISMO*, AND HOPE

The ideological assault being leveled against Chicanas/os is met with resistance. As we look to better understand Chicana/o identity and to move toward empowering interventions, the students reveal potent possibilities. Although the final interviews I conducted with the college students exposed the significant impact of their and their families' experiences with racial confrontation, each of these students integrally tied the concept of change to their identity. These students saw themselves as Chicanas/os with strong ties to their culture and community and with an understanding of the subjugated role of Chicanas/os in this society (as a result of the racism they had witnessed and faced). Within this identity, they included their visions of themselves involved in efforts to make change for the empowerment of the Chicana/o community. The importance of making this change, therefore, was central to who they were and shined a light of hopefulness on the lives of other Chicanas/os whom they might help.

The hopefulness embedded in these students' self-images, however, must be met with an equal measure of reality. Successive generations of Chicana/o students have entered the university with politicized, strong Chicana/o identities that incorporated the goal of seeking change but that were eventually abandoned in losing battles against the institutional forces that demanded conformity and limited the possibility for creating spaces in which transformation can be sought. Ernesto provided a vivid example of the ease with which this abandonment of goals occurs, despite one's earlier commitment to change:

> When I was in high school, I came up [to the university], and there was some guy from Twenty-third Street in [the barrio]. He was going to school; he was going to be a lawyer. He was talking me into going, you know, like all the old *veteranos*[1] do, like, "You got to go to school. I'm

doing this to help out my community, my homeys, and stuff like that."
And I was like, "Oh, wow, that dude's cool." And then three years later,
I found out that he became, like, some rich lawyer in [an upwardly mo-
bile neighborhood], driving a Mercedes.

Although the individual Ernesto described here—and others like that
individual—may be making contributions to the Chicana/o community,
the reality that is being lived by the majority of Chicanas/os implies the
limits of such contributions. The racial history discussed above suggests
a need to redefine and reconstitute success among the Chicana/o populations, as well as a need to avoid trying to place Chicana/o empowerment in the institutionally sanctioned and subsequently gutted entities
of acceptable Chicana/o "resistance."

Rasquachismo is such a redefinition. Although there are a number of
varied interpretations of the term *"rasquachismo,"* it generally refers to
an approach to life that reconceives "lower-class cultures" as powerful,
by invigorating specific cultural icons with reinterpreted significance. As
a larger concept, it encompasses the reconstruction of the underdog into
a subject (rather than an object) who uses her or his agency to transform
and empower the downtrodden. Ybarra-Frausto explains this concept
in his "non-linear, exploratory and unsolemn" description:

> Very generally, rasquachismo is an underdog perspective—a view of *los*
> *de abajo,* an attitude rooted in resourcefulness and adaptability, yet mind-
> ful of stance and style. Rasquachismo presupposes the world-view of the
> have-not, but is also a quality exemplified in objects and places (a
> rasquache car or restaurant) and in social comportment (a person who is
> or acts rasquache). Although Mexican vernacular traditions form its base,
> rasquachismo has evolved as a bicultural sensibility among Mexican
> Americans. On both sides of the border it retains its underclass perspec-
> tive. (1991, 156)

Perez takes these definitions and applies them to Chicanas/os in the educational system as she explains that "to be Chicana/o on one's own
terms within the educational system is to be rasquache with respect
to it" (1993, 277). These ideas and images became vividly real through
conversations I had with Ernesto, who helps us understand Chicana/o
identity, racial formation, *rasquachismo,* and the possibility for transformation and Chicana/o educational empowerment.

Ernesto was perhaps the most successful Chicana/o student I worked
with in this study. As the previous chapter showed, our discussions were

filled with intense stories of a number of aspects of his life, from encounters with the police, gangs, and racist teachers to his travels in Mexico, his family history, and his intellectual emergence.

The story of Ernesto's identity formation begins much like that of many of the Chicana/o students I worked with in Los Angeles. Growing up in an emerging barrio in the Los Angeles area, Ernesto attended schools with a large number of both white students and white teachers. This interracial context played a big role in his identity formation. When we talked about his social sense of self, both through a checklist and in open-ended questions, race was at the center of his identity. As he discussed the influences on this identity, he returned to his school experiences immediately.

Racism and race issues are embedded in each of the stories he recounted from his elementary and secondary school experiences. One of the earliest experiences when, for him, race became a distinguishing characteristic was through ESL classes. Although ESL class participation was technically based on linguistic background, it became a stigmatizing, race issue for Ernesto. As mentioned in Chapter 2, Ernesto's experiences in ESL were, in his mind, racial because it was Chicanas/os who were in ESL, whereas large numbers of the non-ESL students were non-Chicana/o (and specifically white). As Ernesto explained, his racial awareness became clear toward the end of elementary school. In perhaps the most memorable experience he had in elementary school (detailed in Chapter 1), a substitute teacher told him and another Chicana/o student, "Go back to Mexico!" The racist implications of this incident hit home even harder for him because he had been born in the United States.

His encounters with racism became frequent as he entered junior high school. He recalled getting jumped by skinheads at the school because he had intentionally invaded their space in the yard. Ernesto also noted that the school staff exacted punishment differentially, often suspending only Chicana/o students for cutting class, even when white students had been with them. When he began talking about high school, Ernesto mentioned a number of racial incidents with both teachers and students. As with most instances of racism, observers (readers) can interpret many of these events in different ways, suggesting that other means of differentiation might have been used, but in Ernesto's world the means of differentiation was clear. Recall his run-in with a teacher and the principal that was discussed in Chapter 2. His teacher ignored him to the degree that Ernesto had to head-butt him to get his attention, while the principal spoke to his father in what Ernesto felt was a condescending fashion. This incident had strong racial connotations for

Ernesto because it was clear to him that Chicanas/os were seen and treated as second-class citizens in the school, and in the end, he rebelled. He concluded, "Man, fuck white people. I mean, these people are just assholes."

Ernesto remembered other instances of racial confrontations that he had with other teachers as well as a coach. During these high school years he also became more aware of the underlying racism that was present in his earlier school experiences with white students. In earlier chapters, excerpts from our conversations covered both how his white friends had called him "beaner" (as an "affectionate" nickname) and how his understanding of his racial position in the school dramatically affected even his confidence in class. He described how he felt as if he had to apologize for the U.S.-Mexican War and how teachers frowned upon any reference to his own cultural background or interests. These sorts of experiences led him to take a rebellious racial stance that was further solidified when he was assaulted by the police. Throughout these stages in his life, other issues obviously came into play besides race. As discussed in Chapter 1, however, he understood most of these issues as a function of race and racism. When he discussed the importance of class during one interview, he explained:

> And a lot of it has to do with race too, 'cause I remember we were building a skateboard ramp at this Japanese dude's house, but he lived, like, where all the rich white people lived. And we were trying to figure out a way to explain to his dad how we got the wood, 'cause we were stealing all the wood from construction sites. So I remember this guy was like, "I got an idea. We'll just tell him that Ernesto's dad is a construction worker, and he gave us all the wood." So I was like, "Yeah, that's a great idea!" And then I thought about it. I was like, "Wait a second. That's a trip." Like right away they would believe my dad was a construction worker, but they never thought to say, "Well. let's pick whose dad's gonna be the construction worker."

Ernesto recalled other incidents that were based on class—related to school lunch programs and buying gifts—but for him these stories too, in the end, were about race. Making a theoretical point based on his experiential analysis, Ernesto explained,

> You know, it's, like, harder to interpret class oppression. But it's easy to see the racial oppression, since *all* Chicanos are, [the] majority [are], like poor or like low-income. Like you see the race thing. I mean, now I'm

startin' to see, like, the class thing more often. But I still think that in this country—I don't say this too often—but I think the Chicanos have more to deal with along racial lines than class lines right now.

Thus various potential arenas of identity formation had come into play throughout Ernesto's life, but race, as constructed through a myriad of confrontations, was the lens through which issues like class, community, and religion were filtered and understood. This brief look into Ernesto's life exposes the contemporary manifestations of the racial formation process and its damaging impact on Chicanas/os in schools, as well as the means by which Ernesto formed a racial-political identity that allowed him to avoid being crushed by his schools. Much of this identity formation process came in response to the contexts in which he found himself. At the same time, however, his Chicano racial-political identity encompassed his own creative re-visioning of self and community, which in essence is a *rasquache* identity.

In many ways, Ernesto turned traditional constructions on their head, and his doing so helps us understand the ways in which identity, through a racial formation process, can be reconstituted to move Chicanas/os toward empowerment. In our conversations, Ernesto provided several examples of this redefinition. In one case, he discussed his feeling about grades:

> Like I've had classes where I get like a C-minus, and I'm like, "Man, I got a 86 on the midterm. What's up with this, dude? He gave me a C-minus." And I say I ain't even going to sweat it, because if I start getting caught up in grades, then I'm going to be like these dudes who are always like real individualistic. Last week [of class, they ask], "How are you going to grade the final?" And it's like those people aren't here to learn. They're here to get a 4.0 and go to law school or just graduate. So I never complain about my grades.

In essence, Ernesto was redefining the popular conception of the university student's objective from the position of the underdog. Rather than trying to compete to show he was as smart as his peers (as "smart" is popularly constructed), he focused on acquiring knowledge that was applicable to his interests—he sought knowledge rather than acclaim. Although one might criticize him for being naive or for potentially damaging his future chances, Ernesto believed that his future "success" in trying to achieve social change would be shaped by knowledge rather than grades. This redefining is a crucial facet of *rasquachismo* and it is something that he has continuously done at different stages in his life. Looking back at high school, he gave another example:

> We appropriate the cheapest pizza, or the cheapest meal was *our* spot. And even though like the white kids didn't go there because they had money to go to these other places, we hid that, like that was us. We went to go eat at the truck. We went to the truck, you know. And it's like white kids never go eat at the truck. They wouldn't eat that crap. But it was like we made our stuff cool. We made Dickies that cost fifteen bucks cool.[2]

Ernesto and his friends created a social space that was their own and through which they could access power. They made their socioeconomic limitations the symbols of their strength. On an individual basis, Ernesto had done this in other areas of his life to help him feel comfortable with who he was and to move toward his own goals, such as how he dealt with skin color:

> I'm like one of the dark ones, so like it's always a discussion. 'Cause I have an uncle who has four kids, and two of 'em are really light and two of 'em are like really, really dark. So it's always brought up, it's always a discussion, and now I just say, "I'm proud to be browner than white." It sounds fucked up to people who aren't dark, but I guess I'm just turning it around, like I don't have a problem with it.

Ernesto has reclaimed the location of the Chicana/o in society, abandoning popular notions of success and power and replacing them with self-empowering interpretations. Although these actions can be seen simply as survival strategies, they became much more than that as Ernesto applied them to making change. He revealed this importance when he spoke specifically about the *rasquache* orientation to his identity. After first responding to the question of who he was, he later explained the influences behind this identity:

> I like to think of myself as like somebody who cares . . . and someone who takes the underdog cause, thinks about society, and likes to be critical of society and enjoys a good fight, not a fistfight in the street, but I would prefer a open discussion in society. I would *love* to live in Mexico City and be like involved in all the shit that's going on there. But I'm not in Mexico City. I'm here, I'm a Chicano, I grew up here. I would say there's a lot to be done, and I'm really concerned with it. . . . It's from growing up. Talking to my grandfather and my dad a lot. Talking about all the

things they gone through. . . . I've always felt that you shouldn't let wrong things slide. . . . 'Cause my grandfather used to always tell me all these stories [about his difficult experiences as a Mexican in the United States], and I would always think that was fucked up. I always kind of had this feeling inside like "I wouldn't do that to anybody" or "I wouldn't leave anybody hanging."

Growing up with vivid examples of the difficulty of being the underdog, Ernesto—perhaps both consciously and subconsciously—decided to fight for the underdog. His views paralleled those of the Zapatistas in Mexico, whom he had visited and he referred to several times. He described his feelings with this example:

In Mexico they say, "Todos somos Marcos." you know?[3] And they ask Marcos, you know, "Who are you?" And he said, "I'm a gay in San Francisco, black in South Africa. I'm a Palestinian in Israel. I'm a *mojado* in East L.A."[4] I would say like I'm just one person in this fucked-up world and no different from anybody else that's fucked. I'm not in the ruling class. I'm in the dominated class.

Ernesto went on to explain his connection to the oppressed everywhere, creating linkages based on this underdog perspective. In short, he responded to racism by looking at the world through *rasquache* eyes, which allowed him not only to gain a sense of pride but also to redefine the Chicana/o existence and empower his community with cultural symbols that are valued and beneficial. This *rasquache* mentality emerged from the history of Chicanas/os, as Ernesto revealed by his urging that "I think everybody should remember who they are and what got 'em where they are."

As we move beyond defining and understanding the *rasquache* mentality (as introduced by Ybarra-Frausto 1991), we begin to look toward employing *rasquachismo* as a change agent (as suggested by Perez 1993). Ernesto revealed that his *rasquache* mentality was firmly grounded in the pursuit of change:

And that's one of the things my boss told me, because she helped me a lot with my confidence. She went to [the university]. She was a counselor, and she says, "Look, when people talk about issues, they talk about them from conceptual knowledge." She said, "You have practical knowledge of 'em, and that's why people will listen to you." Because I've spoken to like students and stuff, and I don't say things have to change. I say, "This is what happened to me, and this is what we need to do," you know. "Just do something. I don't care what you do."

Although he had created a Chicana/o identity grounded in his contributions to changing and improving things for Chicanas/os, Ernesto was still struggling with exactly what he wanted to do. He would soon enroll in a PhD program and saw himself moving toward applying his education and theoretical analyses to activist work. He debated between becoming a full-time activist, a researcher in communities, or even an applied theoretician. He also considered pursuing his activist interests outside of the United States (e.g., in Latin America). He was caught in the dilemma that confronts many Chicanas/os at that turning point: seeking change but being unsure of where or how to engage in that process. At the same time, however, Ernesto had created a space for himself in the university that was his own, a space that allowed him to not only retain his racial identity but also to inject it with *rasquache* icons and reconstitute it. This reconstituted identity could simultaneously move him toward helping others develop a *rasquache* mentality that would foster self-empowerment and toward pursuing changes that would benefit Chicana/o communities. He had begun a process of empowerment and change that could be passed on to Chicanas/os as communities.

CONCLUSION TO PART 1

Through an in-depth qualitative investigation that engaged Chicana/o students in discussions about their self-conceptions, we have begun to understand contemporary Chicana/o identity formation in ways that have not previously been tapped. The construct of Chicana/o identity includes a multitude of manifestations and continually evolves in fluid, amorphous ways, but the overriding role of race in the experiences of Los Angeles Chicanas/os from an early age results in the predominance of racial-political Chicana/o identities. Although other facets of their experiences are important in students' identity formations and they classify themselves as members of other social entities, the racial formation process results in many of these other facets of Chicana/o identity being subsumed under the construct of their ethnic-cultural or, more often, their racial-political identity.

The objective of this section of the book was to further develop an understanding of Chicana/o identity formation with the hope that it might reveal insights into how identity is linked or can be linked to Chicana/o empowerment, given the overwhelming "failure" faced by members of the Chicana/o community in the schools. By focusing on the intricacies of one particular student's life in this chapter, we have not only better understood the process of Chicana/o identity formation but gleaned possible connections to empowerment.

Ernesto, probably the most successful student among the study participants, revealed how he struggled with racial oppression: he reconstructed his image of himself and the Chicana/o experience, endowing it with a cultural capital that he in turn tapped into as he not only achieved success but also positioned himself to help other Chicanas/os. His story suggests how liberating it can be for students to transcend conventional U.S. conceptions of success and power and replace them with the rich cultural strengths upon which Chicana/o communities are founded. He showed that it is possible for Chicana/o students to write their own stories in their own voices and know that they are valid, regardless of what U.S. norms dictate.

As we turn our eyes to the horizon and walk through the twenty-first century, Chicana/o students, and one in particular, have shared valuable lessons to help us on this journey. It is clear that race is crucial to how Chicanas/os understand and organize their world. One of the fundamental means by which this process comes about is through their experiences with and observations of racism and discrimination. As the statistics on educational failure, along with individual students' stories, suggest, many Chicanas/os are unable to deal with these issues in empowering ways and instead strike out against the mouths and hands of racism, as Ernesto did in high school.

Ernesto's story, however, shows us the possibility for transformation. Ernesto has boldly met the challenge posed by Perez when she proposed invoking *rasquachismo* in Chicana/o educational struggles: "We must creatively continue to exploit unexpected sources in the construction of identities and politics that challenge the norms of thinking and practices within the educational system" (1993, 277). By acknowledging the role of race in Chicanas/os' lives and deciphering the complexities of the racial formation process, Chicanas/os can contextualize their experiences. Through this process they in turn can look within the community for symbols of power and strength and redefine the popular conceptions of "success." By acknowledging *rasquache* roots and nurturing them, Chicanas/os—the inheritors of many southwestern metropolitan and rural areas in the twenty-first-century United States—can embark on diverse paths toward empowerment that lead to the development of their communities and the larger society that depends on them.

PART TWO

INSIGHTS FROM ACOMA
CHICANA/O YOUTH

FOUR

IDENTITY FORMATION
IN ACOMA

In recent years, increasing attention has been paid to the experiences of urban Chicana/o youth. This has left an important part of the Chicana/o population ignored: rural Chicanas/os. To date, almost no investigation of the experiences and forces shaping the lives of Chicana/o youth in rural communities has taken place.

The three chapters of Part 2 strive to understand the lives of rural Chicana/o youth from their own perspectives. Part 2 also takes a different approach, as I transition from developing theory and models and move toward testing them by analyzing this unexplored context. This analysis has led to more depth and detail in describing students' experiences throughout this part of the book.

The present chapter focuses on who these students are and the forces that shape their identities, and the next chapter connects that information to their school performance. These analyses are essential, because although authority figures in rural communities often are confident in explaining the link between who students are and how they do in school, the students suggest that those authority figures do not have any idea who the students are, let alone what leads to their school outcomes. There is a great divide between the central forces that Chicana/o students described as pivotal to their lives and those discussed by authority figures in these communities.

When I was recruited to come to the university in Fowler, Washington, one of the draws my future colleagues mentioned was the large population of Mexicanas/os in Acoma. Everyone explained that much research and innovative work was needed in the many small rural Chicana/o communities of central and eastern Washington State. After coming to Fowler, I was eager to spend time out in Acoma, so I was excited on that

first trip out there. I also had a lot of time to think during that trip, because driving to Acoma takes a while. At best—without run-ins with the
police or getting stuck behind a tractor—it is a two-and-a-half-hour
drive. Almost the entire drive is on a two-lane road that wanders through
agricultural fields. Outside of Fowler they are all wheat fields, but as
you approach Acoma, there are asparagus and hops, apple orchards,
and other labor-intensive crops. Agricultural work is the main source
of employment for the Mexicanas/os who live in the Acoma Valley.
Mexicanas/os support the multibillion-dollar agricultural industry
through their work in the fields and warehouses throughout the region.

Driving out to Acoma felt like driving through parts of the San
Joaquin Valley of California, from which my own family came. The
drive itself therefore began to create a sense of traveling through time.
Those feelings solidified when I arrived in Acoma. It was as if I had become my father a generation earlier in central California. There were
clear social boundaries in Acoma, and it was apparent that Mexicans
could not cross those boundaries. Mexicans lived, shopped, and worked
in their own spaces, and even when they shared certain spaces with
whites, segregation prevailed. Although racism was not as overt as it
had been in my father's time, it hung in the air in Acoma in a way that
is almost indescribable. It lived in Acoma in a way that only those who
have shared the experiences of people of color in similar communities
can understand. One of the students I spoke with at the community
college tried to explain this:

> You always see [it]; if you don't see it, you can feel it. I know I can. When-
> ever I walk into a place or something, it makes you feel really uncomfort-
> able 'cause you know that they're lookin' at you, especially like when you
> walk into a room where there's, like, all white people or something. It's,
> like, I don't know, you can feel it. And then at work you can, like when I
> was working. I worked there for, like, for a year and a half, and then they
> would hire new people, and if they were white, they would always get the
> easier jobs, and they would give 'em more. And it's just everywhere. At
> work, at school, or at home.

A recent public debate in Acoma over racial profiling by the police provided evidence of the borders that exist in the community. A Latino who
spoke in Spanish at the forum explained, "We are more afraid of a police officer than we are of a carjacker or a robber." Although the whites
who attended the forum often disputed this reality, the Mexicanas/os
made it clear that racial profiling was a part of their daily lives.

When I started my work in Acoma, I found that although Mexicans in Acoma were a growing percentage of the populace, they held almost no power. Whites stood fast at the helm of economic, social, political, and educational power. Furthermore, whites wrote and maintained control over the story of Acoma. That is, they described Acoma as a place that was fair and just and where anyone could succeed if he or she just worked hard enough. Thus the dramatic economic and educational limits that Mexicanas/os faced were deemed a product of their own doing. Even more important, the Mexicanas/os who had succeeded were, for the most part, attempting to fit into this social order without making waves. They did not want to be seen as troublemakers, and so most of them avoided addressing the racial divide that they hoped to transcend. To ignore this reality, however, many had to distance themselves from the working-class Mexicanas/os of the community. The few voices that protested the harsh realities of these communities were written off and all but erased from the public landscape of Acoma.

Much of this situation became clear to me during my first visits to Johnson High School, a fairly large and busy campus. As was mentioned in the introduction, its student body was almost evenly divided between whites and Mexicanas/os. Everyone, however, was quite aware that these two populations had very distinct roles in the school. From my conversations with some staff members I got the sense that most staff wanted all of their students to succeed, and many were concerned about the limited success of numerous Latina/o students. At the same time, it was clear that a racial hierarchy existed in the school, and this hierarchy was commonly believed to be a natural function of limited Mexicana/o student effort and family support. Alternative explanations were not allowed in Johnson or in Acoma itself. I found this out just before starting my project at Johnson, when I was asked by the students to speak at a Cinco de Mayo celebration. A few days after inviting me, one of the students called back and said that the event probably would not happen, because the school administration was afraid that it would focus too much on difference and would be unfair to other ethnic groups. The administration suggested planning a multicultural day to celebrate difference and unity. It was obvious from the student's explanation that the administration was afraid that the students might challenge the social order at Johnson and that this in turn might lead to some psychological unrest. This response is not atypical. Most often, when public schools deal with or discuss issues of race and racial difference, the "conversation" is framed within the comfortable confines of culture and cultural difference. Often a host of different cultures are simultaneously covered.

If discussions of race and difference go beyond this sort, they can be uncomfortable, and schools try to avoid that type of discomfort.

When I spoke at the event, I addressed these very issues as I emphasized the historical legacy of Chicanas/os and their strength in fighting for survival. I did little more than point out historical facts and reveal their direct link to contemporary issues. Although I was unsure what impact my presentation would have on non-Chicanas/os, I did not want the Chicanas/os to continue feeling that they were solely to blame for their own struggles and those of their families, something that many had already learned to believe.

The response of many teachers and non-Chicana/o students was that I was complaining and causing trouble for no good reason. Conversely, many of the Chicana/o students were very thankful and appreciated my coming and delivering a message they did not yet know how to convey. I include this story because it displays the social distance between how whites and Chicanas/os understand the experiences of Chicanas/os in Acoma. Many of the whites who heard my presentation were convinced that I was "wrong." Although I spoke only of facts, these facts did not, in their minds, pertain to them, their lives, or their students. Ironically, although they did not know it, their own students disagreed. Unfortunately, the students had little room for voicing their dissent. That is one of the most important reasons that I have done this work. In Acoma, as in so many other communities, Chicanas/os are not allowed to tell their own story.

I found a similar environment at Acoma Community College (ACC). At ACC, however, a group of students had come to college with the goal of addressing the needs of their communities. They had created a support network and used this as a means of pursuing campus change that might benefit them. In particular, the year before my project, they had pushed the college to create a Chicana/o Studies program. Still, with only one professor teaching the courses, the additions were marginal. In fact, students complained that the program was underfunded and understaffed and reflected a lack of commitment to addressing the needs of Chicana/o students. More difficult for the students at ACC was that they lacked a strong sense of community, because they were on a commuter campus, always coming and going between school, work, and home or other family responsibilities. For these reasons, many students had to focus just on making it to class and through a given semester, and significant numbers dropped out for the same reasons. Other issues that were important to these students as Chicanas/os had to be secondary.

Many of the students simply had to focus on finishing school and trying to find a way of bettering the financial situations of their families.

The university was both very different and quite similar to the schools in Acoma. In Fowler, everyone lived in the local area, and there was a tight community of Chicana/o students who had been successful in earlier generations at creating programs designed to meet their specific needs. In addition, this was a college town where economic advancement seemed realistic and attainable. In Fowler, however, the social order mirrored that in Acoma in many ways. Although Chicanas/os and others often vocally protested and although a significant number of liberals were present on campus, power was held by conservative traditionalists who denied the need for the sweeping changes Chicanas/os and others sought. Instead, the traditionalists opted for varying versions of the status quo. My own interactions with students, staff, faculty, and administrators clearly demonstrated that radical ideas and approaches would be tolerated in removed locations on campus but would have little impact on the functioning and nature of education at the university. These contradictions were reflected within the dynamics of the Chicana/o community itself. The students who consciously struggled with these issues chose a number of different strategies to empower themselves. Many mimicked traditional organizations within the university as a means of adapting the status quo to their own cultural background. Chicana/o fraternities and sororities, for example, were emerging as a means of identification for the students. Students were attempting to model the institutionalized paths for social and economic advancement that dominated mainstream social life in Fowler. At the same time, other students challenged the appropriateness of adapting exclusive structures to a Chicana/o community and sought to attack, and to demand the replacement of, these traditional structures. In the end, even the students who attempted to ignore or transcend the significance of race in their lives often found themselves caught in the maelstrom of racial politics.

Although these personal insights may help the reader understand Acoma and Fowler through my eyes, the students exposed these places to their core. The analyses by Acoma students add depth and substance to those of the students in Los Angeles. Because of the added complexities in the Acoma students' experiences, and because so little work has been done on the rural Chicana/o experience, their insights are covered in significant depth in this chapter and the next. After a brief review of the survey findings, their experiences are reported and are organized by each of the sites at which we worked. The rationale for this organization is discussed in greater depth in Part 3, when the experiences of the Acoma students and those of the Los Angeles students are compared. Finally, "Time-out" at the end of Part 2 provides another vantage point on the issues raised in the next few chapters. It is a powerful, personal narrative from one student's perspective that helps the reader understand the evolution of identity and schooling in one student's life.

EARLY FINDINGS

For the survey respondents, two central forces made up their sense of identity: family and school. Ninety-one percent of the students said that family was among the most important aspects of their lives. In their responses, the students explained that they were deeply concerned about helping their families and being able to improve things for them, because their families meant the world to them. This concern stood out as a constant theme and was directly linked to a number of other forces. School, for example, is an arena of identity formation that we would assume to be of importance to any sample of students. Although school was among the most important facets of the students' lives, given that 88 percent of the participants discussed it, the students typically dealt with the significance of school through their need to help their families. The discussion of the role of school did not have depth or detail for the vast majority of students, beyond its importance to the students' families.

Family similarly served as a filter for the other facets of students' lives that the students described as among the most important. Fifty-five percent of the students discussed the importance of jobs (which was related to their social class), 54 percent discussed religion, 52 percent talked about culture, 43 percent talked about race, and 42 percent about their community. In their responses to the survey, however, it was clear that these different arenas of their lives were understood and emphasized through their families' experiences, for each arena reflected what students felt were characteristics of their family lives. One other factor that should be mentioned is gender. Although only 28 percent of the students discussed this as being important to them, that percentage constituted almost half of the female respondents. My own experiences and observations showed me that gender dynamics played a significant role in shaping the lives of these students.

The surveys therefore provided an introduction to some of the forces shaping Chicana/o students' experiences and identities and allowed us to develop interviews that could explore these issues in greater depth. One finding from the surveys that helped us in thinking about the meaning of the survey data was student responses to a general identity question. Students were asked to describe who they are in their social world. Although this question is about identity, students typically answered it with regard to their self-concept and discussed personal characteristics—for example, being determined. The most common discussions beyond self-concept, however, referred to students' race or ethnicity; 22 percent of the students discussed this arena of their social world.

The survey data provided an important framework that could be studied further in interviews. At first glance it appeared that, for these Chicana/o students in rural Washington, the family was the center of their social worlds and their identities. A number of other important arenas of their lives were prominent in their experiences (including school, jobs, religion, culture, race, community, and gender), but the overarching significance of family placed these other aspects of identity within the domain of family. Race appeared early on to be a key factor in the equation of Chicana/o identity formation, but there was clearly some complexity that the surveys could not unearth. To get at that complexity, the project focused on interviewing students in each context.

STUDENTS' ANALYSES: THE INTERVIEWS

High School Students

For the high school students, family was the core of identity. It was from and through this aspect of identity that other identity issues were understood and integrated into the students' sense of who they were. Six of the nine high school interviewees grounded their social identity first and foremost in their families. As they explained who they were and what mattered to them, they focused entirely on two aspects of their families: their families' strength, and their dedication to helping their families. One student reflected the sentiments of his peers when he stated, "Family's like the biggest thing for me in the world. And I'm always there for my mom whenever she needs something. Or my brother. If they need somethin' done, I'm always there to help if I can." Another student related why her family was the most important aspect of who she is and when this first became clear to her:

> If I didn't have my family, I wouldn't say I'd die . . . but, for me, my family is a *rock* that sustains me emotionally, that sustains my effort to

study and my motivation. My family is most important to me. Because if they were not in my life, I know I wouldn't die, but I would feel bad emotionally, in terms of my self-esteem, because I would not have them with me. But I do have them. They give me support, so for me that is number one. . . . When we came here from Mexico, we had to all work together, and all of us would earn money. I knew that together we could make something. (Translated from Spanish)[1]

Speaking so poetically about the meaning of family to her, this student emphasized that for two-thirds of the high school participants, their understanding of who they were began and ended within their families. Of the three high school students who did not place family at the core of their identities, one emphasized her immigrant and language minority status but also highlighted the importance of family, and the other two also addressed family but had faced conflict and a lack of mentorship as they continued to struggle to develop a strong sense of identity in any arena of their lives.

In all the students' discussions, they made it clear that their families were extremely important not only to who the students were but also to what they wanted to be. So family shaped the identities of the students both in terms of their sense of membership within the family and in terms of their sense of the types of occupations they would one day hold. This finding was evidenced in a number of ways. For a few students, divorce had played a key role in their identity formation by leading to greater admiration for their mothers' strength and a desire to support their mothers. One student talked about his mother's and family's influence repeatedly, as in this example:

I'm just mostly doin' it [trying to succeed in school] for me and my family. 'Cause my mom's been through a lot just to keep me in line, and my other brothers and sisters weren't really in line their whole time. So she deserves a break. So that's why I want my own business. I wanna be makin' enough money to take care of her. 'Cause she deserves it. To tell you the truth, she deserves a lot. . . . Just lookin' at her and seein' what she's been through, I need to do this for her. And then there's the fact of my brother . . . how he turned his whole life around. That's something that to me made a big, big difference in my life. 'Cause I seen him turn his whole life around from this big-time gangster to now he's in college gettin' his degree and stuff like that. . . . For him everything's perfect, just about going the way he wants it to go. . . . For me and him, we had not just our mother but older people that looked [after] us [an older sister and brother], you know, like, "This is what happened to us. We don't want this to happen to you."

Later, this student went on to explain that his mother was his biggest influence and why that was so:

> My mom [is my biggest influence]. . . . Just her, with all the struggles she's been through and overcoming so many of them. I want that kind of power that she has. I want to be able to do that stuff. And I hope I am someday.

Here the student described how family becomes so integral to students' identities, as he exposed how the struggles of family members become both a part of who students are and the reason they want to be success-ful—that is, so they can help their families. The students provided countless examples that, though different in detail, were virtually iden-tical in their effect on the students.

The dramatic struggles of their families to survive in Acoma all but demanded that these Chicana/o students fight to help their families. Six of the students had developed a school identity that evolved out of their familial identities and their desires to help their families.[2] These students were very motivated to use school as a means toward achieving financial stability so that they could later provide their own families with comforts that their parents had never been able to afford. The students talked specifically about how their parents had struggled as farmwork-ers and how they wanted their parents to leave this work. One female senior explained this clearly when she talked about her influences:

> My dad and my mom always tell me, "We are here so that you can im-prove your lives. So every time I am studying or doing something, I think of my parents because someday I would like to be somebody and be able to give them some money or give them something so that they wouldn't have to work anymore. So that is what keeps me studying. It's not really for me but for my parents, because they sacrifice a lot for me. I know they make sacrifices for me, and I think that in the future it will be my turn to sacrifice for them. In addition I want my brothers and sisters to see me as an example and say, "I will follow in her footsteps and not hit the streets or get into things I shouldn't," . . . because I believe that I am a role model to my brothers and sisters. (Translated from Spanish)

Throughout her interview, this student constantly emphasized the importance of family and revealed how they are critical to both her identity and her goals as a student. She also challenged the myth that working-class Mexicana/o parents do not value education:

> It has been my parents who have helped me the most, more than anybody it has been them. I study for them, and they work for me. They don't tell me to get a job. . . . My parents are always telling me to go to school. . . . My grandparents in Mexico call me and tell me to study and to educate myself. I have always had my family's support, all of them. (Translated from Spanish)

For this student, as for many others, familial and school identities were tightly bound, for she had also been told directly by her family that she needed to do well in school. Another student subtly pointed to the relationship between her family and school identities as she talked about who she was: "[I am] always trying to do better, always trying to reach the next step. And [I am] also fighting for my family and for myself and, most of all, I think, for my culture." She later described these linkages in a different way:

> Well, religion is important to me, and also my family and my culture. Everything is important to me. They are so special to me, all of them, and like having a treasure—it's all treasure for me. [They are] the big treasure that I think I kinda carry for the rest of my life. And I think I'm good, having this, and I'm proud to have religion, family, my culture, and [to] have school, and I think this is nice. . . . It's just like a ball full of energy, like energy of love, of caringness, that it comes all together like this—like religion, community, spirit, job, and family and culture. It makes me feel good. All this is like one big thing. Like I said, [it's] like a treasure.

As did many of the students, this young Chicana explained how multiple identities combined into a centralized familial, cultural, and school identity that drove her interests and efforts. She and her peers became the future for their families by applying the families' histories and lessons in pursuit of a good education. One of the young men took this idea in another direction and noted how his racial identity, which was linked to his family identity, had shaped his school identity. Asked what had been his biggest influence, he said:

> I think it's the identity—knowing who you are. See, the way it happened is I know now where we stand—the Chicano, Latinos—where we stand. I know where we stand, and I know where I wanna go. And the thing is,

by knowing where you are, you kinda wanna change it. Because it's not too positive. But we got the reputation of being welfare mothers, just picking apples and fruits, being in warehouses, pure manual labor. That ain't true, man. We're startin' to get doctors, we're startin' to get lawyers, we're startin' to get representation in Congress. Slowly, but surely. And, what I want is, I want people to know that. That we're coming up. We're not just stayin' down. And another thing: I know where we are, but we're gettin' stuff thrown at us, you know. And like Proposition 187, you know anti–Affirmative Action, English only. That's all stuff, whether they'd like to admit it or not, [that] is basically [against] us. And I've done my research and I've took the time to notice this. It's only obvious: it's for us.

As this student and others suggested, many students shape their identities not simply around the specific struggles of their families but also around the struggles of Chicanas/os and Mexicanas/os in general. They have witnessed systemic forces that limit their opportunities. Their experiences with and observations of these forces lead them to develop an identity that is grounded in their desire to change their world. Thus, for many students, the familial identity is linked to a racial identity, both of which shape students' school identities and goals. In the case of this particular student, however, he was able to clearly explain these relationships in ways that many of the others could not. His experiences and interests allowed him to tap into readings and perspectives that led him to clearly identify the links among these different realms of his identity formation.

Other students focus less on race but also expose how family becomes the key filter for developing an identity that encompasses other arenas of identity. In fact, for all but the two students who were struggling with identity, other identity arenas such as education, culture, religion, and community emerged through their sense of familial identity. One student provided a good example as she began to talk about important aspects of her identity:

Culture is very important to me, not only in religion [but also] in food, dress, in our way of speaking, in how we express ourselves, and in how we act, in all of these. School is very important to me because I know that it is the path to becoming what my parents want me to be and what I want to be. . . . They are connected because culture is carried in your family, school is tied to family and to culture, to community. If you do not have community, you cannot have school, and if you don't have school, you don't have community. Religion is tied to family, culture, school. . . . In some form you can connect them. So I believe they are connected. (Translated from Spanish)

This student showed us that although family is the core influence on students' identities, a complicated web of forces is continually involved in the shaping of identity, and for many students, identity is much more than the importance of family. Later this student revealed these connections again when she was asked to describe herself. She replied, "[I am] a woman with culture who wants to educate herself, who loves her family, and who hates racism" (translated from Spanish). As the students demonstrated, identity is the complex product of multiple forces operating simultaneously in their lives, and understanding identity requires careful analysis of this complexity.

As this student also revealed, religion plays a key role for several of the young women, because it becomes a more natural avenue for developing a social identity outside of the family (in the larger social world) than is school. This role of religion can be understood as a result of traditionalism and the development of a Mexicana identity as well. Within some families, religion is seen as a more natural way of developing a public social identity than is school success. This does not mean that the students are discouraged from school success, but rather it means that the experiences of their families suggest that religious expression and dedication are, in their eyes, much more realizable than school success, especially for women.

Other issues can equal or surpass the importance of familial identity when they raise comprehendible conflicts for the students. This situation applied for a couple of students through their status as recent immigrants with limited English abilities. They had felt excluded from the world of mainstream students and traditional paths to success. They had often felt ridiculed and embarrassed for their limited English skills and had also come to find that they were subsequently categorized as intellectually inferior despite their strengths in certain academic subjects like math and science. As one student briefly noted,

Sometimes you're embarrassed to ask, because they gonna say that you don't know that word or you don't understand or you don't pay attention. But you really do [pay attention], but you don't understand.

She went on to describe some of the experiences that had negatively influenced her, including things other students had said to her: "Like

'You're stupid' or things like that. 'You don't know anything' or 'You're not gonna go on with your life.'" Later she told how a teacher had contributed to her struggles with her identity around language issues:

When I was in fourth grade, I had this teacher that she never let us go out to eat lunch or have any recess 'cause we have to stay there with her and learn. But she always get mad at us, and she always tell us bad words and stop make ourselves feel good. That doesn't feel good. So I always tell my mom, and she didn't believe me, 'cause she said, "How can a teacher tell you all those things?" . . . [The teacher would say] we couldn't learn what she said. . . . She want us to learn fast the words . . . , but sometimes you couldn't because we didn't understand them. And she didn't want to explain them. So that's why she got mad. . . . [I think she treated us like that] because of our color and we are Mexicans. And she was white. . . . I think [that] sometimes when I remember that, it makes me like sad. How could she tell all of that if she didn't know why we couldn't understand her?

This student struggled with her identity as a language minority student. Because of the conflicts she experienced, she learned that her language abilities defined who she was in the eyes of others in the school, and she developed significant insecurities that made it difficult for her to develop the confidence to pursue her educational goals. As she revealed, these experiences clearly shaped her identity.

Few of the high school students were able to develop a complex analysis of how the school shaped their identities. Still, they did portray an informal system whereby school staff all but forced Chicana/o students to consider the importance of their race in their identities through schooling itself. This process of racialization is reinforced in other arenas of school life. Some students, for example, described differential treatment as they explained that certain school rules had apparently been developed with only Chicanas/os in mind, for it was only Chicanas/os who faced punishment for not following these rules. One student gave some examples:

[The assistant principal] sees every Hispanic here as a gang member, just about. . . . He sees us all as just punks and everything. But if he comes up to this little white boy, [he will say,] "Good job." If you're walkin' around and if you got a three-inch belt that barely comes out or something or whatever and it's just not on the next link, "Oh, you're gang related. 'Cause tuck in your belt." . . . And if you don't like wearin' your pants right at your waist, you wear 'em like between your waist and your hip, and not sag, just a little bit where you're comfortable, if you're saggin', then you're gang related. If you got a big shirt and it's not tucked in, then you're gang related, and if you're Hispanic, then you're definitely gang related. I was playin' ball and I was still considered gang related. I mean, I played basketball, tried to fit in there. It wasn't workin'. . . . And even if you wear a cap and it's cupped, it's gang related. All them white boys out there, wearing baseball caps and everything, and they're cupped and everything, and they're wearin' big old shirts and big old pants, but that's basic, that's style. You see a Hispanic wearin' 'em, [then it's] "Oh no, uh-uh. Search him. Frisk him." We get looked down on for some reason. I don't know why.

This student went on to provide an insightful analysis of the way in which this differential treatment leads to a self-fulfilling prophecy among some students:

The reputation that [the assistant principal] gives, and people like him gave us the reputation that we're lookin' at, and [we] say, "Well, if you call me an asshole, well, hell, I'm gonna be an asshole, if that's what you consider me." So it's just "Well, you're gonna call me gang related? Well, hell, I'm gonna be gang related." That's the way they're thinkin'. They're not gettin' their stuff straight. They're just sayin', "Well, if you tell me this, then I'll do this. You think I'm this? Well, hell, I'll be that."

While many of the students struggled to explain the role of race in high school, several identified a two-tiered system of justice in which certain behaviors and styles of dress were seen as negative and gang-related for Chicanas/os but were seen as innocuous for whites. This student explained the means by which certain students felt compelled to shape their identities around this system of enforcement in school. Again, although many students have difficulty putting this sort of racialization into words, it is common for students to shape their own identities around the racialization they experience within the school. Many feel that they have no other options. Whereas others might see this feeling as a cop-out or an excuse for "failure," these students, in their eyes, had no other options in the school. When we listen to the countless stories they share to support the effect of racialization on their identities, the weight of their collective analysis becomes overwhelming.

Gender also has the potential to play a similar kind of role when gender issues are raised, but such issues usually confront the young women in an indigestible form. In those cases, it becomes part of the subtext and not central to identity. That is to say, although many of the students are aware of gender inequities, these inequities are so inherent to the experience of the students and are so little addressed (as is the case for race for some other students) that such gender issues do not become part of their conscious identities. Still, some young women in the high school discussed the gendered aspects of their identities, as in this example:

> I think that being a woman kinda makes things harder. I mean, not so much as it did in the past, but, like, there are some times where, just because you're a woman, people say things or you feel that you can't do certain things. But my mom always taught me that that doesn't really matter, that if you wanna do something and if you put your mind to it, that you can. So it affects me a little bit 'cause sometimes I let the stereotypes affect me, and I think, "Oh, well, that's more of a man's job" or "That's more of a man's duty." And I'm not happy that I do that. But it's just kinda something that goes along with it. I notice it, so that's, like, the first thing that I could do is notice it, you know, and then change it. So as long as I know that it's going on, at least I can do something about it.

As this student pointed out, gender conflicts are often difficult for these young women to address or even deconstruct, so it is rare that gender becomes a conscious part of their identities.

Conflict along racial lines is the most common of these types of occurrences that influence identity. One student, mentioned above, explained this conflict clearly while discussing why race was an important part of his identity. As was noted earlier, he looked at societal perceptions in general, saying, "We got the reputation of being welfare mothers, just picking apples and fruits, being in warehouses, pure manual labor. That ain't true, man." He then described how race was related to his experience more directly:

> A few times I've been spit at. We were walkin' one time from middle school. We were walking home, and this truck passed by with two *gavachos* [whites]. They go, "Hey, spics" and—boom—they spit at us. And it landed on my sleeve. That made me feel like crap. And *este*, you know, other time I went to the mall that's kinda way up there on the rich side. And that's basically a place where you could play video games. There's a convenience store around there and miniature golf. . . . And I went to the store to buy myself a Snickers bar and a pop. And this lady walked behind me, and she stood lookin' at me. And she just looked at me and seeing what I was

doing. And I grabbed my stuff, and I turned around and I was like, "Aw, this lady prolly thinks I'm a shoplifter." And I told her, "Could I help you?" And she's like, "Oh, I'm just checking what you're doing." And I'm like, "Well, I don't need no babysitter." And she's like, "Yeah, well, I'm just gonna stay here just in case." And I was like, "What?" I just threw her stuff right there. I threw it, man. I was like, "You know what? I ain't givin' you my business. You're stereotyping me already." And that's kinda messed up. That was one of my big shocks right there. When I was followed at the store.

Such incidents stick with students for years. Even when rare, the incidents become central to the identity formation of many students because of the negative and damaging ways in which others make sense of their identities.

Although students brought up the importance of race and racial conflict in shaping their identities, many struggled to make sense of racialization and relied on their families to help them define their sense of who they were in their complicated social worlds. So the family and traditionalism were the key influences on identity. The larger social context—the invisibility of many Chicana/o students in the school and the limits this placed on the students, along with the limited avenues for students to address these issues—also contributed to centering identity in the family.

For a few students, a lack of mentorship was a critical component of their identity development while they were engaged in or expressing interest in doing identity development work, but without mentorship they seemed to be falling through the cracks. The lack of mentorship that students had in dealing with the influences on their identity development made it difficult for them to develop empowering and affirming tactics. Most students attempted to ignore the negative messages they heard about race and inferiority in school and relied heavily on their familial identities for affirmation. They did not have models for developing strong racial identities or school identities that could assist them in challenging the popular definitions of Chicana/o identity with an empowered sense of confidence. Instead, they had to turn to those areas in which they had guidance and role models. In the end, even for those students who focused on the importance of racial conflict in their lives, the familial identity shaped their lives in school and out of school. Within the school, these students focused on the need for their success to help their families, and yet the forces working against that success left many students struggling both psychologically and academically. Again, while

most struggled to make sense of all this, one student provided some helpful insights:

> I guess I would like more people to think like me—and even more ad-
> vanced. To kinda be my mentor, but think like me, you know. Or like a
> teacher and stuff that could think the right way. I mean, to me, thinking
> the right way is . . . using this vehicle of education to head me where I
> wanna go, which is back to my *raza,* and help them get where I am right
> now. And that's where thinking the right way is for me. So I'd like people
> to guide me that way: older people or people my age that I can just hang
> around with. That's why me and Alfredo are real close, obviously. 'Cause
> he's my mentor. I've already told him that. [He] thinks a little more ad-
> vanced than me. He's read way more than I have. And we hang around a
> lot. 'Cause we're always—I mean, we catch each other's slips and things.
> I correct him or he corrects me. And that's what I want. The way it's set
> up right now, there's not too many people like that.

Although this student gave a clear description of his need for mentorship
to help him develop the empowering type of identity he sought, the interviews with students as a whole exposed a wide diversity of needs and
experiences. It is obvious that the families provided a great deal of support and filled many of the students' needs. As the students explained,
the family represented the core of their identities, and it is from this foundation that other arenas of identity did or did not become integrated into
their social identities. School became a critical aspect of identity for the
students because of the needs and struggles of their families. Although
their educational goals often lacked focus and refinement, these goals
were critical to the identities of students because this facet of who they
were was the center of who they saw themselves becoming. Factoring
into these two central arenas of Chicana/o student identity were a number of other forces. For some students, religion was an important off-
shoot, particularly for females. Others emphasized culture as a slightly
broader aspect of identity that was critical to them. For many, race became part of the equation, for they understood their struggles and those
of their families in the context of the racial climate they saw around them
and the racialization that limited the opportunities of Mexicanas/os in
Acoma. Some students experienced conflicts in other realms of their lives
that influenced identity development outside of the family. And for some,
racial conflict was better understood around linguistic issues, because
their limited English abilities led them to be ridiculed or simply deemed
intellectually incompetent. These kinds of conflicts became critical to

students' identity formations. In fact, conflict as a whole seemed to define the Chicana/o student experience at Johnson High School, where some students faced blatant racial or linguistic conflicts and others responded to the conflicts their families faced in trying to advance themselves. This larger context of conflicts led students to shape family identity around a school identity that was intended to empower both them and their families.

Many of the high school students, however, were unable to verbalize an understanding of these processes, and through students' discussions we clearly see the need for mentorship as Chicana/o students struggled with the process of identity development. As the last student mentioned above noted, the complex and often subtle forces that shaped the experiences of Chicanas/os in their schools and communities made it difficult for them to make sense of their experiences and to develop a positive sense of identity without some form of mentorship. While the student who discussed this matter focused on the need for mentorship in developing a critical racial identity, other students needed assistance dealing with racial and/or other forces in ways that they could not yet explain. The community college and university students in the study were able to reflect on their high school years, and those reflections help us understand the experiences that these high school students had only begun to explore.

Community College Students

> I feel like I'm not accepted sometimes, because when I go to Mexico, the Mexicanos treat me like garbage. You know, I'm not Mexicano, because I can't speak fluent Spanish. And I don't know enough like they do about the culture and the background of the Mexicano himself. And when I come over here, I'm not a Mexican American either, because the only way you can be American is if you're European or white, you know. And sometimes I feel like, "Hey," you know, I tell my family, "What am I?"

As this student exemplified, identity was often just as much a struggle among Chicana/o community college students in Acoma as it was for Chicanas/os in the high school. What was almost immediately apparent in discussing identity with the community college students was that race played a bigger role for them than it did for the high school students. First of all, the community college students had finished high school and had begun to understand what they described as the limits that had been placed on them as a function of their race, even with high school diplomas. Looking back at their earlier schooling, they saw how Chicanas/os were affected by low expectations and even how these expectations were covertly couched in the context of language ability. Two students provided examples:

> As a kid, I really didn't think about it, but right now I look back at that. I got into kindergarten, and right there, too, they kind of separated us. I mean, not as much, but they still had the ESLs right here and then the gringos or the Americanized Europeans over here. And so all through my elementary it was kind of like that.

> At school I've always seen, like, teachers specifically give more attention to, like, the white kids or to the kids that are of a higher class. And I guess that's why race is really important. Especially 'cause discrimination's everywhere, everywhere you go around here.

What is most significant about these student recollections is that these experiences with segregation and differential treatment were crucial to how the students developed a sense of who they were both within and outside of the school. As they explained, it was made clear to them that their racial and/or ethnic background distinguished them from other students in ways that limited their educational possibilities. Although many of the students had only recently begun to make sense of this, it was evident that these experiences had shaped their identities for quite some time. As community college students, however, they were beginning to take ownership of those identities in ways that they could not at younger ages.

The community college students were able to frame more clearly the experiences that the high school students were still going through and trying to understand. In fact, some of the community college students sought out others who shared this understanding, and in these support groups they developed an analysis of their experiences together. MEChA (Movimiento Estudiantil Chicano de Aztlán) played this role for four of these students. One student described how MEChA had helped him:

> [MEChA] got me away from all the trouble or skipping that I was doing back in high school, you know, and not really paying attention. It actually said, "Hey, come and learn about this. Come and join our group. We got some love for you." And so it kind of got me back up on my feet.

Initially, the significance of MEChA for many of the students was that the group members saw the potential of these individuals and urged them to strive for educational success. This encouragement was critical to their evolving identities because the support that individuals found in MEChA provided a counterstory to their earlier educational experiences and helped them frame their identities in a new way in which for the first time "Chicana" and "Chicano" did not automatically translate into educational inferiority. Through this process, MEChA helped the students understand what they had seen and experienced. This process was critical in an area like Acoma, where there was typically only one acceptable explanation for Chicana/o students' school experiences and poor outcomes: a lack of student and parent commitment and effort. This support was also much needed because few of the students had encountered blatant forms of institutional racism through which they could challenge that dominant argument. So, for many of the students, race became a critical part of identity, and it was linked to educational goals.

It is also important to note that a few of these students chose a drastically different route in high school, by trying to blend in with their white peers. These students explained that they had tried to hide or erase their ethnic characteristics. They also admitted, however, that they had lost important parts of themselves and simply could not continue on that path. Although the community college students made it clear that they were just beginning to make sense of these critical experiences, they made it equally clear that race had been a critical means by which they were distinguished and forced to understand who they were in the school and in their lives in general. The manifestations of the racialization process they described included hiding ethnic characteristics and attempting to fully assimilate, but these manifestations also eventually led many students to seek a support system that could help them rethink the messages they had received in their interactions with the "mainstream" society. These issues are discussed in depth in Chapter 6.

Although much of the early interviews with these students focused on the struggles around race and ethnicity with which they were then dealing, the family was still a dominant force and central to their identities. As the students emphasized, the family defined who they were:

I've always known that [my family] were the most important people to me. But not 'til I got to college did I realize that they are. And they're always gonna be part of me, and no matter where I go in my school, no matter where I go in my community, no matter where I go with my job, my career, whatever, they're still gonna be there. And I'm still gonna have to be there for them.

In fact, the familial aspects of identity became even more prominent for these students, for these aspects shaped the significance of other aspects of identity such as culture, class, employment, religion, community, and especially education. However, because of the conflicts that emerged over racial identity among the community college students, this aspect of their identity often took a more prominent role in their discussions than did family: race played a central role in their social identity development outside of the home (and it also encompassed community, class, gender, and familial issues). Nevertheless, family identity remained the most important factor to students, especially because it eventually encompassed a strong educational identity. It is important to recognize that the familial and racial identities were not distinct from each other and that they often merged as the familial identity shaped the importance of an educational identity, which then became even stronger through the development of a racial identity that similarly supported and influenced the students' educational goals. One student described part of this process:

> I think the influence for me has been the way all my *familia* has actually worked so hard so their kids can do somethin'. The way I see us going to the fields in the morning . . . it's not necessarily a negative or a positive, but it's that I actually wanna do something about it—I mean, just the way that people live, the way people try here at school, and the way people suffer.

The *mechistas* all strongly emphasized and integrated both the familial and the racial aspects of their identities, most often through their own school identities and efforts to achieve their goals. This combination of familial and racial identity constituted the core of who they are and how they see themselves in their social world. Family represented the heart of their support, along with their inspiration, and family encompassed other facets of identity such as culture, community, and religion. Race, on the other hand, was equally important in that it often defined their lives outside of their homes and incorporated or was linked to other aspects of identity such as community, gender, sexuality, and class. The two forces therefore typically interacted and functioned as a whole as they were synthesized into students' school identities. Each of these students had developed a positive school identity that was the core of what they hoped to become. This identity was informed equally by their families and their desire to support their families and by their racial identities and their hope to address some of the racial inequalities that they had seen in their schools, jobs, and communities. One student gave an example of how these issues had become a syncretic identity. When asked to complete the sentence "Ramona is . . . ," she answered, "Determined." Although this answer focused more on her personal characteristics than on her social identity, she went on to frame her response in the context of her various social identities:

> Determined to always believe. You know, to never forget about God and community. Determined to make our community a better place to live. I mean, it could be connected to all of this. Culture and to keep my culture. School, to finish school. Family, to show my family that I can do better and that I can finish my education. And it could be related to all this.

Familial identities were also linked to a number of other aspects of identity. Two of the female students, for example, transitioned into discussions about gender issues:

> My dad has six girls in the family. And he never thought we would wanna go to college, just because he has this attitude. I guess it's kinda [an] old attitude that being a female means staying in the family, not going anywhere, you know, not going to college or anything like that. I guess just being a female, it has brought a lot of arguments with my dad. I know if I was a male, I wouldn't be going through any of the arguments that I was going with him. But I fought for myself, saying, "Well, just because I'm female, I'm not gonna stay home and do this and do this"—everything that was done by other females just because they were females.

Although the significance of gender and sexism was not emphasized by the female students when they analyzed their identities, some did discuss these issues. As with the high school students, most did not feel that gender or sexism was central to their social identities. Instead, these were issues they had to deal with, but issues that were somewhat accepted as natural, perhaps because they had emerged from the students' own families and communities. Still, the women wanted to be able to address some of these issues by setting an example, and in this way gender was critical to their identities. As one student put it,

I'm a Mexicana, Chicana, female, tryin' to survive educationally to better myself and to somehow someday be myself and all that I can be. . . . If I better myself, I'll be more able to help others in the community, help others within my own sex, be a role model to my own brothers and sisters, to my other friends who are also females, [and] also have my parents be proud of me.

Without question, issues of gender shaped critical aspects of the Chicana students' lives. The female *mechistas* addressed gender issues with the greatest clarity. At the same time, many of the other students did not consider the role of gender in shaping their identities, even when they were asked directly about it. Although that response does not mean that these issues were irrelevant in shaping their identities, this chapter focuses on students' conscious understanding of their identities. Part 3 addresses unconscious identities and the complexities of gender in more depth.

Although the story of the *mechistas* leapt out from these interviews, the diversity of the students in this sample was also quite helpful in understanding the processes of and influences on identity formation for other students. The four *mechistas* fit the "typical" community college student profile in that they were recent high school graduates who had been working and trying to pursue their schooling. The four remaining community college students broke that mold and included a high school student who was taking college courses for advanced credit, a forty-year-old mother who had just returned to school, and two Mexicanos who had immigrated to the United States as adults and were now seeking higher education to help their families. The stories of the identities of this latter group of students varied greatly.

The identity of the high school student who was seeking advanced credit was grounded in his role as a student. Although a number of issues were important to him, the two most significant were that his mother died when he was young (and he had never known his father) and that he had left a regular high school for an alternative school that really helped him focus on his educational goals. Although he was concerned about issues affecting his community and Chicanas/os in general, the circumstances of his life and the needs of his family had led him to ground his sense of self almost completely in his need to achieve educational success. He was a student above all else.

The mother who was a returning student had also centered her identity in her role as a student. She had put other things of importance on the back burner and was both excited and proud about finally being able to dedicate herself to her own development through her schooling. She explained the importance she placed on education when she was asked about the most important aspect of her identity:

> I think educating ourselves is the most important to reinforce, to keep the kids educated so that nobody can take advantage of them. If you're not educated, you're nothing. That's the way I look at it.

She believed that other identity issues were irrelevant if people were not educated. Thus her experiences as a returning student had led her to ground her identity in her role as a student, which in turn was grounded in her role as a mother. Issues of race also mattered to her, but they were not central to her identity as a student. Still, racial issues, along with related gender issues, were an aspect of her identity, for she expressed an interest in learning more about her culture and her origins, as well as in helping other Latinas who shared some of her experiences:

> I would like to show other Hispanic women that if I can do it, divorced two times, left twice with my kids, I'm still going and I'm still gonna do it. . . . I wanna be a role model for Hispanic women mostly. Women that don't know how to get out of a situation that I've been in before myself. . . . If they empower themselves by educating themselves, I believe that they don't have to be [in that situation].

Overall, the identity of this student was grounded in her status as a student but was also heavily influenced by her identities as a mother and a Chicana, because she saw herself using her education to help both her family and other women in her community.

Of the two students who had immigrated to the United States as adults, one was a father, and his identity was deeply shaped by fatherhood. He talked extensively about the need to help children, to provide them with educational role models, and to give them a religious foundation, and he mentioned his interest in helping youth in the community in addition to his own children. Interestingly, his identity was grounded mostly in his role as a student, but, as with all of the other students at the community college, his identity was heavily shaped and influenced by his other central identity—in this case, his identity as a father.

> What influenced me is life. Life and my kids. My kids, my wife. I see the stuff in my life, so I try to get all these things so they can have better things. That's one of the biggest things. And if you don't have nothing, you

cannot give nothing to your kids. Because I'm already thirty-six. So if I achieve a little bit more, I think I can give them something. So that influenced me to do something. And that's my biggest part of my life. . . . It's very important to me that they get what I didn't get.

This student firmly believed that the example he was setting for his children by pursuing his education was the most important thing he could do for them as a father. His experience as an immigrant informed this identity, but because he had immigrated many years prior, his experience was much different from that of the other male student who was an immigrant. That student had immigrated only two years before our interview, and his identity had been completely shaped by his experiences as an immigrant. In fact, though he was a student and involved in his church, his identity was completely centered in his immigrant status. He believed that family was the core of his identity, and it was family and community to which he was most dedicated, but these elements of his identity had been largely influenced by the difficulty he had adjusting to life in the United States, where he felt that the sense of community in daily life and in the church were sorely lacking. The community and customs in Mexico had defined his identity and his life there, and their absence in the United States had forced him to define himself in the context of his experience as an immigrant. As he put it:

I don't like it here, because people are more open in Mexico. For example, in Mexico, you can go out in the neighborhood and leave your home; you can see your friends outside playing, or run into a friend and chitchat, and go to the next block and see two more friends and have fun. For example, I notice that people here do not leave their houses. Oftentimes people are not aware of that here, that they don't interact with the people around them. I see very few people who go outside and talk with their neighbor or organize activities together. All of them travel in their own circles. (Translated from Spanish)

This student went on to describe how these issues were connected to his values, as he further revealed how life in the United States had forced him to define himself as an immigrant: "So I feel that a sense of family, or the concept of the family, is in reality lost here. And I tell you, for Hispanics the family is always the most important . . . before anything else" (translated from Spanish).

Although issues of race, religion, and education were important to this student, he filtered all of them through his central identity as an immigrant. The different way of living and sharing space in the United States exposed what he believed was a critical void in life there. This awareness forced him to define himself primarily as a Mexicano who was striving to provide others with the beliefs that would allow them to live a richer life such as the life he had experienced in Mexico. Thus his identity as an immigrant shaped his goals as well, for he was interested in working as a counselor or in some capacity where he could help youth, who he believed needed the most attention. That is why he was dedicated to his role as a student, which, as with many of the other students in the study, was a key identity that he fit into his familial identity.

As a group, these four nontraditional students showed some of the diversity of Chicanas/os at the community college. Although race was important in the lives of all these students, they, unlike the *mechistas,* had found other issues to be more important in developing their identities. Some had experienced conflicts related to immigration, whereas others were motivated by their roles as parents, and still others were fortunate enough to have had positive educational experiences that led them to develop a sense of confidence and a strong identity as a student.

Clearly, the community college students had arrived at more developed and well-thought-out identities than their high school counterparts. As the students explained, the time since high school had been important to the evolution of their identities. It had allowed or even forced them to reflect and develop a new understanding of their experiences. As college students, they had also made a strong commitment to education, and so their school identities were even more prominent than was the case for the high school students. Family was still central to their identities, but education became a stronger aspect of this familial identity. In addition, their reflection on their earlier experiences led many of them to emphasize the centrality of race in their identities. For the older students, however, their anger about racial issues was less severe, and education itself became more critical to their identities.

As a whole, the community college students also pointed to a critical need. Although often indirectly, each exposed the necessity of mentorship in the identity development process. The *mechistas* made it quite clear that they lacked guidance in making sense of who they were in their schooling and lives in general. They had struggled for years with their identities. The recent immigrants also struggled to find a way to develop a sense of self that integrated their Mexicano identity with a student identity that put them in a position to help others. The older returning student had a positive identity of herself as a student but also continued to fight to give concrete meaning to this identity in terms of her ability to tap into the resources and networks that would allow her to achieve educational success. The high school student who was taking classes at the community college told a different story, for close mentorship from teachers and counselors gave him the confidence and the resources to develop a student identity, as a Chicano, that facilitated his educational success. The combination of the racialization of Chicana/o students with their lack of access to mentors to assist them in dealing with that process played a critical role in the identity development of all the students in the sample, even though some emphasized or deemphasized that identity to different degrees. In the end, it was clear that racialization in Acoma was central to the lives and identity development of many of the students at the community college, and that for them race was couched within familial identity and addressed via school identity, for they all hoped to work toward improving conditions in their communities. Each student and the unique contexts in which she or he lived shaped the way in which these and other identities came together. Although the process was never the same for two students, patterns did emerge. The university students helped expose these patterns through their analyses.

University Students

> I'm not Mexican; I'm not from Mexico. And if I were to go to Mexico, they'd laugh at me. I know this; I've been to Mexico. I'm not American, because I've not been treated equally. I'm Chicano. . . . We're the people that aren't fully accepted anywhere, so we accept each other. We're the nation of outcasts.

The university students exhibited the greatest complexity in their analyses of their own identity construction. These students had developed sharp critical-thinking skills and had been forced to deal with identity issues in ways that their counterparts who still lived at home in Chicana/o communities had not. This may be one reason that issues of race were a much bigger part of their story than for the groups of Acoma students.

The centrality of race emerged immediately and consistently in the interviews with university students. As the students pointed out, when a racial conflict is blatant and obvious or when racial isolation is clear, the situation makes race a central arena of identity for students. Of the students who had faced blatant racism, the one who was most directly challenged by these conflicts had entered gang life; another had become disinterested in those classes in which he had race-related conflicts with teachers; and a third had tried to assimilate, a strategy she later had to abandon in pursuit of transforming the problematic context she had witnessed. Not only did all of these students develop specific strategies for dealing with the racial climate, but they also developed identities that were firmly grounded in their understanding of race. In the excerpts that follow, students provide examples (from early in our conversations) of the way they became aware of the significance of race in the school. The first student focused on policies that he felt had been created for and applied only to Chicanas/os; the second student talked about two specific interactions with teachers that had angered him; and the third student described how she learned English and assimilated quickly to avoid being teased for her use of Spanish. Excerpts from interviews with each of them, respectively, follow:

> The teachers were just real harsh to us in high school. They ragged on us. Anything that they saw, like da-boom, they would get you. Let's say, like, you had a bandanna and you wore it on your head or whatever. Not even like as a bandanna, but just as somethin' to put over your head. They would say, "That's gang related. Get that off." But then at the same time, there's like four or five little white boys wearing their bandannas. "Oh, they're the football team." "Oh, so they're OK." A lot of [us] had a hard time understanding that.

> In my history class, we had to write an essay on Texas and the Alamo and all that part of history. And I wrote it more from the Mexican point of view, how it was more or less taken, and talking about how the land was taken from the people after the Treaty of Guadalupe. The teacher gave me an F on that paper. . . . And she also stated in class that I was gonna go to hell because I was racially mixed.

> I assimilated really fast. I started speaking English, and then I didn't speak Spanish anymore. I just dropped Spanish altogether. I just kind of got tired of teasing and stuff, so I just stopped speaking the Spanish language and I just started to speak English.

What is most significant about these students' discussions is that, without being asked about race or racial incidents, they recounted their school experiences through the lens of race, making it clear that they had learned that this was how their school lives were organized by others, including students, teachers, and administrators. For these students, race became one of the most concrete means for developing their sense of identity.

The four students who were confronted with racial isolation realized at different stages in their lives that this isolation was an important part of their school experiences as they came to understand, among other things, how rare it was in their communities for a Chicana/o to become successful in school. The isolation shaped their understanding of who they were in critical ways, although most had struggled for quite some time before they were able to make sense of these experiences. One student recounted how moving to an all-white school had made him uncomfortable:

> We moved up here. And now it's totally different here 'cause everyone's white. Me and my brother are like the only—maybe a few, one or two other Hispanic students. So that made me feel really isolated and lonely. . . . Whereas when we lived in L.A., it was not a big deal. It's fifty-fifty, you know, black and Mexican. And it wasn't a big deal. You kinda felt comfortable. But moving up here, it's like—just kinda feel like you didn't have nothin' in common with the rest of the people in your classes.

What was crucial for the students in these kinds of early educational experiences was that race was associated with social forces in the school that led the students either to see distinctions in the experiences of different races or to feel uncomfortable in the school in ways that were related to their race. Many students could not easily deconstruct these experiences, even at the time of the interviews, but they made it clear that they had learned that race was related to their identities. One student who discussed isolation in her college experiences explained both how it affected her and how these kinds of experiences (at any age) were related to Chicana/o students' goals of achieving educational success:

> I'm a woman for one, in an animal science field, which is dominated by a bunch of males—"hick rednecks," as my adviser would put it. So in actuality, I'm facing two [barriers]. Not only am I a woman, [but] I'm an American of Mexican heritage. So Mexicans in the animal science field are the laborers, the workers, you know, and so it's very hard to break that stereotype. And so [I] haven't had too much problems, but you hear the jokes and it puts into perspective how other people perceive you. 'Cause I don't see myself that way, but you forget how others might look

at you. . . . I feel, as a woman and as a Mexican American, [that] it makes me want to be a pioneer. So in my family . . . I want to do well. I want them to be proud of me.

Like the students who described racial isolation in their precollege schooling, this student demonstrated that, even without facing specific racial conflicts, students who are racially isolated in school feel the weight of this isolation in their everyday lives. This sense of isolation can be even greater for the Chicanas (particularly in certain fields), because they are often isolated both racially and in terms of gender. Like some of the women at the community college, these Chicana university students rarely emphasized gender as the conscious core of their identities, but gender was critical to their sense of who they would become and to their desire to be role models, because they did not have any role models themselves. Issues of racial and gender isolation shaped identity and became connected with students' familial and school identities as they strove to succeed for their families and for other Chicanas. Both the Chicanas and the Chicanos who experienced isolation defined their own identities within the context of that isolation simply because it was inescapable.

Unlike the isolation described by many of the high school and community college students, the isolation that some of the university students experienced demanded a response in their own identity development. Because of these experiences, race and identity also played a significant role in shaping students' school identities and goals. One student noted:

I'm in this to be a teacher. And so that's, like, my goal right now, but I know that just being a teacher for the rest of my life isn't gonna be enough. So I know that I'm gonna have to come back and get higher education, either a master's or a PhD or something, so that I can make a difference elsewhere, besides just the school district. So, I mean, my whole motivation is so that I can help other Chicano students. . . . I remember seeing the kids, like in my high schools and in my junior high, and they were just, like, lost to the world and no self-worth and things of that nature.

For the majority of the students at the university, their experiences dealing with race forced them early on to emphasize their racial identities, and the specific nature of these experiences led them to pursue educational success as a means of addressing the lack of Chicana/o success that they saw. Also related was that their own familial experiences supported these evolving identities, through the significance of social advancement emphasized within the families.

Race shaped identity in different ways for another subgroup of students. For students who came from mixed-race parentage, race was a central issue in their lives and identities because it was an issue within the home (which was not often the case in homes where both parents were of Mexican descent). Of the racially mixed students, only one was actively mentored by a parent to care about and address Chicana/o issues in his life. His mother had made it a point to raise her sons as conscientious Chicanos. His sense of identity was firmly grounded in his race and was further supported by his experiences in school (he was the student who discussed the racism of teachers early in this section). Even he, however, had struggles that contributed to his sense of identity. As he put it, "Whites don't like you 'cause you're Mexican, and Mexicans don't like you 'cause you're white. And it was always a problem when we were younger, dating people, too." Still, his relative comfort with his identity appeared to be rare, given that the other students from mixed backgrounds struggled with a great deal more confusion. One of the female students, for example, could easily have passed as white, and she did not think much about her ethnic background, focusing on sports and religion in high school. Nevertheless, her confusion over her background made race an important part of her identity, especially in college. She did not explicitly discuss race when talking about her identity until she was asked directly about it. Then she reported:

> Race is important in my life. I would say that race and ethnicity and family and culture kind of roll into one together. Me and [my brother] just having a different dad and him [her dad] being Mexican has always been kind of a point of contention in our family, but it's what makes our family a family.

The struggle of this student was complex, for she had been raised almost her entire life by her mother and a stepfather (whom she calls her dad). Both parents were white. Her natural father was Mexican, and she had had little contact with him, although her relationship with him had improved recently. She elaborated on the difficulties of these family dynamics when she talked about the ethnic label she had chosen for herself:

> When I'm around my friends or my real dad's family, I say [I'm] Mexican. When I'm around my dad and my mom, I say I'm white because they don't

like [me saying I'm Mexican]. . . . I'm confused. Even though I'm strong, I just still limp around my dad. To the world I can tell them who I am, but to my mom and dad I don't want to hurt them or step on their feelings and I wanna be the daughter that they want me to be, even though I haven't figured out what that is yet. . . . In that sense, I'm just trying to keep the family together.

This student revealed the kinds of internal conflicts that dominated students of mixed-race parentage. In her case, her early identity was not related to race at all, but as she had gotten older, she had struggled a great deal with the racial meaning of her background and of her distance from that background. In many ways, at the time of the interview, this struggle defined her identity.

Another female student shared similar feelings, for she was somewhat confused over her background as well, and this confusion defined the core of her ethnic identity. Her larger social identity, however, was more firmly grounded in other arenas like gender, family, helping others, and ROTC. She showed how other aspects of identity could play a much more dominant role, particularly when a conflict emerged in those areas. In her case, the gender conflicts she had experienced as a member of ROTC had pushed her to integrate gender as a central facet of her identity:

I went to [ROTC] camp between my sophomore and junior year, and a lot of times the guys wouldn't want the girls to be there because they [thought], "Oh, they're gonna hold us back. And they're gonna do this or they're gonna do that, and they're gonna have to go get ready." The guys were just total jerks. And that was the first time I ever got kinda ticked off about it. But looking back, I didn't think a whole lot of it, you know, and then after I had [a Women's Studies] class, I was like, "I wish I could go to camp now. Because I would just go off on some people." . . . I've turned into a feminist too in the last year and a half or so. And so that's become more important to me than I realized. And there's just a lot of things you just don't realize that are there, issues that are there that you just don't see 'em until it happens to you.

In this student's case, her race was something that she had never felt forced to confront. She revealed the process by which identity in a specific social arena can emerge. In her case, conflicts with males over gender issues led her to ground her identity solidly in her gender. Although she was concerned about other issues and struggled with aspects of her ethnic identity, gender conflicts demanded that she attempt to address sexism in her life, and they became central to her identity. Her experiences mirrored those that other students had along racial lines.

Interestingly, however, most of the other women did not incorporate gender into their discussions of their identities and the issues that are most important to them. Although two others talked about becoming role models, as with the community college and high school students, that was the extent of their emphasis on gender issues. One student provided a detailed explanation that reflected the conflicting feelings many of the Chicanas had regarding gender issues and sexism:

> I like the role that Mexican women play in our culture. I was writing a paper on this actually the other day in Women's Studies, where, you know, like when I had to get up before and make tortillas for my brother and stuff like that, it made me a stronger person. . . . Gender I guess has something to do with who I am as a woman or as a person. But it doesn't inhibit me. Like I think maybe sometimes my race inhibited me from certain things. But I don't think that being a woman ever has. . . . I don't really think that I've ever felt gender discrimination. I mean, Title Nine's the reason that I'm in college now.

As this Chicana suggested, the complexity of gender and its deep entrenchment in family life often pushed the role of gender into the realm of unconscious identity development (as is discussed in Part 3). For many of the women, gender issues were part of their lives, and they were even frustrated with the sexism in their families, but most saw these issues as inherent aspects of their lives that did not shape their identities the way that race did. For some, like the student above, gender roles were so ingrained in their lives that they simply accepted them. Still, many also strove to serve as role models for other Chicanas, recognizing the need for mentors to help young Chicanas deal with the gender and racial issues they face. It is important to look critically at the complex interactions between gender and race to fully understand the forces at work in these Chicanas' lives (see Chapters 5 and 6).

Another student who came from mixed-race parentage experienced conflicts in a different realm that have become central to her identity. She focused on class issues as the critical component of her identity, because this is where she experienced identity-shaping conflicts:

> We're from like lower, low, low class. And that's been kinda an issue in my life, just because it sometimes seems insurmountable. It's just, like, I don't

know if I can get out of being in the lower class. Kind of a conflicting issue for me just because I have a lot of ideas of what's gonna happen in the future. I think a lot about class. I like to read up on the working class, and I wouldn't call myself a Marxist, but at the same time I would. I think it's an issue that's gonna be a big part of everybody's lives just because of the fact that our upper class is getting richer and our lower class is getting poorer and we're losing the middle class almost completely. I mean, being replaced by technology and there's no jobs. I mean, there's so many kids from my high school that graduate that end up working at McDonald's or whatever they can get at this point. I mean they can't even afford to get an apartment. It's sad to see how it's going, and that worries me a lot. . . . I feel that something has to happen, and I feel like I need to do something.

Although this student did not discuss specific conflicts, as had the student who had to fight against gender stereotypes in the ROTC, it was obvious that being working-class had greatly influenced her identity. She was aware not only of the role of class in her life but also of the critical functions class plays in the larger society, and her identity had evolved to the extent that she was committed to making changes to address the divide between the classes. Later, she told how her ethnic background had played into the equation of her identity development, describing how she had hidden her ethnic identity in elementary school to avoid being ridiculed. She explained many of the forces that can lead to the internal struggles of mixed-race students with regard to their ethnic identity. She was proud of her Mexican background, and it was important to her, but she knew little about it because she had had almost no contact with her father, who was of Mexican descent. In addition, she saw that the few Mexicanas/os in her school faced racist attitudes. Because her skin color gave her the ability to hide her ethnic background, she took advantage of this opportunity because it lessened the degree to which she was seen as different from her classmates. What was perhaps the most interesting finding with regard to the mixed-race students was that race and the limitations forced upon Chicanas/os could lead mixed-race students to ground their identities in other arenas of their social lives, whereas the students who could not escape their ethnicity because of their skin color had to place more importance on race. To a degree, therefore, even those mixed-race students who had hidden their ethnicity were aware of its importance, and ethnicity also played a role as they consciously asserted identities in other realms of their social worlds.

Another mixed-race female had had quite different experiences, because she was dark-skinned and thus was unable to hide that she was half-Mexican. Her ethnic identity had become important to her not only because she had dark skin but also because she had struggled at the cultural level in terms of her affiliation, for she (like many of the others in this subgroup) was frustrated by her lack of Spanish proficiency. In describing her struggles, she exemplified a degree of cultural confusion that many of the students faced over their identities, because being of mixed race or lacking Spanish facility made them feel different from other Chicanas/os. At the same time, these students were often aware of the racial-political forces that existed in their lives and of the need to address them in some fashion.

Chicana/o university students' experiences in dealing with race (be they conflict, isolation, or confusion within mixed-race families) were obviously important to them, given that they described these experiences as some of the most memorable in their lives and some of the longest-lasting influences on their understanding of the significance of race in their identities. Still, as the students who had struggled with identity have shown, their identities were influenced by a number of other factors and evolved over time. Even at the university level, for example, racial identity can be less important than familial identity. One student commented that she was raised to believe that her familial identity was the most important thing she had:

> I just grew up in a family that, you had a family name and you were not to do anything to disgrace it. And so I would be ashamed if I were to come home [having done something wrong].

Overall, eight of the eleven students interviewed at the university emphasized that their families were critical to their identities. Interestingly, seven of these students also discussed the centrality of race. Specifically, three of these students discussed having a familial identity as their central identity, two of whom also mentioned that their racial identity had emerged from that, while the third explained that her familial identity integrated class and athletics. Three other students in this group talked about how race represented the core of their identities, but these students also explained that their families were central to their identities and to the importance of race in their lives. In addition, two other students in this group described their identities as equally grounded and informed by their racial and familial identities and noted that these aspects of who they were were unified in terms of their understandings of their world and their goals. In some ways, these two students help us understand the experiences of the other six just mentioned, for they explain that the interaction between the familial influences and identities of students and their racial experiences and identities is complex and that, although these realms of identity may vary in importance to students in different situations or at different times in their lives, they are both equally involved in the shaping of Chicana/o identity. As these students demonstrated, the racial aspects of their identities became increasingly important in their lives outside of the home as they grew older. Thus the familial identity often evolved through the racialization process that affected student identities. As one student said:

> Family, culture, race, school—I mean, all that's connected, 'cause it's all part of the family. It's part of, at least for myself, how you came up. We have to deal with being broke and being Mexican and then, you know, using school as a means of improving ourselves.

This student summarized the process of identity formation for many of the students by expressing how family is important as the starting point from which other aspects of identity emerge. Later he gave his own example of how the familial identity becomes linked to racial and school identities for many students:

> Being Mexican, I kinda always feel like, being from a minority, you always kinda have to fight all these stereotypes and you have to even live to higher expectations than the average person. 'Cause everyone is looking at you and they always expect the worst from you. So you kinda always have to do your best, at least I have [to] just kinda, like, fight people's images of you or stereotypes of you. You just kinda prove them wrong. . . . So I think that kinda has affected me in my behavior, [to] kinda prove people wrong, that we're not just all uncivilized, lazy people.

The ideas introduced by this student become clearer when we consider that all of these university students who linked their racial and familial identities saw both of these identities as shaping and influencing the development of their school identities, which were also important in their sense of who they were. They saw their schooling and their lives as students as their path to address the negative forces and to support the positive forces that had made these two aspects of their identities so important. This same student expressed this perspective as he described his motivation for succeeding in school:

> I always fed off the fact that my parents didn't have any education, not because they chose not to go [but] because they didn't have no choice. And

so, I mean, we had that choice, and it just kinda felt like you gotta take advantage of it. And so that was a motivating factor. And then also, when you come here and you kinda always have this stigma that Mexicans are lazy and so forth—all the stereotypes, you know. And so I always kinda used that as a motivating factor, you know, to fight it and to prove people wrong. I think I get a big kick outta that. I mean that's why I do good in school, 'cause I just enjoy proving people wrong. And I like the challenge.

This group of university students shared a similar process of identity development. Their identities develop first within their families. As they leave the home, however, they encounter a number of other experiences that force them to develop identities in other arenas of their social lives. Often the racial forces in their lives cause race to become an increasingly significant aspect of who they are. The family experiences, along with the racialized experiences they and their families face, lead many students to focus on the importance of education to them and their families.

Interestingly, all three of the remaining students had identities that were grounded neither in their families nor in their race, and all of these students came from mixed-race families. These students experienced significant confusion and uncertainty over issues of race, and this confusion marked their identities much more than did a strong racial identity. At the same time, the unique and complicated dynamics in their families seemed to have made it difficult for them to develop the type of familial bond that the other students described. This is not to say that these students did not have strong ties to their families, but simply that they did not have the type of familial bond that the others described. As a result, as mentioned earlier, one student had turned to religion to help her develop a strong and positive identity, while for another student who had experienced conflicts around gender issues, gender became a key facet of her identity. Similarly, the last of these three students had experienced a great many struggles around class issues, and class was the core of her identity.[3]

In the end, many of the university students emphasized the need for guidance in dealing with the identity issues that shaped their lives. This need for guidance was of particular importance to them within the realm of school. In fact, many students suggested a need for mentorship in the university environment itself. For example, one student described a confrontation she had had with her soccer coach, who made a racial comment in reference to the music she listened to. As the student put it, "She pointed out to me in a very clear way that I was the only minority." The student said that this had been an eye-opening experience, not because it affected her significantly on the soccer team but because it pointed out to her how she was viewed through her race even when no one had discussed it before that incident. The student said she had never expected this type of interaction in athletics. She concluded, "After that, I was just like, 'Yeah, you're a minority who is a student athlete.'" She realized how alone she was on the team. Her teammates could not understand what she was upset about and even said, "At least she didn't call you a spic or something." After that, the student said, she was much more on her guard around her coach and teammates. She added that one of the hardest things about the incidents was that it had originated with her coach, and the power dynamics involved in that relationship made it unfair and dangerous for her "because for somebody in a power position to throw your racial identity in your face is just wrong."

Another student discussed her lack of support in dealing with similar struggles with racial conflict and isolation, but her struggles had been within her major. Although she did not provide a comprehensive analysis of the impact this isolation had on her, she repeatedly referred to it. She explained how unhappy she was with her department and how hard it was to be the only woman of color in most of her classes and interactions in the department.

> I don't like the chemical engineering department at all here. So I think that's another reason [I'm unhappy]. I just dread going to those classes and I don't . . . I get really frustrated with my department. I think that's the big thing. 'Cause sometimes they'll make little comments about women or minorities or, like, we'll have people come in and they'll say, "You have to have this GPA to get a job with Chevron." They're like, "But if you're a woman and a minority, then it's a lot lower." And everyone looks at me. And I just get pissed off 'cause I just feel like, I mean, I know that's true but I didn't think they really needed to say that in front of all these white males around me. I can't think of anyone down there that I really feel comfortable talking to. . . . See, I don't think there's really anyone down there that's a role model for me.

Overall, in a number of different ways, the students explained how a lack of mentorship and guidance had added to their difficulties in developing an identity that would help them navigate the troubled waters they described.

Finally, one student helped deconstruct the complexity of these processes in his second interview. He noted that identities are informed by and interact with the values students learn. He focused on himself as he explained that the values students learn shape their approach to the issues confronting them and are an interactive force in their identity development. He demonstrated how his values shaped his identity and actions:

> If you're in a city and you see drive-bys every day, I mean you basically got three choices. You can be the ones involved in it, or the ones that just wanna get the hell out, or the one that wants to change that situation. And that kinda goes back to whatever values have been instilled in you. I mean those values come pretty much from, like, family and church, if you're religious. . . . I mean what you see around you is either gonna be negative or positive. Some of the negatives you can make positive, by what you decide to do. I mean, like, my neighborhood in California was all pretty much gangs and a lot of people there dealing drugs. I mean, I could let that be an influence on me negatively and get into that and start doing that type of thing. Or I could just go from there and talk with the younger kids to keep them from following in their father's or brother's footsteps and ending up in prison or whatever or dead.

This student was able to focus directly on the role of values because his mother had raised him to be committed to activism. Taking activist stances and the values behind doing so had shaped his response to the problems he faced, and in that way values interacted with his identity. He felt obliged to address issues of racial inequality and injustice. Because these issues were not something he could ignore, and because he had integrated these issues into his daily life through action, addressing these issues required that he develop an identity that was racially grounded in terms of both thought and action. This student implicitly raised the issue of mentorship, for although many of the students struggled with issues of race to differing degrees, only a few of them, such as this student, were able to integrate racial issues into their identities in a positive and affirming way. Most of the other students had had no guidance in addressing these issues and linking them to their identities in positive ways through their values. Instead, many of them focused on their families and on the values of respect and love for family that their families had emphasized.

CONCLUSION

The story that the Washington students as a whole told is intricate and powerful. The high school students were only beginning to make sense of who they were and what had influenced this. It is clear that their families and their familial identities were most important to them. At the same time, school was a critical component of their familial identities, in terms of their goals for their families. As they revealed, race played a key role within the school, for they were forced to deal with the ways in which the racial organization of school limited their abilities to achieve their goals. Other identity issues were present in their lives, but often in unconscious or suppressed ways, even for important issues like gender and sexism. Most critical was that their discussions pointed to the need to develop some sense of positive identity in any arena of their social lives.

The community college students built on the analyses of the high school youth. They too emphasized the centrality of family, but as they continued on in school, it became increasingly difficult for many of them to ignore the critical role of race in defining their experiences. They also began to develop a broader notion of the racial meanings of their identities as they incorporated other aspects of their lives into their racial identities. Although gender, for example, was still not significant for most of these students, it had become a clearer issue in the identity development of the Chicanas. The students at the community college clearly revealed the psychological impact of race, which was often extremely negative. In so doing, they suggested and even addressed the need for mentorship to help them make sense of all these issues.

The university students helped increase our understanding of identity in general, by exposing the intricacies of the processes of identity development. They showed how conflict influenced identity, as they discussed the development of identities in areas beyond race, such as gender and class. At the same time, these students made it clear that race was the most dominant force at work in the development of their identities. Even for those students who had developed identities in other arenas, the racial forces in their lives often led them to emphasize race over other aspects of their identities. This process was evident among a few of the women who linked the dramatic gender and racial issues they faced in their schooling and tended to discuss gender issues as being racially based. As is discussed in Part 3, these suppressed arenas of identity are distinct from those that are unconscious for other students. In a related matter, the university students also showed that the harsh racial climate in Washington State hindered the development of positive racial identities, and many of these students tended to ground their identities in family as an alternative, occasionally finding ways to include race in those identities. In the discussions of the university students, the dramatic need for mentorship was again exposed. The students' struggles with identity at each stage in their academic lives were accentuated by the lack of mentors for most of the students, to help them make sense of their experiences and to show them how to build a positive sense of identity.

Overall, each of the students painted a unique portrait of life and identity development. With the exception of the few students who had severe family conflicts, family served as the core of identity. As the students described the importance of family in shaping identity, they demonstrated how family took on its own distinctive shape, beyond love and respect. In fact, the racial, political, and economic climate had a lot to do with the specific ways in which family influenced social identity for Chicana/o students in Washington State. Because their families had to struggle financially and often in extreme working conditions, the familial identities of the students were grounded in their pride, and even more so in their goals of improving their families' material conditions. In this way, school became a critical facet of identity for almost every student at each of the sites, because the students saw school as their path to fulfill their family obligations and to create the type of familial identity they sought.

For some other students, their experiences forced them to develop other aspects of their social identities. In particular, race became a critical part of this equation, simply because of the limited opportunities many Chicanas/os faced. Many students sought to develop a positive racial identity by relying heavily on their families, while others attempted to hide or ignore their racial identity in an effort to scale the racial walls of the school. In both cases, race was important to their overall identities. Other issues did not seem to influence identity much for these students, except for gender, which clearly emerged as an aspect of identity in the students' analyses. Most of the females who discussed the importance of gender had integrated gender into their racial and familial identities in their efforts to become role models for other Chicanas, for these students had had few or no role models themselves. The strength of students' mothers also played a critical role, because for many students (both females and males) their mother was their most powerful role model. In the case of the student who had experienced significant conflicts over gender through sexism in the ROTC, gender did become the heart of her identity. As with the students who were heavily influenced by race, her experiences with fighting stereotypes and the negative profiling of women demanded an identity response from her. The same process occurred for one other young woman, who grounded her identity in class because of her socioeconomic status and her observations of economic injustice around her.

Finally, one other unique influence on identity was addressed by two of the community college students: the different stages of a student's life reveal different influences on identity. Two of the students at the community college were older (thirty-six and forty-two years old) and were returning students with families. They mentioned many of the same concerns as the other students did, but their identities were most influenced by their role as parents and their interest in setting an example for their own children. This is an essential finding, because it is possible that these older students can provide models for the younger students that help the latter develop empowering identities.

All of the students revealed what a few labeled as "identities as fighters." They were fighting to help their families and to address the issues that their lives demanded they confront. They were fighting to develop a positive sense of their identity in a world that was often confusing and even psychologically dangerous. Their fight was defined by each of the arenas of identity discussed above, but it was also limited by their lack of help in determining how to engage in the fight. The students suggested that mentorship in identity development would go a long way toward helping them in many facets of their lives. The insights of the students in Washington State fit nicely into the model that emerged from the Los Angeles project. Clearly, power dominates the identity development of these students. The Washington students, however, help us see the critical role of the sociopolitical context, for in this case it significantly shaped the precise manifestations of power and the ways in which identity emerged from that context.

COMMENTARY

It was obvious to me, as an outsider, that race was a critical aspect of social life in Acoma. The racial inequality in employment and education there provided two concrete examples. Interestingly, however, race often did not become the core arena of identity formation among Chicana/o students there. The context in Acoma played a crucial role in this phenomenon, through the dominance of the mainstream ideology that everyone had a fair chance and that there was no racial discrimination. One might expect that a conservative, rural climate like that of Acoma would make racial inequality even more apparent and central to Chicana/o students. In fact, the students who grew up in this climate were bombarded by messages that they just needed to try harder and that they should not raise issues of racism, because racism didn't exist in Acoma. These messages permeated daily life so much in Acoma that even instances of blatant discrimination were not used as evidence of racial injustice by many students. Instead, students often turned to their families and their families' needs as their core arena of identity formation. Although much of the students' familial identities was grounded in their desire to improve their families' lives, that desire was not often framed within a racial analysis of inequality in Acoma. Thus, race was a central axis upon which life in Acoma revolved, but the power dynamics were such that racial inequality was seen as natural and the product of individual choice and effort. So although students' familial identities had evolved in response to their desire to address this inequality, the power inequities were clouded in such a way that few of the students were able to develop a positive racial identity that could assist their efforts to seek empowerment. Instead, for many students a negative Chicana/o racial identity was understood as the only possible Chicana/o identity, and the students insulated themselves in their familial and cultural identities. Thus, although racial inequality was critical to their experiences, their identities evolved around their emphases on familial survival rather than around community and individual responses to racism.

IDENTITY AND SCHOOL
PERFORMANCE IN ACOMA

When we talked about their schooling, the students in Acoma told stories that were often frightening, in terms of both their experiences and the similarities of those experiences. Often the students were unable to fully explain what they thought was happening, because the problems they saw were frequently hidden behind layers of policy and procedure. A high school student provided an example of such experiences when he described how Chicana/o students were tracked into nonacademic classes in his school:

> I started noticing, from my junior year to my senior year, I noticed the Mexicanos were taking certain classes. And it would always be a big group of brown people taking those classes. And it was like, "Why? Why are they always taking that?" It's not just 'cause they were interested. You know, maybe I'm just misaccusing counselors, but I just think [the students] were kinda led that way. I was led in some ways, like they would tell me "Take this class" or "You took wood tech?" I never took wood tech. On purpose I didn't take wood tech. I love wood, but I never took it, because I was pissed because they were tellin' me, when I had to fill in an elective, "Oh, you took wood tech?" I go, "I haven't." "Have you took body, you know, auto body?" And I said, "No, man." So what I would do, I'd give myself a harder class, like I took extra English classes. I took an extra math class.

In the case of this student, even though he wanted to go to college, counselors suggested that he take classes that would actually work against his preparation for postsecondary education. In other parts of our conversations, this student acknowledged that the school staff was supportive for the most part. At the same time, however, he exposed the assumed rules of the schooling game that left Chicanas/os as outsiders. One of those rules was that Chicanas/os took nonacademic classes. Issues like these are of particular concern in light of the following comment from a community college student: "I'd say high school was the most important thing for you. Because that's where your mind opens and that's where your mind starts to set on what you wanna do." As this observation implies, high school is a critical time for students because it helps them define their future. Unfortunately, many Chicana/o students begin to define their futures within schooling environments that limit their exposure to multiple possibilities. Furthermore, these limitations are often constructed around the meanings attached to Chicana/o identity by teachers, counselors and, in turn, Chicanas/os themselves. This form of profiling is a central part of the story the students tell in this chapter.[1]

The negative aspects of Chicana/o school life in Washington State are acute, but they are only part of the story. Many students raised hopeful possibilities. In particular, the students revealed how important and supportive their families were. The Chicana/o students of Acoma challenged mainstream interpretations of their lives. Traditionally, they were believed to be unmotivated for school success. It was thought that they were not concerned with their school outcomes and that they had little if any support at home for school success. I heard these explanations in schools, universities, and communities across central and eastern Washington State. The students themselves, however, told a fundamentally different story. Not only were they quite concerned about their futures and their performance in school, but they specified that their parents were their biggest motivators for pursuing school success.

The meaning of school in Acoma was different from that in Los Angeles. In Acoma, many of the students' families labored in some of the worst working conditions in the country for extremely low wages. The students themselves often spent their vacations working in the fields alongside their parents and siblings. Both the students and their families, for the most part, knew that school success would be the only way out. Still, many forces affected Chicana/o students' opportunities and performance in school beyond their own goals.

This chapter focuses on what the students said about their school lives, the influences on their performance, and, in particular, the role of identity, as well as their suggestions for improving the Chicana/o school experience. Whereas Chapter 2 focused on how six students fit into a specific framework that emerged in the Los Angeles project, this chapter examines how students describe their school lives through extensive examples that are organized around the themes that emerged from their analyses. The student comments from each of the three sites are considered, and then the analysis is synthesized and compared with the framework discussed in Chapter 2. The use of multiple excerpts is of particular importance because little research has been done with rural Chicana/o youth. These excerpts provide an introduction into the students' lives from the students' viewpoint. The interviews were, for many students, their only opportunity to have their voices heard. For this reason, the reader is encouraged to "listen" intently to students' stories, for together the students help us come to some powerful conclusions. To more thoroughly understand the complexity of the students' experiences, some readers may want to skip to the ends of sections and the chapter and then return to the stories. Case studies that build on the patterns covered here are developed in Chapter 6, and "Time-out," an uninterrupted student narrative that analyzes school and identity and follows Chapter 6, offers a final, significant look into students' experiences.

JOHNSON HIGH SCHOOL

When I met with the high school students, I was struck by their commitment to pursuing school success. Although I met with a number of students who were at many different levels, they all made it clear that they wanted to go to college as a stepping-stone to a professional career. The participants included students who were in ESL classes, others who had fought to get into college prep classes, some who had always been seen as good students, and others who had been in a great deal of trouble with school administrators. These students clearly represented a diverse group of Chicanas/os, but it was amazing how similar their stories were in many respects. Most impressive was the importance of their parents to their school lives.

Of the nine students interviewed at the high school, six made it clear that their parents were their primary educational influence. These six focused on the struggles of their parents to survive. In particular they emphasized how important it was to their families that they take advantage of the educational opportunities available to them. Of the three remaining high school students, one discussed the importance of family but felt that the biggest educational influence was the language barriers she faced while attending school and trying to learn English at the same time. Both of the other students lacked family support for their educational goals, and their educational experiences were actually defined by their lack of guidance and support. All of the students made it clear that they lacked strong mentorship. Although all but one of the students had some form of support for pursuing their educational goals, none of the students had an active mentor to help with developing a plan for achieving these goals.

As with the students in Los Angeles, these students and their school experiences were heavily influenced by the larger forces in their lives. The racial-political climate that defined life in Acoma was a major force shaping school life in general for everyone there. The dominance of mainstream interpretations of the role of race in life in Acoma was so overwhelming that it limited the degree of blatant conflict significantly. In turn, these factors constrained the possibilities for Chicana/o identity development, while the lack of strong mentoring further complicated Chicana/o students' efforts to achieve educational success in Acoma. Thus, although the same forces that shape school life for Chicanas/os in Los Angeles were also at work in Acoma, the difference in context led to a different analysis by these students.

Educational opportunity in Acoma was popularly understood as available to all students. As the students revealed, teachers and administrators make it known to everyone in the school that any student could be successful, regardless of race. The key ingredient to success, in the eyes of school staff members, was effort. They had, in their own minds, created a color-blind system. The students, however, told a very different story. They explained that their opportunities were constrained specifically because of their race. The force with which the color-blind ideology was carried out in the school made it difficult for them to publicly address the contradictions they witnessed. As a result, the racial conflicts that they experienced often had to be dealt with alone, simply because others refused to see or acknowledge these experiences.

In Chapter 4 the students showed how their identities had been shaped by these experiences. This entire process of racialization and identity formation is also central to educational success and failure among Chicana/o students in Acoma. The remainder of this chapter will expose the nature of this relationship as it is introduced and analyzed by the students.

The students almost always began their comments in interviews by discussing their parents and the parents' critical role in inspiring the students' efforts to succeed in school. Most students emphasized the struggles of their parents:

> I want something better for me. I didn't want to end up like my parents. I mean, what they done, it's good. I mean, they work every day and

they work for us, and I appreciate that. But the thing is that I don't want to end up in a warehouse or in the fields. I wanna do something better. . . . I wanna feel proud about myself. And it's not really because of money. It's because of my pride. I wanna feel proud about myself.

Students conveyed the importance of their parents in many ways. This student emphasized the desire to do "better" than her parents. Implicit in her discussion, however, was a respect for the struggle her parents had gone through. Although the parents of many students were working-class and struggled in often humiliating conditions, no students were ashamed of their parents. In fact, many students emphasized that they wanted not only to improve their families' situations but also to maintain the strength and work ethic of their parents. As discussed in Chapter 4, one young man expressed this desire after he was asked who had been his greatest educational influence:

My mom. . . . Just her, with all the struggles she's been through and overcoming so many of them. I want that kind of power that she has. I want to be able to do that stuff. And I hope I am someday.

Parents clearly supported and motivated their children in a number of ways, and many parents provided multiple forms of encouragement simultaneously. One student talked about the inspiration he got from his mother's efforts and then mentioned how his mother explicitly reinforced the importance of hard work and even modeled the type of effort he needed:

She tells me, "*Mijo* [Son], wanna live like me? It's a pain in the ass. You gotta make somethin' of yourself." . . . I would be damned if I wasn't gonna try if my mom was tryin' after all that she's been through. I mean, here she is forty years old and she's tryin' to get a GED, the high school equivalence, you know. And I was like, "Screw that. If she's gonna do it and she doesn't give up after all those years, people saying she wouldn't do it, then I ain't gonna stop."

Although this student was inspired by his mother's own educational pursuits, few students had family members who had been successful in school. Still, some students had extended-family members and friends who were pursuing higher education and who also served as a source of support and motivation. Another student talked about her extended family:

> My cousins and other friends from California that graduated from the university down there in California . . . I just know that they're really brains. And they always tell me, "*Mija* [Daughter], you have to stay in school, and we want the best for you. And if you go to school, you have so many opportunities when you graduate and when you finish. And even if you don't major in what you wanted to major, you still have a lot of opportunities out there and you just have to think ahead."

As an interviewer, I was quite moved to hear about the strength of these families and their commitment to their children's education. All of the students who participated in the project at the high school were working-class. None of them fit the profile of the budding college student, as defined in their own schools. Yet these students all expressed a commitment to pursuing higher education, and their families supported these dreams, even though it meant financial losses to the family due to college expenses and lost wages from the students.

As mentioned, not all of the students received strong parental support. One student explained that his family wanted him to get a full-time job:

> 'Cause at home they just don't want me to really come to school. They just want me to work. They're always like, "Just get out of school and go to work." . . . Just to help out with the family. Help out, 'cause my dad, he has, like, two jobs. And he wants me to help him out. I try, I do sometimes. I mean, I would get out to go pick pears or the cherries and stuff like that.

Although this student was the only one in the study who faced this kind of pressure from his parents, some of the students described similar situations with their friends. The economic needs of some families were so severe that they could not afford to wait for their children to complete their schooling, even if the financial rewards would be greater in the future. In addition, many families had never known Chicanas/os who had succeeded in school, and so academic success seemed far removed from their own realities.

Of course, family dynamics for some students were extremely hard on them. One student experienced a great deal of family conflict that deeply affected him both in and out of school. In particular, he was troubled by the anger and hostility of his father toward him. As painful as his relationship with his father was, the conflicts this student experienced did not translate into school failure. In fact, this student did fairly well in school. He used negative factors in his life as inspiration for his own success. As he suggested, parents were not the entire equation. Many students relied heavily on their parents for motivation and inspiration, but even in these instances parents were not able to help their children prepare for college. Most parents did not have the time and skills to help their children with high school work, they did not know how to help their children enroll in the classes that would help them prepare for college, and they did not know how to help their children apply for college. Student success typically required support from other areas beyond the family for these students.

Teachers were the most obvious potential source of in-school support for the high school students. They possessed the knowledge and expertise to serve as a perfect supplement to the motivation provided by parents. In fact, the influence of teachers was the second most-discussed topic when the high school students talked about their school lives. Two students mentioned these influences while talking about their parents. One student described a teacher intervention that included his mother and had made a big difference for him:

> They scheduled a meeting with my mom. And to tell you the truth, I was kinda embarrassed with my mom 'cause she always thought I was doing good. And that was kinda when I turned around. I started kicking back from the gangs. And I started doin' my homework, and my grades actually went up. *Pero* [But] my mom was a big influence on that part 'cause I didn't wanna let her down or nothing. And the other people, I didn't care. It's just my mom. And that's when me and my mom sat down, and she told me, "Look, we came over here and I had you, and my plans was to go back to Mexico, but now that I'm here, I wanna give you a better life. I want the first generation born here to succeed. I don't want you havin' a hard life picking in the fields, going to the warehouses, hurting your back." 'Cause she hurt her back, and that's kinda what woke me up.

This student's experience reflected that of many students at the high school. He had some teacher support, in that teachers made an effort to bring his mother in to understand what was happening with her son. It is interesting, however, that it was his mother who served as the primary influence. For many students, teachers provided some support, but the students did not develop strong relationships with their teachers that might have led to guidance in preparation for college, for example.

Some students did talk positively about their teachers, and although it was rare that they were nurtured and mentored by teachers, any positive experience with a teacher was seen as helpful by the students. Those students who received this kind of support explained that it made them feel great to have a teacher reach out to them and demonstrate that they mattered. Whereas most students did not have strong relationships with teachers in general, at least two staff members on campus were clearly seen as advocates for Chicana/o students. Several students referred to this teacher and counselor as being very helpful. One of the students had this to say about the teacher:

> I have a teacher, he always is there fighting for every student. And he's always encouraged every student to go one step ahead. And always telling you, "Come on. I did it. You can do it too. You're brave, you're strong, and you can do it." And that's what really keeps me up, because when he tells me that I'm brave and that I'm strong, I realize that I *am,* and I go and take those chances in that new experience.

As this student's experience exemplifies, having just one supportive teacher can make a significant difference for students. It gives them confidence both in the supportive teacher's class and in other classes and environments where they might otherwise lack self-assurance. As mentioned, many students in the study did not have this kind of relationship with even one teacher. Although the students reinforced the important role of teachers, they also made it clear that they had not really had the type of support they needed. One fifth-year senior talked about teachers who made being in class hard for him:

> I get mad easy. . . . I hate to be embarrassed, like, in front of the whole class. If I do somethin', you know, they just start yelling at me and everybody's, like, looking at me. I get upset. And I just say things I normally wouldn't. I would just cuss 'em out. . . . [It hasn't happened] a lot. Once in a while when it's a teacher I don't get along with. Or if I feel like they're just pickin' on me or they don't like me or somethin'. And sometimes, when I feel like the teacher don't like me or somethin', I mean, I do things on purpose too, to get 'em mad or something. . . . I would get kicked out 'cause of that. I thought they were just pickin' on me or something. I would hate teachers [if] I felt like they were racist to me . . . in the way they would always be picking only on me. Sometimes I would talk, and they would send me to the office or they would send me outside and they wouldn't let me go back in. You know, there was other kids that would

talk, and he would just give 'em chances and chances. And I thought he was just racist or something. . . . I ended up most times not going to the class. And some of them I would, 'cause I would have friends there that would be like, "Ah, who cares? Just stay here. Do your work." So, but basically those were the classes I wouldn't like to go to.

Many students emphasized that they felt a great distance between themselves and their teachers. In his first comment, this student described how this distance could be bridged by teachers being less strict with the students. His second comment, however, suggested that his relationship with teachers was defined by their lack of understanding of him and his needs. He believed that in some cases his teachers were simply racist. Even for this student, finding someone who could nurture and guide him made all the difference. He later talked about the counselor at the school who worked with migrant youth: "He helped me out a lot. . . . That's when I was skippin' and everything. Counselors, they were pushing me, and I would do better. . . . That's when I wanted to do better." The students explained that teachers and counselors had the possibility of significantly increasing the confidence and comfort of students at school, and that when the students received some support from school staff, it helped their school performance. Similarly, some students noted that negative interactions with school staff had led to disinterest in school and behaviors that often resulted in failure. Others attributed their disinterest in school to a similar disinterest and lack of enthusiasm from their teachers. Some of the students stated that they could do well in school, but when they felt as if there was no reason to put forth the effort, their grades fell dramatically. A number of students were unmotivated in school because in many ways they were disconnected from it. Although they knew school was important and they wanted to live better than their parents, they were not well connected in the school and felt peripheral to daily school life.

It is critical to note that none of the students received any form of strong educational mentorship in any realm of their lives. The support from teachers was often helpful but typically minimal, and that from parents was strong but limited by the parents' lack of knowledge and experience in school. Many students had to turn inward or to friends for support. One student discussed how he turned to a friend for inspiration:

I just had people here and there pushin', but I've never really had, like, this big mentor or anything. . . . My friend surprised me a lot. He got me into school kinda too 'cause he turned his life around kinda too. In middle school he wasn't that great of a student. But when we came here, he changed his life around. . . . Back then, I was the good student and he was the bad. But now it's kinda switched. I seen him doin' things and I realized, "That's what I gotta be doin' too." And he's influenced me quite a lot.

Other students had received similar support and inspiration from a boyfriend or girlfriend, as one student explained when asked who had been the biggest influence on his life:

My girlfriend probly. . . . She would always want me to come to school and do good. She always wanted me to be with her. She's always be like, "No, I want you to pass this, go to college." 'Cause she's going to college right now. . . . She wants me to go to college with her to be there with her. . . . So she wants me to go over there with her. And that's why right now I'm tryin' to do better.

Friends often created a connection to the school in ways that students did not otherwise make. Such relationships could be a big help, and yet, for many students, school was still difficult because their friends also lacked guidance. Furthermore, because students had to rely so heavily on friends and peers for support, shifts in these relationships could have serious effects on them. Students also got involved in negative behaviors because of their lack of guidance. Because they had no one to help them negotiate their lives, they often looked to their peers for options, and that could result in behavior that damaged their school performance. One of the young men described such an experience:

We started gettin' in more gang stuff, and lots of people dropped out my eighth-grade year. In my eighth-grade year I had already seen three or four funerals. And most of them were the people that I seen around my neighborhood, the older guys, who were fighting and stuff. So we knew 'em, so I had been to those funerals, and that's kinda when it was a reality check, you know, it kinda hit me. It's like, "Hey, you're gonna end up there." Then, also the grades wasn't good either. The grades started dropping 'cause, like I said, I started getting involved in—I wasn't officially a gang member, pero I hung around with them. Everybody thought I was. Our grades, we weren't takin' it as serious as we should've. . . . I was just being rowdy. I wasn't doing my homework. I was being rude or stuff like that. Gettin' into fights, writing on the walls, stuff like that. And I was just one of the many that was doin' that.

Overall, friends did not seem to be a determining factor of Chicana/o student behaviors or performance. Instead, the students tended to gravitate toward people who shared their experiences and perspectives. For example, the students never talked about getting pushed into gangs and other damaging behavior by their friends. Rather, they admitted that these actions were choices they had made because those choices coincided with their lack of exposure to realistic alternatives. Involvement with gangs and cliques that were disinterested in school tended to emerge from a student's own disconnection in the school.

Some students, however, chose peer groups that supported their educational interests and often served as the strongest educational support systems in their lives. Three of the students described MEChA as a support system that helped them meet their mentorship needs. Although MEChA is a student organization that is intended to address political and educational issues facing Chicanas/os, at the high school level it typically serves much more of a social function (as a support group). The three students who discussed MEChA in their interviews all had different levels of involvement and varying degrees of criticism of the group, and yet they all turned to the group to help them understand the experiences they were going through and to get inspiration for pursuing school success. The group definitely functioned in this capacity for these students, and yet the limited experience of peers left them still searching for effective strategies to address their concerns and to truly thrive in school. A couple of students provided helpful examples here:

> [MEChA] actually helped school out a lot more 'cause I had people there always asking how I was doing, this, this, and this. And, like, if I needed help, they were there. There were people always around me, helpin' me out. So I think it helped out with school a lot more. . . . I think it helped my grades go up a little.

> When I got involved with MEChA my junior year, when I started doin' all this stuff, it was two guys, they were both at [the community college]. . . . They were involved in MEChA too. And they would mentor me on stuff to do in high school outside the community or how to talk, how to train myself to be able to talk formal, like, when I have to. How to organize and plan and how to not get depressed when something goes wrong, stuff like that. They're some of my mentors also. But, see, that was just only for

about a year and a half. The main one is basically my mom. That's it. It goes back to *familia* always, man.

This last student revealed how MEChA had served as a key avenue for mentorship, which not only helped him achieve his goals but also assisted in the development of an identity that had positive meaning. His story suggests the need for mentorship of students in general, given that the other students simply discussed the lack of mentorship, while their own identity struggles indicated how mentorship might have led them to develop a much more positive sense of identity.

In telling the stories of their school lives, the students emphasized the importance of their parents but also mentioned the benefits of, or their interest in, teacher support. An equally important part of their experience was grounded in their identities and race in particular. Many of the high school students were still trying to grasp the meaning of race in their lives, at least in part because of their difficulty in attributing school experiences directly to race. Thus many students focused on other factors, such as language, which were often more digestible means of contextualizing their experiences. Still, a few students attempted to explain the significance of race in their school lives, as in this example:

> The difficulty is that sometimes when we come down from Mexico, the first thing is that—well, not all the time—but racial things. That sometimes because you're Hispanic, you're Latino or Mexican, they don't give you the same opportunities as the other students.

Although many students didn't always know exactly how to describe what they had seen and experienced, they were confident that race was an important factor that shaped the schooling experiences of Chicana/o students. As seen in Chapter 4, often students understood this racialization through the way language was used as a means for segregating students. In fact, the students who had been in or had experiences with ESL programs were keenly aware of the problematic position of ESL students. Several students talked about ESL and troubles they had had, but few were able to explain these experiences without struggling to do so. Some students went further and described their exclusion from the curriculum:

> Every history class I've taken, we have a page about Mexicans, but what we learn about them is that Mexican-American War, they were bad, they were tryin' to, like, not take over land, when it was just the opposite way.

And that's how we learn. . . . So I think more should be taught about our culture and where we came from and what we've done, what we've overcame and where we're going towards the future now.

In the end, the school influences discussed by the high school students in Acoma fall into the model that evolved from the work with students in East Los Angeles. At the same time, the unique context in Acoma shaped the experiences of these high school students in particular ways. The distractions that students faced in Acoma could often be debilitating. Mentorship could have helped them overcome those distractions, but it was extremely rare. In this case, the racial political climate and its impact on identity were crucial. Because so few Chicana/o students were able to achieve success, and because the Chicana/o community had such limited opportunity to explain and lobby for their needs, most Chicana/o students had to accept what was happening in their schools and communities without question. For this reason, the students had to rely much more heavily on their families. The families provided a great deal of motivation and support, but they were limited by their own lack of schooling and by the limited time they had to help their children in school. Teachers had the ability to serve as mentors, but most did not, although a few staff members functioned in that capacity for students. In fact, these students had clearly learned to understand themselves as "inferior" students in the hierarchy of the school. Few of them were able to encompass their current school life into their identity in a way that led them toward their goals. That is, some students had developed a family-based identity grounded in their desire to help their families and to achieve career goals that would make that possible. At the same time, they did not see this identity as being linked to a positive understanding of their current role in school; instead, they discussed their own struggles in trying to get teacher support or in trying to help others see them as more than below-par ESL students. Many of the students were unable to make a positive connection between high school and their goals and instead seemed to know that their pursuit of these goals would begin after they left high school. The lack of mentorship in dealing with all this made it difficult for them to develop empowering and affirming tactics for school success. In the end, it was complex interactions among multiple forces that shaped the school lives of the Chicana/o students at the high school. None of these forces acted independently of the others, for they overlapped, intersected, and fed each other. Because of this complexity, the students themselves often struggled to understand all the forces that they knew influenced their schooling.

ACOMA COMMUNITY COLLEGE

The similarities and differences between the college students and those in high school in Acoma add depth and complexity to our understanding of schooling in the region. As with the high school students, family was a major influence on the community college students' efforts to succeed in school. One student explained, "I think the influence for me has been the way all my *familia* has actually worked so hard . . . so their kids can do somethin'." Every student mentioned the significance of family members as some form of motivation or support for school success. Being in college had led to additional influences that for many students had been only emerging in their high school years. In particular, several of the students talked about race and its role as an occasional deterrent but also as a motivator for school success. Several students also brought up the role of language and ESL as an inhibiting and often damaging influence on their school lives. All of the students discussed the importance of mentorship, but none had received strong mentorship, although two did receive significant help and support from teachers that clearly led them toward school success.

What is intriguing and hopeful about these students' discussions is that despite the limitations they had faced, several had developed support systems that allowed them to find strength from the very influences that had been damaging earlier in life. In fact, many of the students used those influences as a resource in the pursuit of college success. Nevertheless, it is troubling that the students lacked formal resources and support systems and that this lack led many to struggle in their pursuit of educational opportunities.

When discussing their educational influences, the community college students made it clear that their greatest inspiration came from their parents. As with the high school students, this inspiration came in many different forms. Most often, it was observational. That is, the parents inspired their children through their own struggles more than by sitting them down to discuss school.

One student described this sort of observational inspiration as he discussed how his mother had been the biggest influence on his educational goals:

[My mother is] a strong woman that feels like if her sons, like myself, don't make it, she's not gonna be disappointed, but she's gonna feel like, "I did all this for nothing?" . . . She worked sometimes the fields, and then she went to the warehouse. Or the warehouse, you know, and then night field. I mean, whatever it was that she had to do for us, to keep going to school. . . . [My motivation comes from] just seeing her, I mean, go back home, clean up, go to sleep for about twenty minutes, and get ready for the next work. And seeing her actually start getting her citizenship and getting her GED and have the kids, go to work, and motivating her sons and staying with her sons tight. To me, she's also a hero.

As this student's case exemplified, Mexicana/o parents in Acoma often struggled so hard on so many fronts that their children were driven to help them fulfill their dreams for their families. At younger ages, these students had not always appreciated the degree of effort their parents had demonstrated, but as time passed, this appreciation often became clear. Another student stated that although her parents had not pushed the message of pursuing school directly, they had used their own struggles as a means of conveying this message:

They wanted us to see how it was in the fields. That way we can experience one or the other. You know, either you go to school and get your education or you stay in the fields for the rest of your life. That was one of the reasons that they took us to the fields.

What is striking is the similarities among the different students who participated in the project at the community college. The students each told these stories as they were asked about what had influenced them. They were not asked directly about parents at this point in our conversations. Several students provided almost identical descriptions of their motivations for school success.

Oftentimes, the observational influences of parents were extended to the community at large. The students knew that the struggles of their parents were not theirs alone but reflected larger issues in the Mexicana/o community of Acoma. One student said:

When I look at the statistics of Mexicanos and education, I see that about half of them or more will end up dropping out of school before they can graduate from high school. And I said, "Uh-uh. That's not gonna be me." So that was one of these things that kept me from dropping out, from saying, "Oh, I can't take this anymore. It's too hard for me." One way or another, even though it was hard for me, I still thought I would graduate, no matter what.

At times, the lessons from parents came more from direct experience with the struggles of their families. Many parents purposely took their children to work in the fields in order to push them toward other paths. Although parents were often forced to bring their children to work for economic survival, doing so was almost always with the hope that when the financial need had passed, the experience would serve as an educational motivator. Three students talked about having to leave school to work in the fields and take care of family responsibilities. One student said, "There were days that we hardly had anything to eat, and we had to go make the money."

This burden can weigh heavily on students. On top of this, the young women often had extra burdens of taking care of the males that could be both exhausting and demoralizing. Nevertheless, the female students, like the males, emphasized the struggles of their families as a whole. The severity of their struggles forced the Chicanas to downplay internal familial conflicts so that they could rely on the family as a pillar of support. Still, like the young men, these Chicanas often received direct pushes from their families to succeed in school.

Familial observational influences came in other forms as well. The struggles of Mexicanas/os in Acoma were severe and surrounded them everyday. They saw parents and extended family, including elders, exhausting themselves in the fields. They saw some peers reacting negatively to this reality and getting involved in gangs and other harmful activities. They heard their parents and family tell them that they needed an education, an idea that was reinforced when they had to work in the fields to help their families. For all of these reasons, they had decided to go to college. Their educational goals were critical to who they were, who they wanted to become, and what they wanted for their families.

The community college was the only site where students in the study were also parents. The interviews with these parents often told the other side of the story described throughout this chapter. The parents wanted to set an example for their children about the importance of education and the opportunities that college could provide them that they would not otherwise get. As the father cited in Chapter 4 explained:

> What influenced me is life. Life and my kids. My kids, my wife. I see the stuff in my life, so I try to get all these things so they can have better things. That's one of the biggest things. And if you don't have nothing, you cannot give nothing to your kids. Because I'm already thirty-six. So if

I achieve a little bit more, I think I can give them something. So that influenced me to do something. And that's my biggest part of my life.

In many ways, this father confirmed the insights of the other students who had discussed their own parents' desires. What is interesting is that although it was clear that most parents thought their children's schooling was very important, few were able to participate in school activities, such as PTSA (Parent Teacher Student Association) meetings. Several of the college students mentioned this matter, citing factors like time, limited English ability, and a lack of effort from the school to make their parents welcome. Two students described their parents' situation in this regard:

> Whenever my parents ever got a chance, they would go. But it would be so hard for them to go, because after work they'd have to come home, they'd have to take care of the kids, or they'll have to clean or they'll have to go to another job because they can't afford it, you know, their bills and stuff. I mean, and it was such a low percentage of Mexicanos, Chicanos, I mean, minority groups, going to these PTSA meetings.

> They weren't very involved. And I think the reason for that is because when the school has meetings or something, they do everything in English, and the parents don't really get too much involved, I think, because of that.

The students never emphasized this lack of parental involvement as a factor that made school more difficult for them, but it was obviously important to them. Although they did not explicitly say it, it was evident that they also experienced some resentment toward the school for not welcoming their parents. This too seemed important, because in some ways it defined their own roles in the school as outsiders.

Students experienced several types of distractions that often made it difficult to feel comfortable and do well in school. One student talked about the impact of his family's financial situation:

> The thing that sticks out in my mind the most is, like, the science fair. I remember the first year I had saved enough money to get my project, and the second year we didn't have any money. And I had made it to regionals the year before. The second year we didn't have the money for it and I couldn't do it, and so I just had to back out. I just remember I was in eighth grade, and I remember just crying for, like, two days straight 'cause

I really wanted to do it badly but I couldn't. So it was just things like that that affected a lot of things. . . . Growin' up this way, I think you do, or I did anyway, start to think of yourself as being less than, I guess not having what everybody else had. . . . And then I was intimidated a lot of times by the richer kids. I shunned from tryin' to compete with these people 'cause I knew that they had the resources. You know, they were always gonna be on top. And so that's always been. Now it doesn't matter to me, because if I wanna compete with somebody for something . . . if they have more money than me, well, I'm gonna work that much harder to accomplish that goal too.

This student provided a good example of how the community college students handled obstacles and distractions. Although such obstacles were often overwhelming early in their schooling, their drive later helped them use obstacles as a motivation for success. Still, it is important to recognize that constraints such as these also limited their educational success.

Work and family finances were often difficult for students to deal with, but these were not the only distractions that could be found in the home. At times, family problems made it difficult for students to do their work, even at the college. Most often these distractions came in the form of parental fighting and separation and could become overwhelming for students who had no other forms of support.

Alternative supports for students in such situations can come from teachers. During the interviews, students spent a significant amount of time discussing the role of teachers in their schooling. Like the high school students, the community college students discussed how important teacher support was. For most students, however, these ideas were grounded in having had little support from teachers. Only three students talked about getting some form of strong teacher support. One of these students described his experience with a particular teacher:

There was this guy, and he teaches at Johnson . . . and he got Latino Lit in there, Latino Literature. And this guy, man, I mean, people just thought he was weird. . . . He would say, "Mexicanos, you gotta do this. You gotta stand up for yourself. You've gotta actually go out there and fight for what you guys believe in." I mean, he was just totally for us, and it seemed like the *gavachos* [whites] felt like, "This guy's a sell-out man. He don't really like our kind." And this and that. But it wasn't that. It's just the way he was brought up. The way he seen us struggle. . . . He's seen the racial issues. He's been to these conferences where they don't have no colored people and the way they talk about people. And he would let us know. And he would say, "Hey, you guys are big to me." He goes, "I know I'm not your skin color and I know that I don't have a lot of you guys' pride or dignity or any of your culture, but I know where you guys are coming from. I know how it feels to be discriminated because I get that from my own people." And he goes, "But I'm just here to support you guys. I'm here to talk to you guys, and I'm here to teach you guys." . . . I mean, it was just like, "Man, this guy's bad!"

This was the same teacher whom a couple of the high school students had mentioned as an important influence on their efforts to succeed in school. As this student demonstrated, it meant a lot to students that this teacher would make a commitment to understanding who they were and to supporting them in their efforts in school. From the multiple conversations I had with students at the high school and those who had gone on to the community college, it was clear that this was the one teacher who had made a conscious effort to consider how he could motivate Chicana/o students. That he was white made that effort even more intriguing to students, because they had never encountered that kind of a commitment from a white person. In the case of this student, he had not received mentorship from this teacher in the form of personal support. He had simply benefited from the message the teacher had conveyed to the class.

Another student at the college who had attended this high school found her support from Mexicano teachers. She did not feel comfortable with adults from other backgrounds, and this support proved crucial to building her confidence and preparing her for college. She recalled,

There was always some kinda teacher I could rely on, I could trust. You know, a Mexicano teacher. Since I was so into myself, especially in my early years of education in the United States, I never spoke to any other teacher besides a Mexican teacher. You know, for the same reason that I was never around anybody else besides Mexican people. I was never really comfortable with anybody else besides somebody that was Mexican. So that was good. I thought that was good that there was always some Mexican teacher there. . . . They always encouraged me. They talked to me. They listened to me. They helped me out with any problems that I had. I just felt comfortable with them; I guess that was all. . . . My soccer coach told me about the different scholarships that there was available and actually told me that I could go on to college. I knew I could go on to college, but he showed me how to get to college, how to fill out the paperwork, how to fill out scholarships. . . . He also talked to the other counselors for me. He actually told counselors that I was interested in going on to college, that I was interested in applying for scholarships. He made it easier for me to go to college and to apply for scholarships. . . . He was Mexican as well.

For this student, the specific types of support provided by Mexicana/o teachers made it possible for her to succeed in school. Later she suggested that, without it, she was likely to drop out of school.

If a kid's being treated badly in school by their teachers, I don't think they feel confident enough to—Well, that was me, I didn't feel confident enough to keep going through my studies. Because a lot of teachers were putting me down and because other students were putting me down. The atmosphere has to be positive for you to grow.

This student provided a critical example of the type of teacher support that can facilitate school success for Chicana/o students. Teachers who make them feel comfortable and who understand their needs help students feel confident in their ability to do well in school. Furthermore, teachers who act as mentors and guide students through the steps in their schooling are crucial.

Most students did not get this kind of support, and many had very negative experiences with teachers that overrode the support they received in other areas. Another issue for students was teacher apathy. One student who did not mention negative interactions with teachers, for example, felt that they were unconcerned with her school performance. Her explanation suggested that student and teacher feelings might feed on each other and create a climate in which success was difficult to attain:

The teachers just did their own thing, and they didn't really care whether you did good in school or not. . . . I think it was because I wasn't too involved in school. If I would've been, like, more involved or if I would've been more like a good student, then maybe I woulda had, like, a teacher that woulda pushed me more or something. But I don't think they put too much attention to those who don't care much about school.

Other students shared experiences with discrimination and differential treatment based on race and related characteristics. Several students described experiences with differential treatment that had negatively affected them but that they did not directly attribute to race. For many students, language issues were a much clearer way of explaining the treatment they experienced, for language was the means by which they were tracked into nonacademic courses or made fun of by others. One student's analysis reflected the comments from a number of students: "Because I didn't know English when I was a little kid, I was always picked on by other kids in elementary school. And also in middle school."

Language issues and conflicts around limited English ability stuck out for the students, even after they enrolled at the community college. Many recalled language-related experiences in vivid description and portrayed them as traumatic events of their childhood. Others linked these experiences to race and racism, and some students focused specifically on racial issues as influencing their school performance. One student discussed subtle teacher behaviors and the role that race played in who teachers helped:

> A lot of times, if there's a person there that actually don't understand the culture, they don't understand where you're coming from, he really ain't gonna pay attention to you or she ain't gonna really pay attention to you. If their kid is going there, they'd rather take care of that kid that acts like them, looks like them, or has some kind of special thinking like they do. And a lot of times, they feel like, "I'd rather help this person instead of that person, because they're more of me." And I think that's a big problem, because if you ain't got a person that will actually know who you are or back you up, it's gonna be hard to stay in school. . . . Once you get into that class, you're like a target if you're the only kind. You don't really have a voice, or they're gonna be pickin' on you because they wanna know what you know. But yet, when you ask them a question, they're, like, [not interested].

It is clear that these students were still trying to understand and explain their experiences in school. Several suggested that race was important and even told stories that reflected some form of racial discrimination, but when they tried to explain the role of race in schooling, they struggled. A few students were better able to sort out their experiences, often by focusing on a specific issue. One addressed some of the complexities of the role of race in school as he explained that his lack of self-knowledge had made it hard for him to understand some of what he was experiencing. As he suggested, the curriculum itself often hindered the efforts of Chicana/o students to understand and deconstruct their own experiences.

I can name, like, a lot of experience that I went through in high school that I didn't really know who I was, and because of that, I wasn't really observing. I wasn't really using the intellectuality that I could've back in high school, because of discrimination, and since I didn't really know much about myself, every time I hear somethin' about us, I wouldn't know what to say. I'd be like, "Man, they're prolly right." And so the more history, the more background you have about who you are and the positive attitude once again, it's an eye-opener, man. It's somethin' that will catch your attention. And so that was kind of hard in high school, because sometimes you didn't have the information to realize or to find out who you were. And it was all based on ideology, man. You know, it was who were they? who are you?

Another student pointed to the importance of the curriculum and having Mexicana/o teachers when she was asked what might have helped her in high school:

Having a lot more teachers that were Mexican [would have helped]. And also being taught my own history. I never learned a lotta my own history 'til I got here actually. . . . It woulda been a lot nicer knowing that there was a lot more role models to look up to in history. . . . I didn't think there was a whole bunch of Chicanos that had done anything through the past. And when I got here, I did learn that there was a lot of things that Chicanos had done in the past. I didn't know anything about that in high school. It would've helped me a lot, I guess, knowing that there was people like me that had done a lotta things, not just Anglos. . . . Because I guess I would have more pride in my own self, knowing that other people like me had achieved something. . . . 'Cause my thinking back then was that, "Oh, everything that was done great, it was Anglos only." I never thought something great had been done by my own people. . . . It would've been helpful for me to know that back then.

About half of the community college students raised similar themes on their own in the interviews, and several of them had sought Chicana/o-oriented support systems when they went to college. One student talked about the benefits of Chicana/o Studies classes to her overall school performance:

I've always felt that since I've taken Chicano Studies, I do better in my other classes because of that. . . . I guess 'cause I'm learning new things about myself that I'm very proud of. I'm actually interested in something.

Because I see it's sort of like a correlation. If I like something I'm doing and if I'm doing it because I enjoy it, it makes it a lot easier to take those other classes that are hard, to pass on that energy of enjoyment over here so I can finish this class good.

Several students touched on these themes, explaining that it had been helpful to take classes that covered the experiences of Chicanas/os. Such classes provided the students with a sense of pride and empowerment that translated into greater confidence and interest in other classes. Similarly, the Chicana/o community college students sought other support systems that were grounded in their own experiences as Chicanas/os. In particular, as in the high school, a group of the community college students sought out MEChA as a means of creating a network and support system that could be a foundation for their educational success. One student provided an example by talking about being recruited to come to the college by contacts he had who were in MEChA. He then discussed MEChA specifically (as was relayed in Chapter 4):

So finally I decided to come over here, and as a matter of fact it was [MEChA] students from here that kinda said, "Hey, what are you gonna do? Why don't you go try to see what ACC has to offer for you?" And I was like, "Oh, man." And they, like, just kept pushing me and pushing me. I was like, "All right, all right, all right. I'll go get a application and fill it out." . . . So I finally did it. I got the application. I filled it out. I gave 'em what they wanted. And I got, like, a letter about three weeks later, saying that I was accepted. And I'm like, "That was pretty easy." . . . [MEChA] got me away from all the trouble or skipping that I was doing back in high school, you know, and not really paying attention. It actually said, "Hey, come and learn about this. Come and join our group. We got some love for you." And so it kind of got me back up on my feet.

Several students emphasized how important MEChA was to them as a support group of friends who motivated and helped each other. In many ways, the group served in a mentoring capacity, providing guidance similar to the mentoring that some students had received from teachers in high school.

The excerpts provided thus far have touched upon all of the major themes that the community college students emphasized in their discussions of their school lives. One student, when asked about her biggest influences on her school performance, provided a nice summary of the educational influences that ran through the lives of those at the community college:

> My biggest influence about school . . . My parents having to work in the fields was one of the influences, 'cause I know I didn't wanna go back. And then my mother was an influence too, 'cause she's the one, she wouldn't let me take a year off. So I *had* to go to school. So I thank her for that, 'cause I think that was the right thing to do in the end. I think also, just learning; I think going through MEChA too. That was a learning experience too, because you learn the side of politics that you never really paid attention to. Also, I mean, just to go through Chicano Studies. . . . I guess the philosophy of it; I mean, just to open your eyes, just to learn my different history, that also influences you and you realize more than ever— not because the fields pushed you out—you finally realize "I should go to school." It was like more than ever you feel like "I should." I feel like I should be involved in something. And to be involved, I have to be educated so I can take on these new tasks. So I guess that's one of the influences. I mean, education itself has opened my eyes to show me that I need to learn more.

It is clear that parents were a critical inspiration and source of support, but that parents' limited experiences in school required students to find additional forms of guidance. A few students had benefited from support and mentorship from high school teachers, but most had only yearned for that kind of support. As one student put it,

> I never had a mentor teacher, not even with the Spanish teacher. She wasn't a very good mentor for me either so I can go into college. I guess that's what I needed all along was a mentor. And my mother could take me so far, but they were working in the fields. My mother dropped out of high school in Mexico. But she did have secretary skills and stuff like that, and that was her emphasis. . . . I was kinda lost in a way in all of that commotion.

Even the students who had been mentored in high school lacked this type of guidance when they came to the college. Many turned to each other, relying on MEChA as a support system, while also gaining strength and confidence in Chicana/o Studies classes. As one student said, "You always need somebody to push you, so you won't feel like, 'Hey man, I'm just by myself.'" Even with this support, the students made it clear—both in their own analyses and through their lack of in-depth knowledge of how to prepare for a four-year college—that they needed mentorship. One student discussed these themes while making recommendations for improvements in his college:

> A first step to me would be hiring more Mexicano, Chicano teachers, professors, because we need those professors and teachers to let us know that they're there for us, that they know where we're comin' from, that they understand us. Second is that I think it would be a good idea if we actually had Chicano Studies in every high school and college, to teach you about your history or about things that even others would like to know about you that *you* couldn't even explain to them because *you* don't know yourself. The third thing would prolly be [to] get more books in the library of Chicano Studies, Chicano History. 'Cause there's hardly anything in there to offer you. And to actually let your people know, "Hey, there's books out there. There's things you can go see."

This student touched upon a number of the themes raised in the interviews with the community college students as a whole. Chicana/o students were looking for support systems that addressed their critical needs for mentorship. As the students pointed out, this mentorship needs to come in the form of teachers, peer groups, and the curriculum. The students discussed a variety of experiences and influences on their school lives, and this chapter emphasizes the themes that emerged from their different perspectives. All of the students agreed on the importance of their families as motivators and supporters of their school goals. They also all agreed on the need for mentorship. The students who had had support from teachers made it clear that this support had been extremely helpful and vital to their school success. The students who sought out peer support systems suggested that such groups could serve similar functions. Unfortunately, the limited educational experiences and expertise within peer groups still left the students in need of additional forms of support. Identity issues also played an essential role in the schooling of the community college students. Most had become aware of the role of their race and class early on in their schooling, as they understood that their race and class made them seem less capable in the eyes of at least some other students and personnel in their schools. Their race and class became an important part not only of who they were but also of how they could be helped to achieve their educational goals. As they explained, mentorship and guidance that were grounded in their racialized experiences helped them connect their real lives to their goals. Within this context, gender was important, but most of the students had difficulty fitting it into their analysis of their school experiences.

The dominant story that rang true for all of the community college students was that they felt like outsiders in their precollege schooling. For all but one student, this feeling was related to race (as well as to associated issues of language for many). Only one student did not discuss the relationship between race and schooling (and he seemed to feel like an outsider for other reasons related to his class, his appearance, and conflicts with teachers). The other significant finding is that three-fourths of the students had never had school-based support to assist them in pursuing their educational goals. Those students who lacked mentorship voiced how much they desired it, as well as the "insider" knowledge that they felt they needed to effectively pursue higher education. For the two students who had received supportive guidance from teachers, it clearly had been an essential ingredient for their success in school. These two students seemed to be more confident about their abilities and were performing better in school than their peers who had not received school-based support.

All but one student cited the important role of their families in their pursuit of higher education. These students had all been inspired by their families and the struggles their families had endured, and this inspiration served as the motivation for their pursuit of school success. Three-fourths of the students explicitly stated that they wanted to help their communities and that this desire was another important reason for their pursuit of higher education. For several students, MEChA was a key support system that gave meaning to their schooling by providing a network of friends who shared a vision of improving their community and by helping them on the path to their degrees. Three students mentioned that Chicana/o Studies courses helped them in a similar way by allowing them to make connections between their own experiences and those of a larger Chicana/o community and to connect this understanding to their pursuit of their own goals. For those students who had immigrated as adults, that immigrant status was a key part of their identities and the struggles they faced in the United States that were related to their educational goals. Finally, gender was a significant filter that affected the educational experiences of the women. Although only one student explicitly discussed the limitations she faced that males did not, all of the women made some reference to the responsibilities and restrictions that they faced as women in their families and that made it harder to pursue their educational goals.

Overall, the stories of the schooling of these community college students were similar in many ways. They faced limited opportunity because of the significant racial barriers that they encountered, but those barriers could be overcome through support systems and personal dedication. Clearly, their school lives were shaped by the power conflicts that defined their identities.

THE UNIVERSITY

The lives of the university students were fundamentally different from those of the Chicanas/os at the high school and community college. Most significantly, most of the university students lived about three hours from their homes, in a small college town whose only Chicanas/os were students. Not all of the Chicana/o students at the university were from the Acoma area, but the vast majority were, and living in Fowler was a culture shock for many of them. Although the climate is possibly less conservative than that of Acoma, for most of the students this was the first time they were living without their families and outside of Chicana/o communities. Thus many were much more attuned to race and racial issues in Fowler than they ever had been.

In addition, the university students had had the opportunity to hone their intellectual and critical-thinking skills. Although it is difficult to determine the direct effects of this factor, it evidently had shaped their analyses. These students discussed many of the same issues that the others covered, but they also had a more nuanced analysis and had often had more time to consider their educational trajectories than the other students had.

The remainder of this section provides detailed descriptions of the multiple influences on these students' school lives. Because of the distance between the students and their families and because they were participating in advanced study that far exceeded their parents' expertise, the nature of parental influence was different from that during their precollege schooling. In addition, these students had had more positive interactions with and support from teachers, a characteristic particularly evident among the most successful college students. At the same time, because of the somewhat polarized racial climate in Fowler, race had become a critical issue for many of the students at the university.

One of the strong similarities between the university students and those attending school in Acoma was their emphasis on the importance of family in their schooling. Eight of the eleven university students described their familial influences as the most important to their schooling. Of the three others, one focused on teachers, one on race, and one did not have a significant external, educational influence. Some of the students talked about familial influence in general terms. They had a strong family unit and found strength and support there, as exemplified in the following excerpt from an interview:

> The biggest influences on my life have definitely gotta be my family. Because they've always been there. Not really my dad—he's kinda been an influence, 'cause I've always seen what he's done. Mainly my mom, my brother, and my sister, 'cause when my dad left when we were five, all we had was each other. And that's all we've ever had is each other, and we've always been tight. And so they'd have to be like my biggest influence in life.

Although families were seen as a critical resource, many parents did not have the time and knowledge to actively help their children achieve success in school. Many students, however, described specific influences from their parents and families, and such influences were a distinguishing characteristic among a few of the university students. Even many of the families who had never sent anyone to college pushed hard for it. As one student put it, "My mom knew. I mean, she saw the future. She knew that you're gonna need a college degree to get anywhere." Like this student, many of the other university students felt that they were striving to fulfill the dreams and aspirations of their families. They often felt that they had carried their entire families with them to college. Most did not feel the expectations of their family as pressure, however, and instead saw the fulfillment of those expectations as an honor and commitment they were proud to make.

Some parents were much more familiar with the education system and encouraged their children in different ways. One student talked about his mother and the different methods she used to push him in college:

> My mom and dad come from fairly educated families, and they both have college degrees also, but she's always pushed us towards college 'cause there's just some things that we can't do without college, as far as helping people. . . . College was never a choice. It was "You are going, whether you like it or not." . . . She had a way of making us do things. . . . One summer she made us work in the fields, so we'd know what it was like when we saw the migrants working. . . . You're always gonna have the active influence throughout your entire life. But, I mean, as far as the observations, I mean those are things that can change the way you act your whole life at the same time. I'd say the observations helped back up the active influence from my mom.

What is interesting about the familial support that this student received is that it was well grounded in his race and its educational importance to his family. He explained in later parts of our interviews that his mother had insisted that he had to use his education to help Chicana/o communities, as he suggested briefly in the excerpt above by describing how she provided him both active support and observational influences that exposed him to the needs of these communities. Few students had received this kind of support, which blended the importance of school and their racial background. Instead, almost all of the students had learned, primarily from watching their parents struggle, that it was essential to their families that they become educated. One student described how his family, like many others, had made great sacrifices just so that their children could be educated in the United States:

> One day a long, long time ago, my dad said, "I'm only here [in the United States] because I want you kids to be educated." And it hit me hard. He's away from everything that he wants to be by so that his kids can be educated. And that really was like, *wow,* and even my mother waited 'til she was twenty-, I don't know, [twenty]-four or -five before she even started school. And they all sacrificed to go to school, and it's just really important for both my parents.

The educational influence of families was not always positive. The most common distractions that families created for their children were due to separation and divorce. For one student, her stepfather was a negative influence, and yet she still used that influence as inspiration to pursue school success.

> He's pretty prejudiced and even discriminatory towards my other dad and Mexicans, and since I was part of [my biological dad], I was a bad thing kind of, but not really, but kind of. And so I just always wanted to prove to him that I was good, no matter what. . . . I think that's what influenced me during school.

As with all students, family conflicts could be significant distractions to the university students' pursuit of school success. Interestingly, these students used these conflicts as motivation or simply found ways to focus on schooling instead of the conflict. For other students, the family was neither a distraction nor a support system, so they had to find inspiration for the pursuit of their goals elsewhere. Still others had received positive support from their families, but the financial constraints they faced often made it hard for them to do well in school.

Like the students in Acoma, a few of the university students had to work in the fields to help their families. Although this work was a significant educational distraction, it also served as a motivation for school success. One student described the impact of working in the fields:

> The asparagus—the stress of waking up [very early] in the morning. You got homework, so you forget. And you start remembering when you come back from school, you're like, "Oh, tomorrow I'm going to get on the ball and start doing the homework, or the lab report or whatever." It was stressful at first, but it just becomes a part of what you have to do, a part of you. . . . I remember when I was in elementary, we used to get up at two o'clock. Ten acres of asparagus, to get up at two in the morning, and at two in the morning the sun's not out; it's dark. So Dad would leave the truck on with the high beams, and we pick, and [my cousin] would be driving the truck, turning it and stuff, so we could see where the rows and the asparagus are. And she'd do that till like four in the morning. . . . And we go halfway into the field, and by that time it'd be six-thirty, and at seven o'clock the bus would come. We used to live in a trailer; we would run to the trailer, take a shower, come back in the truck, and we didn't have licenses, so that was kind of fun. And then we'd just stand by the road, and the bus would come pick us up, and we'd wave bye to Mom and then we would go to school. But I don't remember being tired, because, you know, you're so young, I wasn't tired. . . . For as long as I remember, we've been doing it, so it's not really a shock. It's not really a big deal anymore.

For almost all of the Chicana/o university students, their families were their most important educational influence, most often because of their love and respect for their families and their appreciation for the struggles their families had gone through to give their children opportunities to get an education. At times, parents were able to provide more specific and direct guidance, and the students suggested that this guidance was highly significant because it helped them overcome the rough spots in their schooling that other students struggled with to a much greater extent. For a few students, there were times when family conflicts burdened them and even distracted them from school, but many students chose to use such conflicts as motivation to work hard in school. At times, the students also turned to other support systems.

Many of the students, for example, relied on teachers to help them understand how to be successful in school and move up the educational ladder. After talking about his parents being his main influence, one student also discussed how important teachers were for him:

> I've been lucky through school. I've had some really good teachers that motivated me. I mean, I heard a lot of people say stories [like] "Oh, this teacher put me down and said that I wouldn't amount to nothin'" and so forth. And I think that's never the case with me. Maybe [some] teachers didn't really care, but I never felt like that. I think I was always surrounded by teachers that motivated me and then say, "You're gonna be somebody; you're gonna get somewhere." So I think that helped a lot. . . . I'd go to 'em, and they'd be willing to help me and explain things to me. And just by the interaction, I could see that they weren't only doin' their job. They actually cared. And it felt good.

This type of supportive educational environment was something that really helped this student believe in his own possibilities. In addition, it was helpful to him to have a specific person who cared and who made him feel like a real person and not just someone occupying a desk. The same student also talked about one such person at the university who had made his experiences there much easier:

> Once I certified to my major and I got to meet some of the professors—and, again, I've been lucky and I've met a couple. And they're pretty good. One of 'em, I shared my problem with 'em. I talk to her about it. And she's pretty cool, though. She listens and stuff, and she tells me some things. It's just always kinda nice that I can go talk to her about personal things if she's there.

This type of support was particularly needed by students at the university. All of the students who were thriving at the university had a professor or mentor who was helping them. As these experiences demonstrated, mentorship at any stage in school can build student confidence and help students transition into new educational opportunities that are in line with their career goals.

Although the most successful students had received strong support and guidance from teachers, especially at the college level, those who were struggling had lacked this kind of support. Many students described conflicts with teachers that had led to difficulties in school. One student explained his own conflicts with teachers in the course of telling a story about a particular incident with a teacher:

> I was looked down upon by teachers, by most teachers. They were real harsh with me. They wouldn't let me get away with nothing. You know,

like sometimes a kid will speak out of turn and they'll let it slide. Like the average kid—he says somethin' out of turn, they're gonna let it slide. If I spoke out of turn, they'd kick me out of class on the drop of a dime. It's always hard to stay in class. I remember thinkin' like, "Why do I go to class? What's the point of coming if they kick you out after five minutes?" I mean, I walked into a science class and then, this teacher, this Mr. Hell teacher, I didn't like him. . . . He goes, "Do you plan to stay in my class?" And then I go, "Well, do you plan to keep me here? 'Cause I leave by *your* request, not by mine." And he goes, "Get out." I'm like, "For what?" He goes, "I don't like the tone you were takin' with me." And I was like, "Later." So basically I stopped going to classes. I would go every once in a while. But basically I just stopped going. And I was like, "What's the point?"

Repeated conflicts with teachers made this student feel that there was little use in going to school. Although he actively participated in and even instigated some of these conflicts, he felt that there was little else he could do because he lacked the power to have his side understood. Later, he described how he used these experiences to his advantage:

When we were in there, I didn't really see all that was happening, but when I had stepped away, I knew, "Wow, we need school. It's *so* important." That kinda thing. But I think, like, I learned a lot from the negative. I took what I could to use it to my advantage. And I took a lot of the positive, all that I could get.

In the midst of his conflicts with teachers, all he could think about was to find a way that he could feel somewhat in control of the situation and fight back. It was only later that he recognized what had been going on, as he gained some distance from the situation.

What is interesting about the interviews with students who talked about negative experiences in school is how vivid these experiences were for them, even years afterward. For most students, conflicts with teachers were rare. At the same time, the significance of these rare conflicts was immense. Even just one incident could lead a student to feel insecure and to want to transfer out of the school or even drop out. One student who had done well throughout school gave an example:

My French teacher, we were listening to a tape in class, this whole story. 'Cause it was talking about, these people murdered someone and then they went to Mexico to try and hide. . . . The character was trying to bribe the police officer, and then she stopped the tape and was talking, and she goes, "And I think you will generally find that true of all Mexicans, that they're easily bought off and cheap and all you ever see them at is like K-Mart and Wal-Mart." And I got up in class, and I kind of walked out of class. . . . And so then I had a really hard time being motivated to do anything. And then the worst thing was the next year I got her for French *and* Spanish. I had to put up with her twice a day.

Later the same student described the impact all this had had on him:

I wasn't too happy about continuing in high school. 'Cause I kinda wanted to drop out after my sophomore year and take my GED test then and start college then. 'Cause school was just really boring. So I think my grades suffered somewhat 'cause of that, 'cause then I didn't really wanna do my papers for 'em or anything, 'cause it was just so blatant. And I mean it wasn't just isolated to, like, one teacher.

It is important to note, however, that guidance and mentorship could balance out experiences like these. Although this student did not have this kind of support in the school in which the conflicts occurred, he did tell of support he had received in another high school:

I was in the honors classes [in high school], and I noticed in there that they treat students differently that were in there than that were outside of there. But even some of the students that were in those classes, they would kind of treat differently by the skin color still. The teachers would . . . the only one that didn't really act that way was our biology teacher, [who] was Chicano, and he'd be encouraging everyone to go to school and, of course being in biology, encouraging more towards the sciences and becoming doctors and so forth. . . . [He was] always encouraging students how they need to go to school so they can get out, not so much get out of the barrios, but come back and help the people in there get out. And change them and especially with, like, medical stuff, coming back and offering medical help and out in the fields and stuff. And he was also our MEChA adviser there at the high school. And then, as comparison to our English teacher . . . everyone to her, if they weren't white, it's like their opinion didn't matter or anything. . . . Someone had stated something [and] she goes, "A question like that would only come from a stupid beaner."

The negative comments made by teachers had a dramatic impact on this student, but because he received strong support from others (his mother and a teacher), he found ways to survive in what he often felt was a racially hostile climate. Most students did not get the kind of support that this student had received in his first high school, and many of the students who talked about the need for teacher support attributed its absence to a lack of Chicana/o teachers. One student focused on this lack in her analysis and then talked about the lack of role models in the community at large:

> I'd say we're like sixty-forty Mexicans [sixty percent Mexicans] in this school district, and we have maybe five to ten teachers, Mexican teachers. That's it; that is, I mean, *it.* I just feel like that's negative. . . . There's no community leaders. There's no Hispanic community leaders. . . . I just think all these kids are getting this negative feedback of who they are and what they can become.

This issue of role models was particularly important to the university students. They stated that they had felt uncomfortable in many of their learning environments because comments from the teachers, though rarely intended to offend the students, made it obvious that the teachers did not understand the Chicana/o experience and assumed that being Chicana/o was laden with cultural and intellectual deficits. It was because of this sort of teacher ignorance of both the experience of Chicanas/os and the impact of statements that reflect that ignorance that students emphasized the need for Chicana/o teachers. The expectation of the students was not that Chicana/o teachers would be easier on them, but that Chicana/o teachers would create an environment in which the students might feel valued and respected. For the female students, particularly those in the sciences, racial isolation was linked to gender isolation, for they were often the only Chicanas in their classes or departments. These Chicanas sought not only role models who were of their background but also other women of color who could help them deal with the multiple forms of isolation they faced.

A related issue raised by the students was a lack of engagement in the curriculum. Many students expressed occasional or even frequent disinterest in school that they attributed to boring and seemingly irrelevant course content. Like any students, these Chicanas/os noted that their grades suffered when they were bored and not challenged in class. This is important to note because Chicana/o student failure is rarely attributed to students' not being challenged and instead is usually blamed on low skill levels of the students. The students' ability to reach the university suggests that their skills were not the problem.

The issues of race that students described above were not exclusive to interactions with teachers. Many students discussed racial tension within the student bodies of their schools and within their communities, which were significant and often affected their school behaviors, as in this example:

> In the school I came from, there was a lot of racial tension between the hicks and the Mexicans. It came to the point where if you were Mexican, you had to choose whether you were gonna be on their side or be on our side. 'Cause it was just a *huge* thing. And then most people chose to go with us. And then there was a couple that stayed neutral. . . . We're like, "Neutral? What's neutral? Ain't nothin' about neutral." See, 'cause the way we grew up is, it's either all or nothing.

The racial tensions in this student's community had spilled over into the school, shaping the identities of all of the students and forcing them to choose sides. This situation in turn affected much of school life. The same student provided another example of the effects of racial tension when he discussed how he had felt like an outsider in his junior high honors classes:

> It was real strange, 'cause I just felt like, "What am I doing here?" I was never like an outstanding student or someone that everybody recognizes is the smart people. And these kids in these classes were. And I'm thinking, I remember I went back to my sixth-grade teacher and I'm askin' her, "*Why* am I in these classes?" And she's like, "'Cause you're smart." And I'm like, "What? *No*, it's not *true*." I couldn't believe it. It was strange. It wasn't hard. . . . [The students in those classes] cliqued together, you know, like you have little cliques in every school. And they were the same way, like the almost nerdy clique, you know, little preppy boys and stuff. And that just wasn't me. They really looked at me, and they laughed at me 'cause I was always crackin' jokes or doin' somethin'. But then they looked down on me at the same time. I was not someone that they saw as equal. And that was in junior high, and I felt that.

While this student struggled to make sense of this experience as a youngster, he understood that who he was made it unlikely for him to be a success and that his peers quite clearly had the same evaluation of him. For this reason, it was difficult for him to divest himself of who he was outside of these classes and to become comfortable within them. The isolation was disconcerting for him. University students who had grown up in less diverse areas felt this isolation even more so. One student who had grown up in an almost all-white community described her sense of isolation:

> My mom had more bad experiences than I did. Because, I guess, when I was little, one time we went to the store and, like, she got called a nigger. But I never really felt it. I realized it more in high school, that people just didn't say anything, all those years they just thought I was, like, black or half-black. So it's just not very known up there. People are very ignorant still.

This Chicana student was one of only a few people of color in her school and her community. Resistance was not an option she considered. She believed that her best strategy was to prove herself to everyone around her:

> I always wanted to, like, set a good example, 'cause so many people have negative opinions about different races. They think, "Oh, they're just a bunch of," whatever. So I wanted to show them that I'm a part of that race and I act like this. I think that was important to me to always like set an example, since there wasn't any other ones in my school.

During her high school years, this student struggled silently with the effects of this situation. She recalled that she did not have significant conflicts, but she did feel isolated. This isolation became clearer to her when, as a college student, she reflected on her past experiences. As she put it, "I don't think I was ever treated differently by [my friends], but they were always, like, really ignorant."

While feelings of isolation and discrimination were common to many of the students, a few of them were able to develop positive social relations in their schools that pushed them to succeed. It is of concern, however, that even those who received this kind of support in high school could struggle in college when they lost that support. In addition, for many students, the conflicts and issues that they saw emerging in high school continued in college. One student provided a couple of examples of how race had become significant in her university classes:

> I was in one of my classes and we were watching that stupid movie *Stand and Deliver,* and my professor was asking questions about the movie, and the question was something like . . . "Do you think it was right the way he

used to talk to his students?" You know, how he used to call them burros or something like that. And this little white kid raises his hand. . . . He said something like, "Well, maybe that's the way those people are. Maybe they like to be talked to that way." And I just got so ticked. So I said something. . . . I was really mad, and I was really sarcastic about it. But, I mean, if I hear something like that, I'm not gonna sit back and not say anything. . . . I mean, we deal with these issues all the time, because I have my ESL classes and my bilingual classes and most of the kids in there are from Washington. So they've seen Hispanics to a degree. They know that we're there and that a lot of Hispanics don't speak any English. Another time I was in another bilingual class . . . we were talkin' about minorities and not even Mexicans in general. But she [the teacher] was like, "Well, we just have to remember," something like, "As a teacher, we just have to remember that they're just like us, that they're not any different." I'm [thinking], "I can't believe you just *said* that." And she was sitting next to me too. I was just [thinking], "I'm not gonna say anything, because I know that you didn't mean anything rude by it." . . . I was [thinking], "Well, what do you think? We're green men? We've got three eyes and five legs?"

These types of experiences in the university could be very damaging, because the students felt that higher education should not permit such ignorance, but then the students actually found that this ignorance was even supported by university practices at times. For students who did not receive strong mentorship, other forms of support became even more important in such situations. Students who faced racialized conflicts in their classes and daily lives at the university had to find means of dealing with these conflicts in ways that allowed them to continue to do well. Many students discussed the importance of receiving support from other Chicanas/os, as in this example:

I met my one friend, my really good friend, up here and she's Chicana, and she was like, "We gotta go to the [Chicana/o-Latina/o] center. Let's go to the center." And we came in here, and everybody was just so friendly. They're like, "How're you doin'? Yeah, you're the girl on the soccer team, huh? We've been waiting to meet you." And I was just like, "Yeah, I know. I've been hearing so much about you guys." And so I just felt so welcomed. I had never felt so welcomed as I did when I came here. I mean, I felt welcome in the athletic department, but it was like, "What position do you play? Where are you from?" Everything was based on what I was gonna do on the field. And, like, after the games they're like, "Oh, you had a really good game." . . . And it wasn't like, "So how're you doing?

How's life? How's everything else? How's school?" It wasn't, but when I got [to the center], it was like, "Oh, so you're on the soccer team? That's cool. That's cool. So what classes are you taking?" And it was just [that] they cared more about me as, like, a person. . . . I just felt like I could've been like a D student with absolutely nothing going for me, but the fact that I was in college and I was Chicana and that I came in here for help was a reason for them to love me. And so it was really cool. It was really cool. I mean, I never really felt as welcome as I did when I came in [the center], anywhere else on campus.

Although many of the students did not have mentorship in the college environment, some of them, like some of the community college students, found support that met at least some of their mentoring needs through formal and informal groups of peers. Still, the importance of guided mentorship became even clearer when the students discussed their goals. Many exposed how family, school, and identity combined to form their sense of who they would become. These insights suggest the importance for students of being able to tap into mentors and support systems that will help them achieve their goals. One student had extended her goals to encompass other students who she knew needed the very type of support that the participants in this project said they needed. She described her motivation for doing so:

Being a Mexican is really important to me. . . . The community where I was raised from, like, sixth grade on has really gone to hell. I mean, kids are dropping out of school left and right, and they're just abusing drugs and they're out there. And that affects me a lot.

Another student expressed her desire to be a role model simply:

I wanna be like a role model for people within my family and just society in general. 'Cause I know, especially with engineering, there's not very many females of color that are in engineering. So I wanna be able to prove that it is possible and for people in the future to be able to look at me and say, "Oh, it can be done."

Again, the drive and dedication of these students were impressive, but, as in the case of the last student, they often did not have mentors who could help them realize their goals. In fact, this last student was struggling in her major because of the very factors she hoped to address by becoming an engineer. Clearly, multiple forces influenced the school lives of Chicana/o students at the university. The interviews with these

students demonstrated once again the complexity involved in understanding the forces that had shaped their school performance. For almost all of them, their parents were the most important educational
influence, most often through their struggles to provide for their families. Teachers were also a critical influence. Whereas some of the students had thrived on the support they received from teachers, many students had been deeply affected by negative interactions with teachers.
The discussions of these negative experiences led to a larger explanation
of the fundamental role played by the larger racial-political climate in
Acoma and Fowler both. In the end, these students pointed to strong
linkages between identity and school performance: the same forces that
helped define who they were were vital to their understanding of their
lives and their possibilities as students. In a couple of instances during
an interview, one student in particular pointed to some of the most extreme ways in which identity translated into school behaviors:

I didn't like school because of the fact of how we were treated. And it was-
n't just me who was treated like this. It was my friends too. And so it both-
ered me. It made me not want to be there, basically. You don't go to a
place where you don't feel wanted. . . . We were not given a comfortable
feeling at school. It was always, everybody's staring, everybody's looking,
people talkin', you know, doin' the same old, same old. And so that made
me think of what I do about school. And the community, you know,
they're all about themselves. The mentality of the general community is,
"If we don't talk about it, it's not happening." They didn't think there was
a gang problem until they got slapped in the face with it. They didn't think
there was racial discrimination and this and that until they got slapped in
the face with it. And so it's like, "Let's pretend it's not there, and maybe
it'll go away." And, I mean, at school you can't pretend. When you're in
the jungle, you can't pretend.

Race, ethnicity—I think that's a major part of my life 'cause I was surrounded by it growing up. I mean, when you look in the mirror and you
see you're not like everybody else, it's gonna affect you. People fear me,
and they don't know me. I mean, if you were to know me, you would
know that I'm nothin' to fear. You know, piss me off and it's a different
story. But just to see me and, like, to walk a little bit more to the left or
walk a little bit more to the right or walk around me—you don't need to
do that. I ain't even like that. Just 'cause I'm a big Mexican guy, people
tend to be a little touchy. "Oh, don't mess with him. He's gonna kick your
ass." And this and that. I ain't even like that. . . . I think there was a time

in my life when that made me a lot harder, like made me a lot tougher. I had to be tougher, because everybody's expecting it. They're like, "Oh, you don't fuck with [him] or else he'll kick your ass." And so what do you have to do? You have to show 'em, "OK, fine. You wanna play; then let's play," [that] kinda thing. It affected me like that.

Although this student's experiences were not typical of the university students in the study, they did reflect much of what the students had seen happening in their lives. Their personas in the school were defined by their race. In turn, this racial categorization influenced how other students and school staff interacted with them through the filter of expectations. In the end, many Chicana/o students felt that they had to define themselves on those terms. Some chose to fall into the categorizations, and others chose to challenge them, although the latter were still defined by others—and even by themselves—within this framework. In Acoma, because the options seemed to be so limited, many students withdrew from school and turned to their families for their complete sense of identity and self-worth.

Racialized, contextualized mentoring was crucial to the students who received it, but it was not common among these students, simply because the opportunity to be mentored by someone who understood these complex forces was rare. Still, any mentoring in itself allowed students to create a bridge between their educational goals and their experiences and racialized identities, and that bridge could be quite empowering. For many students, inconsistent mentoring was a serious problem. Some students had struggled for a great while until they received mentoring. Others had received mentoring when it was too late for them, and still others had benefited from earlier mentoring but then struggled later in its absence—in college, for example.

Overall, family was the core of the university students' drive and support for school success, which was always contextualized in the family experience and thus was often linked to issues of race as well as to issues of class and gender (or other key forces), for power conflicts played a dominant role in both identity development and schooling. These identities helped students ground their educational goals and served as a key source of motivation. The degree to which students achieved success seemed to be shaped by the opportunities they had and often by the degree and nature of support they got. Strong mentoring was helpful, especially when students could link it to their identities in an empowering way. Other forms of support were also important, though, and could make a critical difference for students.

CONCLUSION

The experiences of the Chicana/o student participants in Acoma and Fowler were ridden with contradictions and conflicts. There was a great diversity of experiences, and yet there were also clear patterns. The framework that emerged from the project in East Los Angeles was applicable to these students' lives, but the unique context in Washington State provided additional insights (which are discussed in Chapter 7). The students' analyses can be broken down into six key points.

1. The family was the most important aspect of life for these students. Their families gave meaning to who they were, to what they wanted to be, and to how they viewed school. With only a few exceptions, the family is the overriding influence on the students and their goals in school. In particular, mothers and their strengths were often seen as the pillar of family support and inspiration, suggesting the critical role that gender plays within the familial dynamics. In addition, students' observations of their communities and the struggles of others to achieve success there served as another source of motivation.

2. Teachers played the most important role in students' school lives. Students understood their abilities and possibilities through their interactions with teachers. For this reason, positive interactions with teachers were very empowering. Even more so, mentorship from teachers led to tremendous self-confidence and success. Although some students had positive experiences with teachers, the majority of students did not have positive interactions or support from teachers, and many students had negative interactions with teachers. These negative interactions, even when infrequent, were often debilitating to students and led them to tune out or even drop out of school. Furthermore, the negative interactions often outweighed the positive in their effect on students, unless the students had strong support and mentorship. Still, many students used these potentially harmful experiences as their motivation for pursuing school success.

3. In the racial-political climate of Acoma, race is defined as an insignificant issue by those in power and is discussed only when Chicanas/os raise concerns, in which case their complaining is seen as the key factor that limits their own success. Despite the clear social, economic, and educational separation, segregation,

and inequality that exists in these communities of Acoma and eastern Washington, the popular discourse defines the area as a place that offers equality of opportunity. The differences in student outcomes are understood as a product of Chicanas/os not taking advantage of that opportunity. As was the case in earlier times in California and other regions, the members of the Chicana/o community in Washington State have such little access to power and positions of influence that they have limited opportunity to challenge this interpretation of their economic and educational opportunities. Still, their experiences in the workplace and the schools suggest that equality of opportunity is but a myth.

4. The forces that shape the racial-political climate also defined the experiences of Chicanas/os through their interactions within their own communities and within the schools. These experiences shaped students' understanding of their social identities. Early on in their school lives, many of the students saw that they were devalued in the schools through their segregation via tracking, through school policies that were directed at them, through the informal exclusion of their parents from their own schooling, through their own isolation (for some), and through direct conflicts and confrontations with authority figures (for others). Some students responded to this negative environment by challenging it with a strong racialized Chicana/o identity. This identity, however, is difficult to maintain in Acoma. Instead, many students turned to their families as a source of psychological sustenance and grounded their identities much more in their families. The dramatic contradiction between their experiences and the popular explanation of Chicana/o outcomes forced many students to define their social identities in an arena where the popular discourse was not able to affect how they saw themselves.

5. Mentorship was the key to success for Chicana/o students both in Acoma and at the university. It seemed critical that mentorship be specific to the needs of each individual student, but some patterns also existed. Foremost, students needed mentors to help them develop confidence in their potential and abilities. Second, students needed mentors who could help them deal with the obstacles they encountered during their school lives. For many, their primary difficulty was that the number of opportunities they had was limited because of their ethnic background (whether as the result of subtle tracking, linguistic isolation, or more blatant

discrimination). Mentors who could help the students understand what was happening were much needed, but even more important was the mentor's ability to help the students translate that understanding into acquisition of the required knowledge and skills for succeeding in school. The desire of Chicana/o students to learn about their own history and people was just one interest that mentors could exploit to help Chicana/o students. A critical part of this mentorship was to help students transition into subsequent phases of their school lives, for this was an area in which many students confronted significant problems. This aspect of mentoring could include helping students with the application process for college but also needed to encompass helping them transition into the new environment and finding new mentorship that would facilitate their success in that context. Finally, some students needed help addressing family conflicts, which often were a distraction and which students who received guidance seemed to deal with well.

6. Not every student fit perfectly within this general model. Although it applied to the experiences of the vast majority of students in the study, other students would not have applied the model directly to themselves. For instance, most of the few students who might initially have said that the model did not apply to them were mixed-race individuals. Interestingly, however, most of these students expressed a significant degree of confusion over and struggles with their own identities and the meaning of their race and ethnicity in shaping who they were. In fact, many of the forces that shaped the racial-political climate defined their own confusion and even their choice to understand their identities in another realm of their social lives. For many students, their non-racial identities were quite racialized. Still, some individuals shaped their identities around other aspects of their lives that were more demanding, such as gender. For Chicanas, gender was clearly a powerful force in shaping their experiences, and although many of them struggled with its role in defining their identities, these Chicanas could benefit from mentorship that helped them integrate gender into their identities in more empowering ways. Most of the students who emphasized gender placed it in the arena of race. Regardless, contextualized mentoring needs to respond to the specific identity-shaping power conflicts that students face, which can be in any number of areas of their lives.

LESSONS FROM ACOMA
STUDENTS FOR SCHOOL
SUCCESS

The previous two chapters provided an in-depth understanding of the lives, identities, and school experiences of Chicana/o students in Acoma. That detailed analysis is of particular importance because no one has researched the experiences of this population, and very little research has been done with rural Chicanas/os in general. This chapter looks closely at a few individual students to help frame the overall findings of Chapters 4 and 5. Their experiences reflect what is now happening in rural areas across the country with emerging Mexican communities.

As the information from student interviews demonstrated, the racial power structure in Acoma controlled the understanding and discussion of race in the community and left little room for resistance. The lives of Chicana/o students were explained for them, without their input, and with the confidence that their input was not needed. This chapter focuses on a few case studies to reveal how students in this environment were able to survive.

Specifically, I chose to look at students whose experiences reflected those of the majority of participants in the project. In addition, I looked for students who had developed survival strategies that might be applicable to all of the participants in this project and to students in Acoma in general. Three women at the community college told quite similar and compelling stories of their struggles over the course of their schooling. Together they have provided some critical insights into surviving these travails, and their stories are the heart of this chapter. I also have included the perspectives of two males whose stories addressed different issues and can help us understand survival strategies more completely.

The objective of this chapter is not to provide a detailed analysis of each person and her or his life, but rather to understand the students' struggles and how they overcame them. In the end, the goal is to prescribe means for addressing Chicana/o students' needs, based on that understanding of the students' experiences. Each of the students told a different story in a different way, addressing unique aspects of life in Acoma and the racial power structure. When their stories are taken together, the combined story and message are powerful. Readers are encouraged to carefully read "Time-out," at the end of this chapter, for an understanding of many of these issues through a first-person, in-depth look at one student's life.

RAMONA

At the time of our interview, Ramona was finishing her first year at the community college and had about a 3.6 GPA in her first two quarters. Born in Mexico, she had migrated to the United States with her family at about the age of three. Her parents had little education and worked as laborers in the agricultural industry. Although Ramona was doing well in college, she reported that her school performance had fluctuated a great deal over the years. Early in the interview, she talked about teachers and their role in her schooling (in an excerpt partially included in Chapter 5):

> I haven't really had, like, close relationship with any teachers. . . . I know at some stages in my life it was because of myself, and at other stages it was because [of] other people. . . . I think it was because I wasn't too involved in school. If I would've been, like, more involved or if I would've been more like a good student, then maybe I woulda had, like, a teacher that woulda pushed me more or something. But I don't think they put too much attention to those who don't care much about school.

Ramona struggled a little to describe her relationship with teachers. She knew that it was not strong, and she also knew that she simply had not cared much about school at different times. Although she briefly mentioned that these aspects of her schooling were not all her doing, in the end she attributed her lack of connection with teachers at that stage in her life to her own lack of effort. In many ways, her initial response reflected the way students are taught to understand why some students do not do well in school: they are not putting forth enough effort. Later,

Ramona began to look more deeply at what was happening in the schools (in an excerpt also included in Chapter 4):

> At school I've always seen, like, teachers specifically give more attention to, like, the white kids or to the kids that are of a higher class. And I guess that's why race is really important. Especially 'cause discrimination's everywhere, everywhere you go around here. . . . 'Cause, I mean, you always see [it]; if you don't see it, you can feel it.

While Ramona began by blaming herself for her lack of success in school, she was also aware of discrimination and its role in school. Her analysis depicted the turmoil Chicana/o students faced in Acoma as they struggled to make sense of the reality they saw and the contradictory popular messages that inaccurately attempted to explain that reality. Those popular messages did not accept racism and discrimination as explanations for Chicana/o school failure. In Acoma and eastern Washington, crying racism was seen as blaming others for one's problems and not taking responsibility. It is ironic, then, that although Ramona and some of her peers exposed racism, they also did not see racism as a reason for them to give up or even as the cause of their struggles in pursuing success. In fact, she and her peers took sole responsibility for improving their and their families' lives. Ramona expressed this sense of responsibility when she discussed the impact on her of her experiences with and observations of racism:

> In a way it makes me think that they just think they're better or whatever, and I guess it influences, like, my education too. 'Cause, like, I now want to show them that anybody can do just as good as they can.

Many students who encountered racism and discrimination in Acoma found that their only positive response was to use those experiences as a motivation for success. For some of the students, a critical path for effectively doing this was through the support system of MEChA. As Ramona pointed out,

> Right now mostly what has been influencing me a lot is MEChA. Because a lot of the goals from MEChA are, like, education, get educated and stuff like that. So that has been an influence on me. . . . There's been people pushing me in MEChA and everything. . . . They're always worried about who's doing good and who's not.

Although Ramona did not elaborate on many of the themes she introduced, her story helps us begin to see how some Chicana/o students in Acoma survived. The key for Ramona was to acknowledge racism and use it as a motivation, simultaneously relying on a support system that was grounded in the same approach to schooling. She did elaborate on the importance of this approach as she outlined what she thought needed to be changed:

> I think we need more role models. 'Cause I think, like, a lot of the people that are coming to school here are Mexicanos, and we need to see more Mexican instructors. We need to see more courses taught about the Mexican people. I think it's really important because, especially if you're in the valley, there's so many Mexicanos. And I think that not just Mexicanos but everybody should know about the Mexican culture and everything, because a lot of people who aren't Mexican don't know much about the culture, don't understand them much. And I think that's a lot of the reason why there's so much stereotypes and stuff. And I think we need a lot of that.

Like many of the students, Ramona was beginning to put together an analysis of her experiences that she could use as a foundation for her future efforts in school. In some instances, her analyses lacked depth or were not supported with examples, perhaps because she was still making sense of much of what she had seen. It is important to listen carefully to the analyses made by students like Ramona, however, because they reveal the difficulty many Chicanas/os have in struggling first for education survival and later for success. Furthermore, the type of emerging critique that Ramona highlighted made it easy for whites in Acoma to ignore the counterstories of Chicanas/os who attempted to challenge the racial hierarchy in their lives. It is therefore important to see that Ramona was not alone. In fact, her peers told stories that were strikingly similar.

CHELA

Chela was a second-year student at the community college when she participated in the project and had been getting mostly Bs in college. Chela, a native of Mexico, had come to the United States in the fourth grade. Her parents also had little education and worked in agriculture as laborers. Beginning school in the United States as a fourth grader with no English skills had shaped much of Chela's school life.

As seen in previous chapters, ESL is a common theme brought up in students' discussions of significant early school experiences. Chela provided a critical insight into the ESL experience. She explained that she felt isolated via ESL and showed that this was not just an instructional isolation but a distinct separation that continued long after mainstreaming and was a means by which Mexicana/o youth were silenced. Chela emphasized that her shyness was an issue with which she had struggled in elementary school. In many ways, she, like Ramona, initially blamed herself for this struggle. Later she began to formulate a different analysis:

> When I was shy, I was shy for a reason. I was shy because I didn't feel comfortable around my surroundings, and that was because I was Mexican. I felt like I wasn't considered very high. I wasn't comfortable with my surroundings, and as I grew comfortable with my surroundings, I became more outgoing.

Even in this discussion, Chela still indicated that it was her actions that allowed her to overcome this shyness, deemphasizing the role of the context in which she found herself. When she was asked about why she wasn't comfortable, however, she went deeper into these issues:

> [I was hearing that] because I was Mexican, because my first language was Spanish, I could not do well in English or I couldn't do well in math or I couldn't do well in this and couldn't do well in that, just because of that. And that was the reason I tried to prove 'em wrong. And I did end up proving them wrong.

Like Ramona, Chela used the differential treatment she experienced as a motivation for succeeding in school. When asked about this, she said she had sensed lowered expectations from students, teachers, and administrators and then described how these lower expectations had affected her:

> I was extra hard on myself. If I did something wrong, if I didn't get a good enough grade, I felt that it was because I didn't study hard enough, and I became very, very unsure of myself. Because after a while I just started to believe that it was true that I couldn't do as good as other students because of my race and because of my language.

As Chela began to talk about the effects of low expectations, she still framed her discussion in a positive light, describing how she pushed herself very hard. Then, however, for the first time, Chela discussed the negative effects of these experiences, commenting that she had to fight not to believe the messages others told her about her limited potential and ability. As the conversation progressed, Chela exposed more of the negative psychological impacts of these experiences:

> When I got to high school, I tried not to talk too much Spanish, because I didn't wanna seem to others that I could speak Spanish. I talked Spanish only when I was only with Mexicanos. Only with them, and no other person that didn't know Spanish, especially not around teachers. I would never talk Spanish to any of the teachers, because they might say, "Oh, she only, she knows Spanish." They would perceive you as less, not a less person but, like, with less knowledge if they knew that you spoke Spanish or were still associated with the Spanish language or whatever.

Chela thus provided a critical explanation of the subtle messages conveyed that related to language and race and how these carried over to teachers' understandings of students' intellectual abilities. She was quite aware of how teacher expectations affected the opportunities of students and how race and language shaped those teacher expectations. Chela knew that pretending not to know Spanish would give her a better chance of getting support and guidance from her teachers. In addition, simply being Mexican was understood as negative in the world of school. Chela went beyond hiding her Spanish abilities and also tried to become "American." She mentioned this as she talked about herself and an older sister:

> We had a hard time [downplaying] the Mexican side of ourselves and trying to blend in to the American. We did, but we were putting our Mexican side behind us even though we still looked Mexican and stuff like that. But we just acted like Americans. Tryin' to blend in, you know. . . . It wasn't working for us, just tryin' to be *gavachos*.

In a follow-up interview, Chela discussed this in a little more detail:

> Back [in high school], I guess I try to always be more, I guess more on the Anglo side. And just try not to dwell on the Mexican side and close that side of myself. . . . Shut out that side. . . . A lotta Mexicans weren't treated very well there. . . . I [felt that] to be respected, I would have to be more at the American side, you know, [the] Anglo side. I guess that's what at least I did back then.

When asked if this strategy had worked, Chela replied,

> No. I was still being treated just Mexican. And it felt even worse because I felt like I was betraying my own people. I never stood up to 'em back then. And I feel pretty guilty about that. I still do. It didn't work at all.

No one had ever explicitly told Chela that being Mexican was not good in the world of school, but she nevertheless received this message very clearly. Furthermore, it was conveyed with such force that she felt compelled to act on it. Her entire persona in school was transformed by her understanding of the limits that being Mexican placed on her. Later she provided an example of one way in which she received the message:

> I remember one time we were talkin' about Pancho Villa in history, and I didn't wanna say that he was kinda related to me. They say we are, I don't even know, but it's kinda been passed on through my family that we might be related. And I was the only person that was a Villa. And I felt kinda weird talkin' about that because it said on the history book that he was a bandit and that he just crossed over from the Mexican border to the U.S. to kill Anglos, and I was like, "Oh, my gosh. Ewww." And, I mean, he did that, but now I know that was just one part of that. Now I know that he was, mostly with the Mexican side, he was considered a hero. And I'm proud, if we're relatives, I'm proud to be his relative. But back then I was like, "Oh, my gosh." Right there was said that the race Mexicanos was bad, I mean, wasn't good. That being a Mexicano, that they were considered bandits, lazy. And I didn't wanna be associated with them because of that.

For Chela, school was a psychologically dangerous place. She learned that who she was made her both a target for school failure and a potential social outcast. Her own family, for example, was possibly linked directly to a legacy that the school and society had derogatorily deemed dangerous. This incident affected Chela's entire self-image in shocking ways. As Chela recalled,

> In high school, I still had an accent, and it would make me feel uncomfortable, having that accent. Other people didn't, but I did. And it was weird. It's one of the things that brought me down, I guess, made me feel down.

When asked if there were other things that had brought her down, Chela mentioned the following:

> My skin, like I talked to you about before. That used to be a big thing. Even back then, I used to work a lot in the fields and I used to be really, really dark-skinned because of the sun. And now that I don't, I'm a little bit lighter, but back then I was. And it just made me feel like I maybe wished I wasn't that. I wished I was a little bit lighter or didn't have that accent. I wished I was somebody else, not myself. And that just made me uncomfortable with myself.

Chela felt that who she was—her skin color, her accent, her cultural practices—were, in essence, bad things. The psychological turmoil Chela struggled with was something she did not resolve until she got to college. Even then, the damage that had been done to her was clearly still having overwhelming effects. Her honesty helps us see the real power of racialization on Chicana/o youth.

What made the difference for Chela academically and in getting into college was mentorship. She was the only project participant at the community college who had a teacher who significantly helped her navigate her way through the educational process. As mentioned in Chapter 5, Chela relished her luck in always knowing a Mexicano teacher she could count on for support:

> There was always some kinda teacher I could rely on, I could trust. You know, a Mexicano teacher. Since I was so into myself, especially in my early years of education in the United States, I never spoke to any other teacher besides a Mexican teacher. You know, for the same reason that I was never around anybody else besides Mexican people. I was never really comfortable with anybody else besides somebody that was Mexican. So that was good. I thought that was good that there was always some Mexican teacher there.

Most important of all, Chela's soccer coach in high school walked her through all of the steps of transitioning into college. As she explained (in an excerpt in Chapter 5), she would not have gone on to college right after high school without his support.

In college, Chela sought similar guidance and turned to MEChA for this support. Whereas Ramona emphasized the academic support she had received in MEChA, Chela talked about how MEChA helped her deal with the identity struggles that she had experienced in high school:

> Well, in high school I kinda lost myself there. I kinda didn't wanna associate myself with my ethnicity. I was tryin' to be more with the other people besides my own race. And when I got to college, I had started being more with my class, my race, because I'm in MEChA. Another reason was also because I started losing myself. I didn't know who I was in high school, and when I got to college, MEChA helped me understand who I was, and it was good to be my race and to be Mexicana.

In her final reflection on high school, Chela addressed some complex and covert issues. She explained that in Acoma it was a common strategy for students who were seeking success to try to hide their ethnicity and race, because the popular ideology suggested that that was the only way to be accepted (as she implied earlier). Chela began to explain, however, that this tactic was not always healthy or successful, and in her case it was both unsuccessful and psychologically damaging. As she concluded her discussion of MEChA, she revealed that this support helped her overcome some of the psychological stress that accompanied her previous educational tactics:

> MEChA has influenced me a lot into thinking that who I am is important. Being Mexicana is important, being Chicana's important. Not only because we have a human right to be important but also because our ancestors actually fought for us to have what we have and it's our turn for us to actually do that. And better yourself in the future.

Through her brutal honesty, Chela exposed the complex psychological forces underlying the racial and interpersonal conflicts that occurred in school for so many Chicana/o students in Acoma. Her willingness to be self-critical gives us a glimpse into the internal processes students go through, as well as the strategies they invoke for succeeding in school. Like the students discussed in Chapter 5, Chela wanted to be successful in school to help her family. Early in her U.S. schooling, she saw that this goal might not be possible, as she discovered that being Mexican was considered an educational deficit by many. In response, she simply tried not to be Mexican. The toll this took on her was significant, and in college she finally found some peace through her affiliation with MEChA.

MARI

Mari was also in her second year at the community college when we talked. She was born in the United States, although her father had been born in Mexico, while her mother, born in Texas, had been raised in Mexico. Her mother had completed high school in Mexico, her father had little education, and both worked as laborers in agriculture.

Mari's story is similar to those of Ramona and Chela, but Mari often cuts to an even deeper level. She was one of the few students who talked almost directly about a racial power structure. She began this analysis after being asked why she was quiet in school.

> I was really quiet. I guess all my life I've been afraid of white authority, you know, and it's the truth. 'Cause I remember thinking that I was scared of white authority. And I don't know why. But I know that I was.

As she thought more about it, Mari told a story that explained this fear:

> There was this one teacher, my brother was telling me—he was little [in first or second grade]—and he goes, "I made this teacher fall." And I didn't know my parents signed this paper that he couldn't get punishment, nobody could whack him. And they [took] me aside and told me that I could not tell my parents and I *should* not tell my parents that he was gonna get a spanking for dropping this teacher. And I remember, I think, a Mr. B—he was the one that would whack us, right? So that was a sad part in my life, I think, 'cause knowing that I couldn't tell my parents. I don't know why I couldn't think for myself at that time. They told me I couldn't tell my parents. He goes, "You can't tell your parents," I forgot the reason why, but I believed him. And my brother got a spanking that he should not have. And to this day my parents don't know. . . . So it was, like, to this day I won't forget that.

For Mari, it was important not just that the corporal punishment occurred but also that she felt helpless to challenge the authority of the teacher. Even though she knew it was wrong, Mari felt obligated to listen to the teacher and not tell her parents. This blatant and severe experience leaves little room for alternative interpretations. The more subtle experiences in many ways are even more traumatic, however. Particularly when the students are younger, they often struggle to make sense of experiences that are shrouded in subtleties and innuendo. Chela discussed this sort of experience a great deal in her interviews. Mari also shared experiences that were more subtle than her brother's spanking.

For example, later she talked about her experiences working in a lab and the negative messages she received there:

> They were saying school's the way to go. But at the same time they were saying, "Oh, I don't think [being a] biotechnician is a good way for you to go." And I'm like, *"What?"* . . . Let me tell you, every kind of racial thing that ever happened in the fifties or sixties was happening to me in there. I didn't realize it then. I didn't. In a way, I knew it was wrong, but I didn't understand why it was wrong. Like it wasn't until I took Chicano Studies that I understood that my own mentality was distorted. My own mentality was letting them push me around. But I don't have to listen to them anymore. I guess I made the white the most important thing. They knew that they were. I guess that what I'm trying to say is that basically, in my mind, they were smarter than me, [and] therefore I should listen to them because they were smarter. And I don't think that now. But then I did.

In one short story, Mari unpacked a complex set of forces that operated in her daily life. She enjoyed working in this lab and thought it was interesting work. Her supervisors, all of whom were white, urged her to continue her schooling but also pointed out that the biotechnology field might not be the most appropriate for her, despite her interest. At the time, although she wrestled with their comments, she believed their assessment. At the heart of this belief was her fairly tacit acceptance of white superiority. As with the teacher who spanked her brother, Mari knew deep inside that they were wrong, but she still accepted their analysis of her potential.

Obviously, Mari did not put all of these ideas together until she had had a significant amount of time to deconstruct her experiences. As she explained, having the opportunity to examine issues of race in Chicano Studies classes helped her to analyze her previous experiences more critically. As Mari and the other students made clear, the power of dominant interpretations of Chicana/o students' potential and abilities was so overwhelming that it was exceptionally difficult for students to make sense of the contradictory messages they received. Most students accepted the dominant narrative that explained their lives.

Mari spoke about these issues extensively. She later went on to discuss the psychological impact that the dominant racial ideologies had had on her:

> Race, race and ethnicity—that's an important issue to me because I was in junior high and surrounded with all these white folks. I didn't know

who I was. I was always lost in myself. You know, I hated myself then. It's funny, I never understood why, but I hated myself then. But yet I wanted to be like them. I felt sorry for myself around them 'cause I didn't have what they had, you know, little vacations. No, I had to go to work. I felt sorry for myself. Those are issues I wanna tackle in life.

Mari's analysis is strikingly honest and self-critical. Although she suggested that earlier in her life she would never have been able to clearly understand all that was happening to her both in her interactions and within her psyche, she had since spent a lot of time struggling with these issues. She made it clear that the racial power structure in Acoma all but demanded the survival strategies that she had chosen; strategies that she thought were appropriate but that were also creating severe psychological pain. Wanting to be successful, being Chicana, and knowing that Chicanas could not be successful had left her actually hating herself. Mari pulled no punches in this self-critique. She had hated who she was because of the implications of what it meant to be Mexican in Acoma.

Like Ramona and Chela, Mari found a great deal of solace and strength through her involvement in MEChA once she got to college. When we discussed what had been the most important influence on her life, she started there:

I would say MEChA in a way because . . . I was put into a position where I was like, "OK, you gotta do it. You gotta start talking to people. Get out of this nutshell. Move on." And I guess my biggest influence about myself to feel as confident as I do now is that I was pushed into a position where I was forced to talk. I was forced to challenge myself. I wasn't doing that for a while, I guess. I wasn't challenging myself like I should've. I mean, maybe 'cause I didn't know how to challenge myself. I didn't know how to do it. And it wasn't in me or, I don't know, it's just [that] I had to be pushed into it or else I wouldn't have done it.

Interestingly, whereas Ramona talked about the academic support of MEChA and Chela focused on its support in developing a strong racial identity, Mari emphasized the leadership skills she acquired in MEChA. Together, these three women suggested that having a strong support group that helps students feel comfortable in an academic environment allows them to tap into the specific types of support that they need. As Mari began to describe her evolution through MEChA and her introduction to others who had helped her understand herself and her experiences, she discussed the importance of this evolution of thought:

> Another thing that's important to me was my way of thinking. How white my way of thinking is. How I went through that little black box where the teachers teach you one way, you know, take away everything and you come out like a processed product; you know, to think that the government's perfect and wonderful and beautiful. That stuff really aggravates me. That's important to me too. Just to see the kids understand that it's not great. Democracy isn't pretty. And it's capitalism, and if you let it, it'll take advantage of you. Things like that.

Mari suggested that there is a force at work that can limit Chicana/o students' abilities to contextualize their experiences. Furthermore, she challenged the racial power structure that her experiences revealed as so limiting. Considering the dramatic impact that this power structure had on her early in life, it was amazing that she had become as confident and successful as she now was.

The lessons that Mari, Chela, and Ramona shared are important for understanding how other Chicanas/os can be helped to succeed in Acoma and eastern Washington. First, it is clear that racism, discrimination, and racial hegemony shaped life for Chicanas/os in Acoma both in and out of school. The most powerful and potentially damaging manifestations of this reality were the multiple ways in which the self-esteem and confidence of Chicana/o students were attacked. Although this sort of attack often happened in subtle ways, the impact of living in a community in which those in power had organized daily life on the understanding that Chicanas/os cannot succeed was often overwhelming. Students became withdrawn and insecure, and most unsettling is that they even learned to hate themselves for being Mexican. In fact, they often adopted the very beliefs that were terrorizing their psyches.

Chicana/o students did survive this trauma, however, in large part because of the mentorship and support they receive. One student was fortunate enough to have had Mexicano teachers and a coach as her support system. The coach in particular was vital in helping her prepare for and transition into college. Still, none of the students had mentorship specifically to help them address the racialized, psychological battles they had been fighting throughout their schooling. In fact, it was not until college that the students found this support in MEChA. Although each used this support system in different ways, MEChA's being grounded in efforts to assist Chicanas/os in empowering themselves through education helped these students begin to make sense of their own histories.[1] Similarly, Chicano Studies classes also helped them develop analytical and intellectual tools to assist them through this process.

Together, these three women at the community college pointed to the importance of achieving a sense of internal/psychological, racialized empowerment to accompany students in their pursuit of educational empowerment. The reality of life in Acoma suggested that many Chicana/o students experienced racial-psychological trauma that significantly and negatively affected their efforts to succeed in school, especially given that the school was a critical site in inflicting that trauma. In addition, the students needed mentorship in preparing for the transition into colleges and universities, because many suggested that their skills were still being honed and explained that they had little guidance in this. Although Mari, Chela, and Ramona were all on paths toward educational success, those paths had been difficult and extremely rocky at educational, personal, and psychological levels. As the students only hinted occasionally, gender was also involved in this process. Race was the most dramatic arena in which power was exerted against the students, and so it was often their focus. Still, gender was tightly bound into their experiences and identities and also needed to be a focus in their mentorship.

ANGEL

Angel was in his first semester at the university when we first sat down to talk. Like his parents, Angel was born in the United States. His father was a lawyer, but he was raised by his mother, who did not get beyond high school and who worked as a truck driver for a delivery service. Angel was an example of a student whose conflicts in school became too great to overcome. He began by talking about his first serious conflicts in school:

> In junior high, I think it's when the teachers really started labeling kids. Labeling *me*. But I got labeled real quick, real quick: "class clown," "gangster," this and that. "Oh, he doesn't take nothin' serious." And in junior high the teachers were real mean to me. . . . That made me hate school. Any person in authority, I didn't like 'em, because they had shown me that this are what people in authority are like. I lost all respect for my teachers basically.

As he discussed at other points in our conversations, Angel seemed to be understood by those around him mainly on the basis of his appearance.

He was tall, big, and dark, and he knew that some people see him as mean-looking. He attributed his being labeled to this perception, because although he liked to joke around in school, he never had any conflicts with teachers or other authority figures until he got to junior high. The conflicts he experienced with teachers then became the heart of his understanding of schooling. He described the continuation of this process into high school (in an excerpt also included in Chapter 5):

> The teachers in high school, they had already labeled us from junior high. "Those are the gangsters. Don't cut 'em no slack." And it's like they were trying to get us out of school. . . . You know, it's like, "Why can they look right at us and make rules *just* for us that apply only to *us* and not apply to everybody?" Everybody thought it was real fucked up in high school basically. . . . Like the average kid, he says somethin' out of turn, they're gonna let it slide. If I spoke out of turn, they'd kick me out of class on the drop of a dime. It's always hard to stay in class. I remember thinkin' like, "Why do I go to class? What's the point of coming if they kick you out after five minutes?"

Angel was not an innocent in his struggles in school. He often challenged teachers in ways that left them little choice but to punish him. At the same time, Angel's actions typically came as a result of his own observation of injustice. This was a critical issue to Angel. He cited several ways in which Chicana/o students were treated differently from whites, and he rarely let the issue go without making it known that he saw what was happening. Angel also described how this context and the injustices had led to his disinterest in school. In another detailed analysis, he provided additional examples:

> I think that a lot of the rules and regulations were made for us. . . . It was like a policy that applied to everybody, but it was mainly applied for us. . . . It would piss me off, 'cause we all knew what was going on. "We don't want your belts hangin'. You can't wear pants this size. And you can't wear this type of clothing. And anybody wearing three of the same, say, three of the same hats, one of 'em has to take off their hat." You know, stuff like that. Real stupid stuff that was implied to the whole school but was applicable only to us. You know, I mean, "No wearing bandannas." I had a bandanna one time. Just had it on, just tied it back, and I went to school. And then this teacher said, "Take that off right now." And then I'm like, "Why?" He goes, "'Cause it's against school policy." Da da da. "Take it off right now." And he was just tellin' me. And I looked to the

side—we were in a gymnasium, and they're havin' an assembly. And then there was this white kid right there wearing a red one in his hair. I said, "Look at his. I mean, you come here to tell me to take off mine, but yet you don't tell him to take off his." And then he goes, "Well, you're goin' to the principal's office." And I go, "For what?" And then he was like, "Well, for disobeying." I go, "You're full of shit." And then I went to the principal's office. Just [with] little things like that, I mean, we were always treated differently. Always. . . . They say, "We're fair, and we're this and that," but why all these regulations for us? . . . [They were] push-out regulations, you know, regulations to push kids out of school. . . . [It's] them telling you, "You can't be who you are." And so, you know, "Fuck this. I'm leavin'." That's what they say. That's the mentality. And they do. They leave.

Angel began to explain why many Chicanas/os, including himself, had opted out of school. They saw that the school had created a two-tiered system of discipline whereby Chicana/o characteristics were almost used as a model for inappropriate school behavior. Although Angel understood that the school staff themselves did not always see that, he provided examples that showed how, if these types of rules were applied to whites, they would be seen as ridiculous:

You got all these white boys preppy wearing polo shirts. I mean, you don't see them saying, "Hey, we notice they're all wearing polo shirts. Look at that little guy on the horse." I mean, they weren't putting rules and regulations [like] "We don't want no polo shirts."

Contradictions like these were too much for Angel and some of his friends to tolerate. Angel made a case that these policies and practices, if understood through his eyes, all but demanded resistance. As he saw it, school did not seem a realistic option for many Chicana/o youth. Reflecting on why he eventually dropped out of school, Angel talked about the role of expectations, a subject raised earlier by the women at the community college:

Authority, I think that has a lot to do with the opportunities that you're given and the chances that you're given. And I think that in school I wasn't given a whole lot of chances. Not chances that are mostly given, you know, the chance to succeed. The chance, the hope, you know, you're not given the hope. You know, that "Hey, you can do it." I wasn't given that. And so I think that that's the reason that I did poorly in school. There was no one to say, "Hey, you're gonna do somethin' with your life." It's always bad.

One of the factors that later led Angel to pursue his education further was a teacher who did try to help him. The teacher, as Angel explained, thought Angel was very bright and was upset at how he was treated by other school staff members:

> I never knew what it was like to have a teacher look out for you until I got into high school. And I had one teacher look out for me. I had never known that, never known a teacher to see potential in somebody that's got this label, "Always a bad kid. Watch out for this kid." Because he even told me, he said, "Angel, they had a faculty meeting before you came, and you were one of the kids to watch out for." They blatantly [said], "Watch out for this kid." You know, "Don't let him go on anything." They were literally trying to get me out, to get kicked out of school. 'Cause they didn't want me there. So it's hard.

The support of this teacher gave Angel confidence and encouragement, but it was too late for Angel to save his high school career. He had experienced too many injustices that he could not reconcile and had tuned out for too long to recover. Angel dropped out.

Still, he knew he wanted to continue his education and eventually ended his involvement with negative forces in his life, such as gangs, and enrolled in a special program to get his GED. This program changed his life. He received strong support from his teachers and became confident in his intellectual abilities and potential. After he completed the program, he applied and was admitted to the university.

By his second semester at the university, I knew Angel quite well. We talked often, and he enrolled in two of my classes. I was impressed by his intellect. He was extremely intelligent and insightful. At the same time, his work often did not reflect that intelligence. In another interview, he had already explained why:

> What blows my mind is that it's just grades. I mean, I don't even think I'm here for scholastics, you know, academic achievement, anything like that. I mean, that's not my purpose for coming to college. I mean, I understand that it's required, to get that little piece of paper, but I don't agree with the fact that just 'cause you got an A and you got an F, the person who got an F is takin' away less from the class than the person who got an A. I think that person who got an A knew how to work the teacher, knew what the

teacher wanted. The person who got an F just didn't. And because in my classes right now, whether I get an A or whether I get an F, I'm getting from that class what I'm gonna get from that class regardless. I really just don't agree with grades.

As an instructor and having seen Angel learn and grow in class, I had to agree with him. His contributions in class were always among the most important and demonstrated that he was among the most engaged students. Clearly, however, his belief conflicted with the rules of university life. It seemed to me that his critical analysis of schooling in his earlier years had translated into a unique approach to learning that continued to put him at risk. The conflict between his own approach to learning and that of the university only worsened, as he detailed later:

> Just the other day, I went to philosophy, got pissed off, wasn't learning anything. This guy was talking and talking and talking of what philosophy is—"This is why it is; this is what it is"—instead of letting us get a chance to discover for ourselves. And so halfway in class I got up and walked out. Talking about rationality versus irrationality. You know, [in] philosophical class you would think you got a chance to think. . . . He was tellin' what's rational and what's irrational. [And I said,] "Who's to say what's rational? What may be rational for you may be irrational for me. And what's irrational for me may be rational to you." I go, "You can't say that." [And he said,] "Oh, I don't wanna deal with that right now. That's a deeper question." And then this one little kiss-ass raised his hand . . . and he goes, "I think we should give each other the respect that we deserve, and this is how a class is supposed to run: one person is speaking, the rest of the people'll be listening." And then I said, "What?" I go, "I don't mean to bust your bubble over here, but just 'cause that's the way it usually is, does that mean that way is right?" And I go, "Just because that's the way that you learned, maybe they learned in their groups. Maybe talkin' to each other about the subject, maybe that's better for them." And I go, "You can't say that there's a right or wrong when you don't know." I go, "Is your right more right than their right?" And everybody's like, "Ooooohhh. Oohh." . . . I was figuring, "OK, I'm here. I'm like lookin' at the book. This guy's talking. It's like, this is in the book. I mean, are we here [to be] lectured at? Why don't we just get the book on tape?" That's what he was doing. And to me I just saw very little point to what he was doing.

Eventually, Angel could no longer reconcile the distance between what his education was and what he wanted it to be. He left the university.

I had him in a class during his last semester. Although he had no interest in doing the class work, he did submit his final analysis of the class:

> I have found more than Education in this class. No book could ever teach me nor could any research ever show what I have walked away with. I Have Truly Learned. It's like I have tapped into a POWER. A Power that we all have, but most of us rarely use to its full capacity. The Power As A Human Being To "See Life," to hold It In My Grasps. When a tree is no longer a tree in a physical sense, when an apple is more than just a mere fruit, when an arrangement of chairs is not about the chairs at all, but about Life Itself . . . This is what changes a person, this is what inspires, what motivates, what leads to not only the discovery of a different world, but a Discovery of a Person Inside You. "This Is LIFE." [2]

In the end, the conflicts Angel had with school were too great for him to tolerate. Although he demonstrated intellectual strength and growth, his choice to leave school had a negative impact on his future, for it limited his options, particularly in eastern Washington. Angel's story is not as hopeful as those of Mari, Chela, and Ramona. His conflicts were much more violent and physical, perhaps because he was a male. Still, men and women such as these can find ways to avoid this type of conflict. They can also find ways to overcome the deeper intellectual conflicts that may underlie their efforts in school.

CESAR

Cesar was born in the United States and was raised by his mother, who came from Mexico with little education and had worked in the agricultural industry most of her life. Because Cesar attended the university after graduating from high school, we developed a relationship that extended well beyond the project.

Cesar shared many of the experiences described by Angel above. Cesar had felt the sting of differential treatment in the school through ESL and tracking and was highly critical of the policies and practices that led to fundamentally differential school experiences for Chicana/o students. He had also been involved in harmful activities outside of the school—through his association with a gang—that had seriously affected his school performance. Unlike Angel, however, Cesar decided to challenge the injustices he observed by succeeding in school. He explained how this decision came about:

> That's when MEChA came along. My tenth-grade year, I was here and the MEChA group was here. I started doin' all right in grades, but there wasn't no pride there. I didn't have a meaning for it. It was like, "OK, let's say I graduate from high school. Then what?" You know, "Who am I really?" . . . And that's when I started reading books on my own. That's when I started goin' to the library. . . . I would read the good parts, or to me the interesting parts, and take notes. And I would freak out because some of it I didn't know, and I'm like, "Is that how this happened? Is that how it really happened?" And *este,* then I started gettin' pretty pissed off at my history classes *porque* they never teach us that. I remember they taught me—let's see, twice I read one paragraph on Pancho Villa, and their version was he was a villain and he messed with the United States. But he was slick enough that he got away. But he was a villain. He didn't do no good. And then I started reading books, and I found out, "Well, look, he's a revolutionary leader of the north. He fought for the *pobres* [poor], and the United States interfered, so he went over there and did his thing." That was bad of him, that was his wrong, but they just counted what he did wrong and that's it. And it was just a paragraph. So these guys over here, even our own *raza,* they're gettin' taught that Pancho Villa was bad. They only have about one paragraph on Benito Juárez. Well, you know how he separated state and church and stuff like that. And César Chávez, I think one page maybe. And that's like, "Come on, man." We're like, back then it was like twenty-somethin' percent of the population here, and it's like we need to get taught more than that. And *este,* before I was kinda shy around people. Then I started gettin' a little more outspoken, 'cause if they say somethin' I didn't like, I'd say, "No, no. That's not true." And I started challenging my history teachers. And what's funny is, sometimes they'd get mad and sometimes they'd like that I was challenging them. And they'd bring it to an even deeper level. And sometimes I didn't know what to say, so then I'd go back to the books and start reading a little more. And that's what started interesting me more. And then MEChA, that was the first icebreaker. Then, at the end of the year, *este,* I started going even more to those meetings. And they started saying, "We need to look for officers for next year." And people had already heard me, how I argue or contradict the teachers sometimes—and usually come out right—about the history. They're like, "Well, let's nominate Cesar," and I didn't want to, but they nominated me for president. So during summer I was all shaky because I was gonna be leading a group. And come

summer, I started reading more books. I got a copy of the school policy and started reading things about that. What they can do, what they can't do. What we have the rights to do, what we don't have the rights to do, and how to go about that stuff. So that was my homework, then, the whole summer. Then come my junior year; that's when I started taking a leadership position.

Cesar described the process by which he used his observations of inequality as his inspiration for taking his education much more seriously. Even after he knew that school was important and that he had to stop engaging in harmful behavior, his schooling had little meaning for him. MEChA began to provide that meaning. It helped him understand that he could educate himself on issues that were important to him and could use his schooling as a means to address the issues he saw in his daily life, as he explained in more detail:

> What I blame for how I'm doin' right now is basically that I found out about my culture. Because I found out my identity. Because in a way that got me pissed off so much that I wanted to learn more and get involved. 'Cause the way I started gettin' involved in school activities was, I'd see something that was kinda negative towards our *raza*. So I'd get involved and try to change it. And I did, in a few cases. Then there are other cases that leave *raza* out. ASB [Associated Student Body] officers are only white. Not that it's bad, but we need some representation out here too. There's seventeen hundred students, [and] we're about six hundred Chicanos, Mexicanos, so I started gettin' in there. . . . And it all started out with me tryin' to learn more about my culture.

Cesar made it clear that his identity was critical to his understanding of his role in school. Before he dedicated himself to his education, the negative identity that others attached to Chicanas/os influenced him as he tuned out of school. Later, when he had the opportunity to learn about who he was and to create a positive racial identity for himself, these became his reason for succeeding in school and, as he mentioned, defined who he wanted to become:

> My career plan is to graduate from a university with a double major in Chicano Studies and Political Science. And then from there, go on to graduate school in Political Science and then get my doctorate in Political Science. That's what I really wanna do. But two years ago, three years ago, that wasn't even on my agenda. . . . It's from me finding out where we

stand. It's kinda like the way I look at . . . it's kinda like something picking at me. A sharp point picking at me that I have to do something. Otherwise, I won't be happy. . . . My whole focus, I would like to make a
change. 'Cause I don't like where we're standing right now. I just definitely
don't. And I imagine myself as, whether it be running for office or just out
in the community making changes for the good. And not just with our
people. Other people, other minorities are out there suffering the same
way too. That's where I'm happy. 'Cause that's what I want to do. And I
know they're strong goals and it's gonna take a while, but, shoot, it's
worth it.

What is most striking is that Cesar had developed these goals without
any strong mentorship from a teacher or professional. He had carefully
assessed his own life, what he wanted to see happen and then looked
into how he could do it. In the process, he had relied heavily on other
students in MEChA to expose him to the experiences and resources he
needed. *Mechistas* at the community college, for example, helped him
develop his skills as a leader and provided mentorship. In a later interview, Cesar focused specifically on identity as the core of his motivation:

> I think identity is what helps you academically in school. In our case any-
> ways. 'Cause that's the only thing that I've noticed. It does help a lot. And
> of course there's people that don't know about their culture and make it.
> But that's one of the things that helped me out. I can only speak for my-
> self 'cause I been through it. But learning about my culture is what made
> me mad and want to get educated. And I think that's the way other people
> will be. 'Cause when you're being taught to be ignorant your whole life
> and then all of a sudden you ram into the truth, it's a big shock. And so
> all of a sudden you get pissed at the system and you just wanna go through
> the system so you could change it. You know, not necessarily I wanna be
> a communist or somethin' like that, but I think if someone's a gangbanger
> or something like that and they're over here screaming—without even
> knowing what it means, where it came from, and how it should be used,
> they think they know what it's from, you know—"Brown pride." *Pero*
> they don't really know where those words derive from, and I think if they
> find out where not only those words derive from but more about their cul-
> ture, days, different events and think of why we are how we are, I think it
> would really change their lives a lot. Not only their educational and aca-
> demic goals and stuff like that, but their life. . . . And if they found out
> about their culture, it's kind of like, remember the whole taco? Right in
> the beginning it's just a tease because the beans are down at the bottom.

It's like that when you learn about your culture a little. You taste it, but not all the way, so you just wanna get more. That's the way I look at it. Just want more and more. That's the way I am.

For Cesar, the key to success was reconstructing his identity so that it was empowering rather than debilitating, as being Chicana/o was portrayed through the policies and practices in his schools. He suggested that providing students a channel to develop positive racial identities is a critical first step in their seeing school success as attainable. Furthermore, Cesar made it clear that having a support system to help students through this process is fundamental. These support systems ideally would include a number of types of resource people, but even when they consist only of peers, they can make a significant difference in students' lives.

CONCLUSION

The five students discussed in this chapter are all unique in many ways, but they also share strong similarities. Given the diversity of Chicana/o students beyond these five, the analysis they provided must be applied to the larger context.

Although all of the students in the high school, the community college, and the university responded differently to the contexts in which they found themselves, they made it clear that the racial-political climate in their communities is dangerous and damaging to many Chicanas/os. Whether they had run-ins with authority figures, watched siblings struggle with discrimination, heard stories from others, or chose to disassociate from their community as a survival strategy, their analyses leave little room for doubt that race is a crucial lens through which Chicanas/os are defined and limited in Acoma and the surrounding communities. Furthermore, we have to recognize that gender is a critical component of this climate, for males are often dealt with more violently and females face an additional and equally powerful layer of discrimination.

As the students in these last three chapters explained, a number of types of responses to these contexts are possible. Some students deny that race is an issue, believe in equal opportunity, and try to fit in. And for some, this strategy works, at least for a while, but as Chela and Mari suggested, it can be psychologically painful and can lead to growing distress that, in the end, must be confronted. Others withdraw from school by physically or psychologically leaving. This strategy allows them to divest from any commitment to an institution that considers them outsiders or even inferior. This tactic can be psychologically safer, but it significantly limits opportunities for these students. Other students respond to these school climates through conscious and severe rebellion, challenging and even verbally attacking school staff and administrators. As Angel indicated, this response can be even more psychologically invigorating, but it also leads to significantly limited opportunities. Some students choose to ignore the negative messages they encounter, though acknowledging the severity of the messages, and instead these students focus on their own educational goals as a means of proving wrong those who expect their failure. This strategy can be effective, but it can isolate the students who choose this path, for they have few sources of support for their efforts. Finally, some students engage in a type of informed resistance. These students are committed to addressing the racial injustices they see, and they use their schooling as a means of achieving this goal. They challenge the status quo, but only in ways that allow them to maintain their good standing within educational institutions so that they can continue to maximize their opportunities for educationally empowering themselves. These students typically develop their resistant stances through tapping into support systems, particularly peer groups such as MEChA.

The five students highlighted here demonstrate that, regardless of the approach that students take toward their schooling, any type of mentorship significantly increases their chances of succeeding in school. However, given that many students are struggling to make sense of their role within the racial-political climate in which they find themselves, support systems that help them achieve a positive and empowering sense of racial identity are particularly crucial. And for the female students, support systems that also address the gender politics they confront are even more helpful. Even when Chicana/o students have no other form of mentorship, support systems such as these go a long way toward helping them develop strategies for achieving their educational goals. Ramona, Chela, and Mari showed that this type of support system—MEChA, in their case—gave them the opportunity to create a shared vision of their importance as Chicanas who were pursuing higher education. In addition, each of them was able to use the group to develop the specific skills and awareness that she most needed. Still, the struggles these women experienced were significant, and they continued to deal with them in college.

Cesar received similar support from MEChA, but at a much earlier age. This earlier exposure to this support system allowed him to move beyond the development of an empowering identity and on to the process of channeling that identity into his own educational advancement. His story also suggested a means of addressing the serious concerns raised by Angel's experiences. Angel never had a support system to help him develop a strong sense of identity that incorporated or addressed the injustices he had seen. He took that struggle upon himself and relied on his identity as a gang member to help him see himself as a powerful person rather than as the problem others understood him to be. Angel's experiences in college and his dropping out take our analysis to another level, however. Angel's case suggests that we may also need to provide avenues for Chicana/o students to rethink and address the fundamental educational contradictions that underlie their experiences in schools. Angel challenged many of the core principles of education that represent what he believed were the fundamental injustices in his life. In particular, he critiqued schooling as competition rather than creation. One of his comments in our last interview hinted at a need shared by all of the students:

> I think the most important thing to me right now is kinda just succeeding. You know, I mean trying, just tryin' to make it. That's kinda what I am tryin' to do, just takin' it day by day and just trying. I'm just gonna fight. I'm gonna fight it. And it's a constant fight, to get up every morning and go to school. It's a fight. I'm fighting. . . . Fighting what we see as injustices and the unfairnesses and the unequalness, just fighting for it. I think when we stop fighting, that's when there's somethin' wrong . . . I've had to fight every step of the way. Every step. And then there's just walls after walls after walls after wall after wall comin' up. And it's just like I never wanted to feel sorry for myself or anything like that. But, I mean, now I begin to realize what I came through to get here, as [opposed] to what a lot of other people come through. I mean, it's easy for a lot of people to stay in school, just to make it here. I mean, it comes easy for 'em. But I think for me it was just like one of the biggest struggles of my life just to get here. I mean it was just like it was a huge fight.

In some ways, the analysis Angel made of his own identity is applicable to all of the students in the project, because they are all very much engaged in their own fights. Some are fighting for their families, some are fighting for Chicanas/os, some are fighting for Chicanas and women specifically, some are fighting just to make sense of themselves within the confusion that reigns around issues of race and ethnicity, some do not know what they are fighting, and some are fighting for all of these things at once. Angel's analysis helps us understand the role of power in shaping identity among Chicana/o students in rural Washington State. As with the Los Angeles students, the Washington students typically developed their identities in response to power. Their experiences illustrate that when Chicana/o students are confronted with a clear message that they have no power in a certain social arena of their lives, they are forced to make sense of this lack of power and to incorporate it into their own identities. Context, however, plays a key role in both the degree to which the inequity is visible and the shaping of individuals' means of making sense of this disequilibrium.

In summary, these five students covered a number of critical issues that confront Chicanas/os in schools. Most important, they exposed the tight connection between identity and school performance. For many Chicana/o students, race is a critical factor in this equation. These students also emphasized the need for mentorship and support systems to help Chicana/o students address the relationship between their racial experiences and their school lives and life goals. Thus, mentorship becomes the heart of the recommendations that these students made in both indirect and direct ways.

ERNESTO SANCHEZ'S AUTOBIOGRAPHICAL ANALYSIS OF IDENTITY AND SCHOOL IN ACOMA

Ernesto Sanchez enrolled in a class that I offered at the university in Washington that dealt with identity development among Chicanas/os. I offered the class while I was working on the project described in this book. The students were asked to write autobiographies that focused on their identities. Ernesto's paper covered many of the themes I was finding in my research. I should add that I had not talked about that research when he submitted the paper. Another important point was that Ernesto was the only student in the class (and the only person I had met at that time) who had attended all three of the schools used as research sites for the project.

At the end of the semester, as I thought about the class and the project, I decided to ask Ernesto if I could use his paper in this book. He graciously agreed. What follows is the paper almost exactly as he submitted it. With his permission, I made only a few minor changes in punctuation and cut a few paragraphs toward the end in which he talked about the class readings.

The importance of this work is that it is Ernesto's analysis of his world exactly as he wants the reader to understand it. It requires no further explanation, nor interpretation.

ERNESTO SANCHEZ

AUTOBIOGRAPHY

FEBRUARY 9, 1998

"YOU SPEAK REALLY GOOD ENGLISH FOR A MEXICAN KID": IDENTITY POLITICS IN CHICANO/MEXICAN YOUTH

"You speak really good English for a Mexican kid" are words which impact a young child in ways that even he does not understand until he has time to reflect upon his life. Until a person understands the oppression and racism that are present in American society, one cannot comprehend the significance a simple comment, a look, or even a seemingly innocent compliment plays in the formation of a person's identity.

I was born in Coalcoman, Michoacan, Mexico, on March 1, 1976. I was the first child of Jorge and Lucia Sanchez. My father was 23 when I was born, the son of Carlota Sanchez. My father was only 2 when my grandfather, Agustin Sanchez, left my grandmother. *Al Norte* he came, and in *el Norte* he remained. My grandmother was left with five hungry kids to feed; the children, with bitter memories of what could've been. This is the first trauma that my family suffered at the hands of *el Norte*.

I was only 2 years old when my parents made the difficult decision to travel to *el Norte*. Leaving elements of what they were behind—family, memories, their roots—moving on in search of a better life for themselves, but more importantly for their children. It is often looked upon as a merely positive thing for immigrants to move to the United States, but rarely do we see the impact of that which is left behind. In leaving Mexico my parents left a piece of themselves, a piece of who they were, a piece of their identity. My forefathers, Pancho Villa, Emiliano Zapata, and Cuauhtemoc Cardenas were replaced with Abraham Lincoln, George Washington, and the Puritans. Confusion.

Our journey to *el Norte* came to its first stop in Los Angeles, a popular stop for many of the immigrants who come from Mexico and Latin America. We lived there for about 2 years. My earliest memories are of Los Angeles. I remember the kindness of the people there, both Mexicans and Centro Americanos; their willingness to help those who were less fortunate. They too had been there once and understood the meaning of a helping hand. I have fond memories of Los Angeles and can remember sadness when we undertook the second phase of our journey, a journey that would end in Washington . . . Cowiche, Washington.

It was here that I saw my first apple tree and remember my first trips to Church. Living in Cowiche was a sort of artificial freedom. My parents both worked and my grandmother was in charge of taking care of us. I remember their long days at work and a life that would compare to that of any 19th century settler of the west. We lived in poverty and in isolation, tied to the land and dependent upon it for survival.

Living in Cowiche, I remember going to church and the preaching of *el Padre Duffy*. We only lived about a 5 minutes walking distance from the church and were regular visitors on Sunday. I remember *el padre* coming to my house and bringing us *galletas* and catechism books. Learning to pray was important in those days. Learning was important.

It was during our stay in Cowiche that I first made my entrance into the educational system. I started Epic Head Start when I was only four years old; my sister Anita started at 3. One thing that I remember is that I had a Chicana teacher and that Spanish (the language of my people) was used fluently throughout the day. I felt comfortable in her classroom. My parents were at ease about leaving me there. But the time was short-lived and we moved to Acoma only days before my entrance into grade school. I remember kindergarten being a total culture clash for me. I did not speak the language and soon found myself feeling as if I did not belong. I dressed different, spoke different, and looked different than the majority of the students at my school. I can agree with Richard Rodriguez (rich-heard road-ree-guess) when he says that it was not until he started school that he found out that he was a Mexican.

I cannot say that I was sheltered before I was enrolled in grade school, but I can say that I was never prepared for the emotional trauma that I was to endure at the hands of the educational system. Some will argue that children cannot make racial distinctions when they are in kindergarten. I will argue that point with anyone. I was quick to recognize that I was different than the rest of my peers. We dressed different, we looked different, and most important, we talked different.

The issue of language in grade school was very evident. We associated with those who could understand us. For me, it was the Mexicans: my comfort group, *mi Raza*. I was never enrolled in any ESL (English as a Second Language) courses in grade school and as a result suffered during the first part of my educational career. I had no basis of English or grammar to use as a stepping-stone, and was given a sink-or-swim option to learn English. I survived the first couple of months at the school only because of the fact that I had cousins who were at the school that were able to help me and encourage me to go on. Others were not as lucky.

It was while I was in grade school that it became increasingly evident that I was different, but I continued to accept it as nothing out of the ordinary. One day this realization would change. While I was standing in line to check out a book one day, a librarian came over to me. She must have heard me speaking to someone, and made the remark, "You speak really good English for a Mexican kid." I remember feeling the words cut through me like a knife. I was speechless and a swirl of emotions swept through me. What did she mean by this? What did it mean to be Mexican? Were Mexicans supposed to speak English bad? It was the most painful compliment that I had ever received and it was not until much later that I realized why I had been so uncomfortable with the statement.

By the end of my first year in school, I was one of the best students in the class. This continued throughout my grade school years and followed me into middle school. In middle school I was, you might say, confused. I was always at the top of my class and as a result was in a pool with a great majority of *gabachos*. I made several *gabacho* friends when I was in 6th and 7th grade in middle school. In retrospect, I can say that it was because I felt alienated from my *Raza,* viewed different because I was a high achiever. Similar to Rodriguez, I wanted to fit in. After all, wasn't this my crowd now that I was making the grades that were so out of reach for my Chicano brothers and sisters? I figured that I would befriend those who thought like me, who achieved like me.

When I look back on my middle school years, I remember feeling uncomfortable with the *gringo* children. I was never comfortable to express my ideas and often forced to accept apologies without emotion when they accidentally said something that was not cool. I also had Mexican friends, and due to the fact that I had befriended some *gabachos* they looked upon me differently. I was often in a bind with my Mexican friends who knew I was like them, but at the same time different. I was in a dilemma, one that pitted my *Raza* against my scholastic gains.

During 8th I finally made a decision to associate myself with those who were like me. I felt much more comfortable around them and finally I found an avenue where I could express my ideas without negative criticisms. I found myself at ease. It was during 8th grade when I was given the option to enroll in Honors classes upon entering high school. I agreed and the very next year I was at Johnson High School.

At Johnson, a distinctive change was to occur within me that would affect my life in negative and, at the same time, positive ways. It was during high school that I realized that in order to be successful you either have to be white or act the part. I was neither white, nor did I want to act white. I remember going into classes full of *gabachos* and being taught by *gabachos*. It was a very humbling experience for me. I was always made to feel as if I did not belong. I was not given proper attention, always the last one to be helped, always the one who was least desirable when choosing groups, always picked to answer questions that the rest of the group did not know the answer to. I was on the spot.

I heard and experienced racism and had no idea how to confront it. I had to be twice as good, make twice as much effort and accept my inferior status to continue.

As a result of my experiences in these classes I was discouraged with the program, and it was during my first year in high school that I received my first "F." It was in an Honors English course. I just did not have the *ganas* to continue with the bullshit that was being fed to me every day.

I dropped out of the Honors Program and was enrolled in regular classes. They were full of Mexicans and I felt a comfort that had not been present since middle school. But once again the tables were turned against me as I realized that these teachers didn't give a shit about me. I was just another Mexican. Regardless of what I did or accomplished I was just another Mexican, a stupid-lazy-troublemaker. I remember the friends that I used to hang out with and the often-scornful eyes that would be focused on our every move as we walked through the courtyard during lunch. Always suspects, we were forced to be on guard. Where was the home away from home feeling that the school is supposed to provide the student? I struggled with this eight hours a day, five days a week.

Pandilleros is what they saw us as. Mr. X, Mrs. Y, Mr. Z [school administrators]. It made no difference to them whether or not we were honors students or whether we were here to get an education to try to better ourselves. We were Mexicans. Being Mexican was our crime, our only crime. I remember how we were not even allowed to have a conversation with more than two or three persons, because it was suspect to gang activity. Race had a great deal to play with this suspicion. I remember white students only feet away from me in large picnic-type gatherings and yet the Mexican was always suspect. The Mexican was always the problem.

I began to be labeled as a *pandillero* time and time again, by teachers, administrators, the police, and the media. Mexicans were trouble. I remember when Ramon, Federico, Juan, Fernando, Roach and other friends used to be into bicycles and would go riding around the east side. Innocent, we were just out having fun. I remember being pulled aside by police and getting searched for no reason. I remember the first time we were labeled gang members by the police and were given the honor of having our pictures put on the Yakima Police Department's Gang files.

One day, I left home a Mexican and came back a gang member. The two terms, which to an ignorant mind would be interchangeable, meant totally different things to the young man who would transform his identity around the latter. Experiences and what others perceive you to be go a long way in the formation of an identity. Eventually the *bycicleteros* were forced to fit into the mold that was laid out in front of them—La Raza Fourteenth Street. *Norteños* to the bone, or so we thought. An identity given to us by the system is what we cherished, took pride in, and admired.

I remember going home each night and watching the news. How many more of my friends would I see on the news today? I saw friends get shot, stabbed, and even die because of the gang. Many who had no alternative but to follow the steps that were laid out in front of them by the same system that is supposed to guide and protect us. I wonder if guidance and protection only comes to those who are of a certain color and class status.

I now know that the system forced me into a gang. It was not my parents, as many believe. My parents were always there for me when I needed them. What they could not provide for me is a safety shield from discrimination when I left for school. The only regrets that I have about joining a gang are that I was too naïve to understand the reasons why we were labeled as *pandilleros*. Never once did I fully believe that this was my goal in life.

My senior year in high school I found M.E.Ch.A. *(Movimiento Estudiantil Chicana/o de Aztlán)*. And although it was only a social organization at the time, in it I found a fresh new approach to what I was accustomed to seeing and hearing. I made M.E.Ch.A. a regular function after school and as a result, I was able to stay out of trouble for at least a couple of hours. I was sick and tired of fitting into the mold that was set out in front of me to step into. I wanted something more to come out of my life.

Gradually, I was able to stay away from the gang and spend more time in M.E.Ch.A. I did not identify myself as a gang member any longer; I was a Mexican. I began to see the negativity that was associated with the gang and the digression of our people, our young people, into nothing more than outlaws and inmates. I began to watch the news not to see how many of our people were on trial, but to search for positive portrayals of my *gente*. I found none; no role models to fulfill my desire, my need for redemption.

During my senior year at Johnson I was fortunate enough to attend a conference at the university that was dedicated to the late Cesar Chavez. It was a very important experience for me because it was the first time that I saw my culture, language, and history so openly celebrated. I had finally found the role models that I had been denied. I met poets Ricardo Sanchez and "Flaco" Maldonado, but most importantly I was able to see that my *gente* had a history in this country. We had the right to be here. This experience was very important to me as an individual and very important in the identity that was to be formed within the barriers of my mind. A renewed pride in my people had been awakened.

During my senior year in high school, I was never under the impression that I was going to make it to college. I was going to graduate and that was it. I was never encouraged and helped by my counselor, who only called me into his office one time during the four years that I was in high school. That visit with my counselor was to see if I was eligible to graduate. I was never encouraged to apply for scholarships, apply to any colleges or universities, or apply for financial aid. A ten minute meeting in return for four years of high school.

During my high school graduation, I was able to see the extent of my *Raza's* problems. Out of the several hundred *Mexicanitos* that had started school with me, only about 50 or 60 were graduating. Of all of my close friends, I was the only one to graduate. It was a sad day in my eyes. It was a sad day for my people.

I graduated and was obsessed with the idea that I was going to work and make lots of money. It was only a dream. I started to work some dead-end jobs and realized that I was going nowhere. I was determined to do something about my problem. Several months later I was in college. In January of 1995, I started ACC (Acoma Community College). It was a very important step in the formation of my identity. It was here where I began to take classes in Latin American, Mexican and Chicano History, and it was here where M.E.Ch.A. took on a totally different and identifying feature for me. I began to read and explore all that was related to Chicanos/Mexicans. I was inspired by the stories of Cesar Chavez, Jose Angel Gutierrez, Rodolfo "Corky" Gonzalez, and Reies Lopez Tijerina. I was learning of the struggles for justice and equality that my people fought and continue to fight today. I had discovered the role models that would guide the path that my life would follow during the next several years. I realized that injustice is not a thing of the past; my life and the lives of the thousands and thousands of Chicano youth that drop out of school each year, due to the institutionalized racism present in the public school system, were a clear example of it.

During all of my years in the public school system I had never heard of any Chicano/Mexican other than Cesar Chavez. I was always lacking role models, people to look up to, people like me. I found those role models during my stay at ACC. I found that role model in the Chicano Studies Instructor at ACC and it was through him and my experiences with M.E.Ch.A. that I learned what it meant to be Chicano. An identity which is always changing, hard to define and yet so near to the hearts of so many who know that our *gente* are in a state of crisis and are engaged in the struggle to break the binds of oppression that have held us subservient for so many years. I learned that Chicano is a state of mind. You can be born a Mexican-American, but to actually call yourself a Chicano requires that you understand that your people are in a state of crisis and it requires that you make a decision to devote your life to the betterment, the self-determination of your people, the Chicano/Mexican people. I will never call myself a Chicano, but I will call myself a Mexican with a Chicano ideology. I can never negate the fact that I was born *del otro lado,* and unfortunately I can never go back and live as a Mexican.

. . . I am from a working class family that struggled throughout the years just to try to put food on our table. . . . I know that if it had not been for my family's class status I do not feel that I would have been blessed to work in the fields. Working in the orchards of Acoma gave me a sense of identity as much as any book I read, or any class I have ever taken. It builds character and determination by reminding you of all of the obstacles that you must overcome in order to be considered an equal in American society.

In relation to gender, I did make the distinction that Rodriguez and Navarrette may have benefited from male privilege while making their way through high school and college, and I can relate to this. Being a male, I believe that many privileges are afforded to us. If I had been a female, I probably would not have been as involved in activities and organizations such as M.E.Ch.A. I would have probably been restricted as to when and where I could go. I would have never been able to make field trips such as the one I took to the university. I know this because I have five sisters and saw the burden that was placed on them for being women.

. . . The fundamental concern that I would like to address is the lack of pride within our community as to being Mexican. This is a fundamental issue and can be seen in the way that our youth are constantly being brought under the influence of the gangs and how we as a people are not comfortable in saying, "YES I AM MEXICAN," or "YES I AM CHICANO." I believe that if I would have believed in myself and taken more pride in what I was when I was younger, many of the identity problems that I went through would not have been present, or would have been present to a lesser degree. Learning early in life that it is fine to be a Mexican would not only help to boost the morale of our people at a very young age, but would transcend into the overall productiveness, and self-confidence of our people.

The way that I propose to do this is by initiating an after-school program for young Chicano/Mexican students that would focus on building awareness and pride in the Chicano/Mexican Ethnicity. This would be done through personal narratives (such as the one that I am doing right now), history lessons, cultural activities, and social gatherings in which the youth, the program coordinators, and the parents could meet and discuss the program and give feedback on the progress of the program. The incorporation of the works by Richard Rodriguez, Ruben Navarrette, Roberto Rodriguez and Gloria Anzaldua would be beneficial in getting the children to think abstractly and critically with respect to their own personal struggles. This program would address the problem of the low confidence evident in today's Chicano/Mexican youth, but also prepare the children for college by exposing them to the experiences of those who have already been there, making them believe that they have the right and an obligation to be there for their people.

One very important aspect of the program would be the incorporation of the children's parents' experience and frustrations when dealing with the issue of identity. This would be very important because the children would realize that it is not only them who are struggling with identity, but that it is a struggle that knows no age limits and affects us all in some way. This involvement would allow the parents to get involved and open a dialogue between the student and his/her parents with respect to the program and with respect to identity.

I believe that this is a very realistic approach, all that is necessary is the *ganas* and the commitment of several individuals who are willing to educate our *gente*. The program would probably run after school and this would give us the advantage of recruiting latchkey kids who would not only be more susceptible to the influence of the gang, but also more susceptible to the isolation that often leads to identity struggles.

I have envisioned starting a program like this for several years now, but I always seem to run into the roadblock which does not allow me to go any further due to the fact that I have never received sufficient backing from other students like me. One day last year, I even proposed it to the principal of an elementary school in Acoma, and got a yes from him, but the problem was that it was only me, and that would be robbing the students, not only of a gender balanced environment, but also of differing perspectives on identity formation. I still have hopes and dreams to start my *escuelita* and I realize that if I give it enough time and thought it will work out.

PART THREE

UNDERSTANDING AND TRANSFORMING THE SCHOOL LIVES OF CHICANA/O YOUTH

RACIAL PROFILING, IDENTITY, AND SCHOOL ACHIEVEMENT
Lessons from Power Conflicts in Diverse Contexts

Racial profiling has been attacked as the most blatant example of the racial divide in the United States today. African American and Latina/o communities in particular have protested the informal policy that makes DWB (driving while black/brown) an offense in many areas. These protests are a response to the greater frequency with which black and brown drivers are pulled over by the police than are other drivers. In California, the San José Police Department (SJPD) monitored the ethnicity of drivers who were pulled over during a six-month period in 2000 and found that this frequency difference was indeed the case. The reason given by the officials in the SJPD was that the black and brown drivers were concentrated in communities where the police force was required to have increased officer presence because of higher crime rates. Within a few months, however, a scandal broke out in one division of the SJPD when officers were told to pull over anyone who was black after the next bank robbery attempt in the area.

The debate over racial profiling is complex and often convoluted. The point of introducing the concept here is not to enter into this debate. Instead, I want to use this popular concept to help frame the students' analyses and to emphasize the impact of racial profiling on youth. In Chapter 1, Diego described how racial profiling can affect youth. After he was pulled over for, as the police officers explained, driving while brown (in the wrong community), he had to deal with this with regard to his own sense of self and identity.

Many Chicana/o youth live and go to school in areas in which they can be physically or psychologically attacked simply because of the color of their skin. When they drive in or out of their communities, when they walk in their neighborhoods, when they go to the mall, when they apply for jobs, and when they go to school, people are profiling them. This is not always a conscious process on the part of employers, police officers, and teachers, but it certainly happens. The students' stories in the previous six chapters have made this clear.

The ways in which Chicanas/os are profiled in schools are multiple. They are profiled according to skin color, dress, linguistic abilities or patterns, test scores, specific behaviors, friendship groups, socioeconomic status, parental involvement, or, most often, some combination of these characteristics. The result of this profiling is typically the same: Chicanas/os are expected to perform in certain ways because of characteristics that often have nothing to do with their intellectual abilities. In fact, schooling itself is based on profiling to a large extent. In order to make their jobs doable, teachers often feel obligated to categorize their students and shape the learning environment to meet the different needs of these categories of students. Profiling occurs every day in schools around any number of student characteristics. Although most teachers admit to knowing how students will perform in class based on what are often very quick assessments of their students, few teachers believe that these assessments are based on race.

My own work as a teacher and with other teachers since leaving elementary teaching suggests that few teachers *consciously* sort students on the basis of race. Yet these same experiences have made it clear, as the students themselves have shown throughout this book, that teachers *unconsciously* categorize students on the basis of race in ways quite similar to the racial profiling that occurs in law enforcement.

These processes are significant because teachers represent both authority figures and the gatekeepers into the realm of knowledge and success. When these authority figures base their actions on stereotypes, the impact of those actions is overwhelming for many students. Just as the police often use racial profiles to determine who are potential criminals and who does not need to be pulled over, teachers use racial profiles to determine who will and will not benefit from opportunities to excel in school. Again, it must be emphasized that this is typically an unconscious process on the part of teachers. In fact, it seems that the profiling that teachers do simply reflects that of society at large. A brief look at legislation in California in the 1990s and its relationship to schooling helps provide a context for understanding these ideas.

Although California has a long history of proclaiming itself a mecca of tolerance, it has an equally long history of simultaneously and informally limiting the opportunities of Chicanas/os. During the 1990s, California politicians, educators, and community leaders supported the passage of Propositions 187, 209, and 227 under the flag of fairness and equal opportunity, but what actually happened in the schools was a quite different story.

Proposition 187 was passed by Californians in 1994 under the slogan "Save Our State." The legislation and its supporters emphasized the importance of ending the provision of social services to undocumented residents in the state. A key component of the initiative was the verification of the legal status of all students and their parents and the denial of education to "illegals." In the schools, Proposition 187 took on a quite different meaning. Students clearly felt that lines had been drawn and that they were seen as the enemy (see Trench and Simón 1997 for examples). In many instances, the messages were not even subtle, as, for example, security guards denied "Mexican-looking" U.S. citizens entrance into their own schools.

Proposition 209, passed by Californians in 1997, was an effort to end the consideration of race as a factor in awarding state jobs, contracts, and school admissions. Among the most-contested aspects of the initiative was the proposal to end the use of race as a criterion in determining admission to the University of California. The most ardent supporters of Proposition 209 explained that everyone should have the same opportunity to gain admission into the university and that all special preferences had to be ended. Although the logic behind the argument made sense to many, it ignored the reality of the multiple "preferences" incorporated into the admissions process. Few voters ever had the chance to consider the complexity of the educational issues involved. The proponents of the legislation expressed no concern that athletes, as just one example, would continue to be admitted to the University of California under a set of admission criteria different from that used for the rest of the applicant pool. Ironically, during the debate over this issue, the *Los Angeles Times* released information about several University of California applicants who had gained admission, after initial rejections, through lobbying from the same trustees who opposed affirmative action policies. Thus, while university officials continued to recognize that admission into the University of California should not be based on strict criteria of grades and test scores, the voting populace and the Regents of the University of California did not believe that the unique life experiences of, for example, a young Latina—who had survived abject poverty, constricted educational opportunities, racism, and other forces that limited her academic achievements—should be taken into consideration in university admissions. What voters and school personnel alike have typically failed to acknowledge is the significant degree of educational inequality that exists, as well as the skills and intelligence required for many Chicanas/os to make it within this system of inequality. In the United States, we see the segregation in our schools as natural, commonsense, and understandable. The educational and economic opportunities of Chicanas/os are limited, and then the school itself forces the unequals it created (e.g., whites who are often nurtured and Chicanas/os who are often expected to fail) to compete as if they were equals. This system is the most virulent form of not only maintaining inequality but also creating a justification for the differences that are then explained as natural.

In yet another twist in this tale, Proposition 227 was designed to end the provision of bilingual education in California schools and was passed by the electorate in 1998. The proponents of the measure said that bilingual education was not providing limited and non-English speakers with the English-language skills necessary to function effectively in the school and the workplace. The proponents focused on the high costs of bilingual education and on research that suggested that English immersion was a more effective way of teaching English to non-English speakers. Although the proposition was framed in the context of public desire to provide the best educational opportunities possible for students, this goal was clearly lost in the political shuffle. Research into the effects of bilingual education has never conclusively shown that English immersion is more effective, and it often shows the opposite. In addition, few proponents had addressed the issue that bilingual education in California schools had typically been poorly implemented. In fact, the problems frequently attributed to bilingual education are reflected in schooling at large, although no one argues for the eradication of public schooling. Furthermore, since voters had little exposure to the key issues surrounding bilingual education, the proposition essentially boiled down to whether or not voters wanted to pay for other people's children to be educated. The animosity of parents and even school staff toward the bilingual education programs became apparent after the proposition passed. Shortly after Proposition 227 went into effect, not only did certain schools abandon every effort to provide students with guidance in their native languages, but these schools also got rid of all school materials that were not in English, often discarding expensive library books in Spanish.

The discord between the rhetoric behind Propositions 187, 209, and 227 and the daily manifestations of the popular support for these measures is significant. It mirrors the discontinuity between the popular messages that Chicana/o students hear in schools about how all students can succeed in California schools *and* the students' experiences, which reveal a number of limitations on their opportunities to excel in school. This discontinuity underlies the dramatic struggle facing Chicana/o communities. The vast majority of voters who supported Propositions 187, 209, and 227 undoubtedly believe they did what is best and probably even what is best for Chicana/o youth. They accept the rationales behind these measures as "right." This position is possible because they cannot conceive of the world in which so many Chicanas/os live. They cannot see the world through Chicana/o eyes and believe that, in fact, Chicana/o perceptions of their own lives are wrong. This book does not attempt to argue directly against the reasons voters had for supporting these measures. Instead, it focuses on the power of the story Chicana/o youth are telling and asks the readers to listen. Even the more "liberal" opponents of the legislation need to pay close attention to what these youth are saying.

What many of us have failed to address in looking at the issues that face Chicanas/os in the schools of California, for example, is that the racial climate in which we now find ourselves is having a significant impact on Chicana/o students. Chicana/o youth in California today are often painfully aware that they are not seen as equal to other children. Many immigrant and U.S.-born Chicanas/os alike quickly learn that they are not expected to succeed in the schools. The effects of these experiences are devastating and receive far less attention than the policies that this racial climate produces.

What is evident in the example of California is an intricate system of racial profiling whereby many associate looking "Mexican" with being undocumented, seeking special benefits that have not been earned, and trying to find an easy way through the education system because of a lack of the skills needed to succeed. Others associate looking "Mexican" with language difficulties, disinterest in school, and interest in working with one's hands. Still others associate looking "Mexican" with being a troublemaker, a gangbanger, or a class clown. There are countless variations of these profiles of Chicana/o students, but it is rare that looking "Mexican" is associated with having the intelligence and determination to succeed in school.

For many teachers I have worked with, being Chicana/o means that a student does not care much about school and will never rise above the working-class status of her or his parents. Again, these messages may not be created by teachers, but they are often re-created and made understandable to youth through daily interactions with these teachers. The teachers most often are not conscious of all this, because they learn racist profiles through popular racial discourse—as defined in the campaigns for Propositions 187, 209, and 227, for example. These notions are also grounded in media representations of Chicanas/os. The role of the media is particularly significant for Chicanas/os because they are the most segregated ethnic group in the United States. The result of this segregation is that relatively few non-Chicanas/os have the opportunity to live and interact with Chicanas/os and see them as three-dimensional people, families, and communities. Instead, many non-Chicanas/os develop an understanding of Chicanas/os that is static, flat, and grounded in media portrayals of Chicanas/os as uneducated, unmotivated, social leeches who are often involved in crime and social irresponsibility. A recent documentary, *Farmingville,* demonstrates these kinds of perceptions among non-Chicanas/os, as well as how they act based on those perceptions (Sandoval and Tambini 2004). This image prevails despite the recent popularity of Latina/o entertainers, such as Jennifer Lopez and Ricky Martin, who are seen as being cool but not like "all those other Latinas/os."[1] All of these forces work together to shape popular understandings of Chicana/o youth. In turn, these understandings affect how teachers and others interact with Chicanas/os. Still, it is essential to note that many teachers do not fall into the trap of racially profiling students. In every school I have been, there is at least a small group of teachers who consciously fight against these very forces. The critical issue that many Chicana/o students reveal, however, is that even an occasional confrontation with racial profiling—or, for some students, just one encounter—has a dramatic affect on their identities and demands a psychological response.

As the students explained throughout this book, these issues are a big part of their lives. These issues are not the only factor influencing Chicana/o schooling and identity development, but they are often the most significant. Students are also profiled in other arenas of their social lives. The issues most often raised by the students are related to gender, class, and sexuality. In addition, students who do not emphasize these other factors are surely influenced by them. For example, many Chicanas (and Chicanos as well) who do not discuss the significance of gender in their lives are surely affected by it.

UNDERSTANDING RACIAL HEGEMONY

The objective of these first few pages of this chapter has been to validate the analyses of the students covered throughout the book, and to do so in a way that demonstrates their connection to larger social forces. Now we are prepared to consider one of the key concepts of this book: racial hegemony. Racial hegemony is the dominance and virtual impenetrability of the popular belief that equality of opportunity for all racial and ethnic groups exists in the United States, despite dramatic evidence to the contrary. This hegemony is manifested in the way that society and social institutions structure opportunities. The previous example from California politics and, more importantly, the students' analyses throughout this book demonstrate the existence of a clear racial order that is both unjust and rarely contested in this country in any systemic way. Despite the daily indications of this injustice and inequality, the dominance of the popular perceptions just discussed do not allow, for example, Chicana/o youth to have their voices heard and their realities accepted as truth. It is vital to understand this situation as racial hegemony so that we can recognize that the issues covered in this book are not simply individual experiences with racism perpetrated by other individuals. Rather, an institutional process of educational racism allows individuals and schools to create inequality and to feel that it is acceptable, even natural.

The goal of the rest of this chapter is to create a more complex framework that explains the social forces that shape Chicana/o social identity development and school performance and the relationship between the two. The metaphor of racial profiling and the concept of racial hegemony provide a backdrop for this framework that should facilitate deeper understanding of the workings of these social forces. The analysis that follows comes directly from the insights of Chicana/o students.

THE ROLE OF POWER CONFLICTS

Chicana/o students' social identities are influenced by a number of factors, and the process of identity development is ongoing, so it is difficult to freeze students' lives in order to categorize them in a certain way. Still, in terms of the process of identity development, one central force seems to be at work for all of the students in Los Angeles and Washington. As discussed in Chapter 1, power defines the evolution of identity for these students. When students are confronted with the fact that they are disempowered along a certain axis of social interaction, they are forced to address this disempowerment in their identity formation. For example, in the case of Diego getting pulled over by the police (as mentioned above and in Chapter 1), the officers made it clear that because he was Chicano, he did not have the same rights that others did. As Diego himself explained, he had to deal with this. He had to find a way to make sense of it in his own mind. He had to address his racial disempowerment through his identity formation. In his case, Diego felt compelled to affirm his Chicano identity through resistant stances that challenged the racism he continually encountered in and out of school. Students in these kinds of situations can choose any of a number of paths, but their identities are still being shaped by this power differential. This is the most conscious way in which identity is shaped for Chicana/o youth. They may be disempowered in other ways, such as with regard to class, for example, but if they face a confrontation along racial lines, race almost always takes a dominant role in their identity formation. Still, later in their lives they may face a confrontation along another axis of their social lives to which they have to respond. This is often the case with Chicanas who become increasingly attuned to and confronted with sexism as they get older. As the Chicanas at both universities suggested, these women develop identities that synthesize gender and race as they attempt to become role models for other Chicanas, for example. In contrast, there are other students who do not blatantly confront power conflicts and whose social identities are therefore defined by the social realms they inhabit. Although such cases were rare among the students interviewed for this project, these students tend to be withdrawn from school and to define themselves primarily within their familial contexts. Finally, the age of students is a vital element of identity development. This factor became evident in the Acoma project when older returning students at the community college made it clear that their identities had evolved beyond their peers' identities. Most significantly, being parents had led these older students to ground their identities in their goal of serving as role models for youth, which was linked to their understanding of the racial-political climate as well.

As I have been suggesting, it is necessary to understand that race is not the only factor that influences the identity development of Chicanas/os. Every day countless forces influence their ongoing identity development. Surely, many of these influences affect identity formation only on an unconscious level or in a minor way. This book therefore focuses on students' own understandings of their identities and of the forces that they recognize as important in their lives. Because of the degree of racial profiling that occurs in their daily lives and the dramatic impact that even a single experience with racial confrontation can have, race is the most significant realm of identity development for the vast majority of the Chicana/o students who participated in this project. Even gender among the females did not come up nearly as often as race did, although that finding seems to result from the role of gender and sexism within Chicana/o students' own families. As many of the females noted, sexism and constricting gender roles shape their lives in significant ways, but these aspects of gender are seen as inherent to their families and culture, which they love. The contradictions related to gender are difficult for many females to sort out at a younger age. For this reason, they often choose to ignore it and consciously focus on the role of race in shaping their identities. Although the starting point of this analysis is to understand the identity issues of greatest importance to students as the students themselves define them, the role of unconscious and suppressed identities is also critical and is addressed in more detail in the next chapter.

THE ROLE OF CONTEXT

Just as significant as the power dynamics that students confront is the sociohistorical and sociopolitical context in which these dynamics emerge. This context defines the impact of power by determining the rules of social life in the area and what individuals can and cannot do. Identity development in Acoma, for example, is fundamentally different from that in Los Angeles. Many of the students in Los Angeles chose to define their identities along racial lines in response to the power dynamics described above. Race was the core of their social identities because, in their lives, race profoundly shaped their opportunities. Furthermore, they had ready exposure to others who had defined themselves in similar ways, often for one or more generations. Finally, they frequently saw that they had few options for social advancement in the contexts in which they lived, and many of them had little hope of advancing beyond the socioeconomic positions of their parents.

In Acoma the students described a similar racial dynamic whereby Chicanas/os were exceptionally disempowered. The social landscape, however, was fundamentally different in eastern Washington State. Most important, the dominance of the mainstream interpretation of the Chicana/o experience was so overwhelming that alternative, Chicana/o interpretations were almost nonexistent. The dominant racial order left no room for anyone even to suggest that racial inequality existed there, let alone injustice. Even the efforts of some students to promote pride in their Mexicana/o background were seen as troublemaking and inappropriate and were even cited as examples of reverse discrimination. For this reason, there were almost no role models of Chicanas/os who had developed a positive racial identity and challenged the status quo. Most of the successful Chicanas/os in Acoma were in the mainstream and either accepted or did not challenge traditional explanations of Chicana/o outcomes. Because of all this, the vast majority of Chicana/o students did not know how to develop a positive, affirming Chicana/o identity. This situation was fundamentally different from that in Los Angeles, where students had multiple models of racialized Chicana/o identities and where those identities were much more acceptable, such that race became the public social identity for many students, while family was a much more private aspect of identity and removed from public, social identity. Thus, in Acoma, although race was fundamental in students' experiences, for many students it was not consciously the core of their identity. In Acoma the power dynamics forced students to turn to their families for a positive sense of identity. In addition, because so many of the students' families in Acoma were struggling under harsh working conditions, the students knew that they could help their families through school because even just a high school diploma could get them out of the fields, whereas in Los Angeles a high school diploma would not translate into greater opportunities than students' parents had. In Acoma, therefore, most students grounded their social identities in their families and the need to improve their financial conditions, and they strove to address these needs through their own schooling. In short, the racial-political climate defined their identity options in significant ways along racial lines. The severity of this climate forced most students to turn to their families, whose experiences in this climate in turn led the students to build their social identities around school identities. Thus, the students in Acoma struggled with a great deal of internal turmoil and conflict that was not as evident among the Los Angeles students. Overall, the history of Chicana/o resistance and alternative explanations allows students in East Los Angeles to challenge the racial-political climate there, which defines them in negative terms. In Acoma, students' identities are shaped by the same forces, but the lack of alternatives to their negative portrayal demands that most students withdraw from the public sphere and rely on their families for their sense of social identity.

As the students in Acoma suggest, the connections between Chicana/o students' social identities and their school lives and outcomes are strong. First, school itself is an essential element in identity formation. Through the demonstration of the power dynamics that dominate school life—as illustrated in the example of racial profiling—Chicana/o students typically learn that the school understands them through their supposed racial characteristics. Most students must shape their own identities in response to these experiences. Many of the students in Los Angeles lashed out at these processes and rebelled in school, resulting in their school failure and marginalization. Other students felt they had little hope of succeeding in school because of these messages and simply tuned out, just squeaking by for much of their school lives. Some students, however, used this racialized reality as their inspiration for pursuing school success as they strove to prove wrong those who questioned their abilities. In Acoma many students simply tried to ignore the racialized messages conveyed to them in school, and they sought school success. In fact, many of these students faced psychological turmoil because their efforts to succeed demanded some degree of acceptance of the racial profiling of Chicanas/os in Acoma. A few of them also attempted to turn this racialization on its head and use it as the driving force behind their pursuits of educational empowerment.

FIGHTING BACK AND MENTORS

In the end, whatever their identities and whatever their school lives were like, all of the Chicana/o students who participated in these projects took on identities as fighters. Several in fact described themselves as fighting against racism and other obstacles to attain their goals. In some way, they each responded to the power dynamics that created border identities for them. All of the students also recognized that school was the path toward winning their fights, although many did not know how to connect their roles in school to their central identities in realistic ways.

For students in both Acoma and Los Angeles, one other factor is essential in understanding both their identity development and their school performance: mentorship. The most successful students were those who had been mentored through their schooling and had help in making the transition to the next level of schooling. Similarly, the students with the most positive and strongest identities were those who had been helped to understand and deal with the forces that shaped their identities. Most compelling of all is that the students who had mentorship that linked identity issues and school issues seemed to be the most successful and the most dedicated to their schooling. They were also the most self-assured and confident in their own identities.

This is the ultimate message of this book: identity and schooling are intimately connected, and Chicana/o student success is significantly enhanced when students receive mentorship that actively addresses this relationship. It is not that students who did better found mentorship, but rather that students who found mentorship—specifically mentorship that linked school and identity issues—developed the means by which to succeed in school.

The first two sections of this book described some of the unique experiences, identities, and outcomes of Chicana/o students in each context. Clearly, these students have multiple possibilities. At the same time, each of these students fits into the framework described here. The racial-political climate in each community shaped the way teachers understood and interacted with the Chicana/o students and how the students understood themselves and their schooling. These factors in turn affected the identity development of the students. Because this process occurred around school life, identity also affected students' approaches to school. For this reason, identity and school outcomes were closely connected for all of the students in Acoma and Los Angeles, although the processes were always unique.

EIGHT

CHICANA/O STUDENT
EDUCATIONAL EMPOWERMENT

The students themselves spent a great deal of time making suggestions about how to address the needs they laid out in our discussions. Mari's suggestions in the following interview excerpt unpacked much of what has been covered in the first two sections of this book:

> I'd reinvent the whole school system. Make sure there's mentors there and have people that care. And I don't want any teachers that are too tired to teach kids. If they don't wanna teach, just quit the job, find something else, weed 'em out. Have people that care and make sure even to reach out to the *cholitos*. They're good people too. . . . They have respect and it's in there, and a lot of people don't see that. And it pisses me off when some of the teachers are gonna right away judge them. These are good kids. But if you're gonna judge 'em wrong, of course they're gonna retaliate against you. So *para mí* [for me] that's a big thing, 'cause I guess that's why I wanna go to high school, [to] grab some of those kids, sit their butts down, and tell 'em.

As mentioned in Chapter 4, Mari wanted to see schools that care for and nurture Chicana/o students. As her first sentence above suggests, attaining this goal is a difficult task that requires, in her eyes, a reinvention of the entire school system. In the introduction this was a pivotal issue, because much of the past research on Chicana/o schooling relies heavily on proposals for dramatic, systemic change to address Chicana/o students' educational needs.

Schools are not the only site from which Chicana/o empowerment might emerge, however. This chapter focuses on the multiple strategies for addressing the needs of Chicana/o students that have been uncovered throughout this book. The students described realistic ways of addressing Chicana/o students' needs that individuals, communities, and even schools can initiate immediately. This chapter presents issues relevant to parents, teachers, and peers who want to help Chicana/o students, and then it emphasizes an intervention program that can more comprehensively assist Chicana/o youth in empowering themselves. These ideas are presented in such a way that they can be adopted immediately by Chicana/o youth and their communities in any context. The process described is powerful because it not only allows students to address the issues covered in this book but also helps them develop strategies for meeting the many needs they might have in schools.

PARENTS AND FAMILY

Despite the traditional portrayal of Mexican parents as unconcerned about education, this was rarely the case among the families of students who participated in these two projects. In fact, parents were often Chicana/o students' strongest supporters or motivators for school success. The students discussed two kinds of familial support. The first, and the most common, is observational influences. Many students find motivation and strength from seeing the struggles and commitment of their families to provide their children with opportunities to achieve success. Parents who strive to motivate their children should know that just by setting an example of hard work and commitment to helping the family, they are having an important effect on their children.

Even more helpful to students is direct influence; when parents reinforce these messages by explaining their own struggles and the need for their children to take advantage of all the educational opportunities they might have. This direct influence does not require that parents have succeeded in or completed school themselves, but simply that they make it a conscious part of their parenting to reinforce the importance of school with their children. This type of support is extremely helpful to Chicana/o youth.

Parents of Chicana/o youth are often burdened with multiple jobs and a great deal of stress in their efforts to support their families. For many of them, providing an observational influence and an occasional direct reinforcement are all that they can do. Parents should know, however, that their children often need other kinds of help too. In particular, Chicana/o youth often embark on their identity struggles alone and need guidance in making sense of the link between their identities and the world of school. The dominant pattern that the students brought up was the difficulty of making sense of their own familial desires for school success along with the messages they received about the link between race and educational ability. While parents want their children to do well in school, schools as institutions and school staff as individuals often tell these youth that they will not succeed and even that they are not wanted in school. These conflicting messages are hard to make sense of, and many Chicana/o youth simply give up trying to do so, because they do not know how to overcome these low and negative expectations. Immigrant parents and those with little formal schooling may not always be familiar with these issues, but they should know that whatever assistance they can provide in their children's efforts to establish a positive identity can go a long way to helping their children advance in their schooling.

One way parents can help is by discussing their own lives and struggles with their children. Some of my conversations with parents have helped me understand why these kinds of discussions between parents and their children do not often happen. Many parents do not want to talk about their experiences with discrimination, for example, because they hope that their children will never have to know what it feels like to be degraded in that way. They want to protect their children from the pain these experiences caused them. Unfortunately, as the students explained, many Chicana/o youth have to deal with these issues and often in even more complex ways than did their parents. Students who have parental assistance in making sense of the role of race in their lives are often the best prepared both for succeeding in school and for developing a strong identity.

Of course, students' identity struggles are not always related to race, and parents need to be just as attuned to helping their children deal with other issues that may be crucial. Certainly, some of the strongest and most successful Chicanas were those who had guidance from their mothers in dealing with the difficulties they would face as young women and as members of a racialized minority group. Parental guidance in dealing with the forces that shape life as a Chicana—that is, as both a young woman and a person of color—is much needed.

Furthermore, in attempting to help their children develop positive identities, parents can address any number of important aspects of identity, such as class and sexuality. Generational differences between parents and their children can be difficult to overcome as parents try to communicate with their children, especially when those differences are compounded with cultural differences, as, for example, those between Mexican parents and their American-raised children. Parents can, however, be aware of the issues that youth are facing in their lives and can find multiple ways of helping their children, such as looking for other potential mentors. Finally, as one student explained in Chapter 5, the values parents teach can greatly help their children deal with these issues. When parents help their children see that it is OK to stand up to injustice and to fight for fairness, it is much easier for their children to deal with the power conflicts that shape their lives.

Most students feel as if they have no one to talk to about their identity struggles. Whatever parents can do to help their children deal with their identity struggles will go a long way toward helping them succeed in school. The final sections of this chapter provide a model that parents can adapt to their own discussions with their children.

TEACHERS AND SCHOOL STAFF

Because the parents of Chicana/o youth often do not have extensive experience in or knowledge of the educational system, the students frequently rely heavily on teachers to help them choose their paths for pursuing school success. At all of the schools I worked in, Chicana/o students found a great deal of strength from positive interactions with their teachers. Students spoke fondly of simple things, like teachers who just showed they cared or who gave them positive encouragement. Teachers who are looking for ways to help Chicana/o students can begin with easy things, like providing these students with support, concern, and encouragement. This sort of help, of course, begins with earnestly asking the students themselves what they need from teachers.

Most Chicana/o students have few places to turn for guidance in navigating the educational system and, for example, in preparing and positioning themselves for the transition to subsequent levels in their schooling (e.g., college or even high school). Chicana/o students who received this type of guidance from teachers found it exceptionally helpful and explained that it facilitated their successful climb up the educational ladder. Typically, the students who had this support were lucky. That is, they just happened to find a teacher who took an interest in them and found the time to counsel them through school. None of the students spoke of formal guidance measures, such as assistance from counselors, that helped them prepare for educational advancement. Typically, counselors were a nonentity in Chicana/o students' lives, or when they did interact, students saw counselors as a barrier, for the counselors encouraged them to take classes that would not lead to educational success and even discouraged them from enrolling in classes that would prepare them for college.

A fundamental concern for Chicana/o students is that even when they had support from one or more teachers, negative interactions and conflicts with other school staff overrode the significance of that support. Some students found it difficult to believe in their own possibilities for success when they were psychologically attacked by others in the school. These attacks were often unconscious and even occurred in the name of normal policy and practice. Nevertheless, issues like tracking and differential enforcement of school policies felt like a slap in the face to many students who could not reconcile the support they received from a given teacher with these other, negative experiences. More typical, however, was the student who did not receive teacher support and still had to deal with what felt like a racially unjust or hostile climate.

One issue that emerged in all of the sites was the silencing of Chicana/o students. Living much of their lives in schools in which they were devalued, many students indicated that they had little opportunity to be truly heard. As some of the examples mentioned suggest, no one heard their concerns about tracking or the unequal enforcement of school rules. No one heard their desire for a curriculum that did not degrade their heritage and that instead addressed their historical struggles and perseverance.

Teachers, counselors, and other school staff who want to help Chicana/o students succeed in school should consider innovative ways to address each of these issues. These Chicana/o students need support, encouragement, guidance, the opportunity to develop their own voices, the chance to learn their own history, and help in dealing with the messages they receive in and out of school that tell them they cannot succeed. As with the parents, teachers who can help students deal with their identity development within the context of its relationship to their educational goals can provide the best support for them. A model for doing this type of work is discussed in the final sections of the chapter.

School personnel are typically overburdened already, however. While we might want teachers to be able to do all of these things and while we should applaud those who do, we cannot expect this response from teachers, particularly given the climates in which they often have to teach. Still, schools that are concerned with addressing the needs of their Chicana/o students should look for ways to address these issues. Suggestions for doing so follow in subsequent sections of this chapter.

PEERS

In the past, a great deal of emphasis has been placed on the role of peers in influencing Chicanas/os and other youth to engage in negative behaviors (e.g., gang involvement). In the projects covered in this book, the Chicana/o students told a very different story. Few discussed peer pressure that led them into negative behaviors. More typically, students who did get involved in gangs and in other behaviors often deemed negative explained that they had developed negative views on school and their own opportunities and had gravitated to others who shared these beliefs. Furthermore, all of the students who later withdrew from these activities were able to do so with little difficulty, contrary to the typical portrayal of gang resistance and pressure on members to maintain strong ties.

Since parents had limited experience and knowledge as to how to help their children through school, and since most students did not have mentors or even teachers who provided guidance through school, many students depended on friends to provide a support system in their pursuit of their educational goals. Some students had just one friend who supported them or served as a role model by working hard in school. Other students had a group of friends who were all pursuing educational success and thus supported and motivated each other and even provided an atmosphere of friendly competition that helped push them along.

Formal student organizations were most often cited by the students as an essential form of peer support. In particular, MEChA played a crucial role for many. The organization served multiple functions for students. One of the things students most appreciated about it is that it provided a comfortable environment in which they could interact with other Chicanas/os who were pursuing school success. The students explained that in MEChA it was good to be Mexican and to be trying to do well in school, a feeling that they did not experience anywhere else. In addition, MEChA and the environment that it fostered acknowledged the issues that many Chicana/o students found themselves forced to address. In particular, these students did not have to explain to members of MEChA that race was an important issue in their school lives, because others understood this and did not question it. Although MEChA is known for its radicalized politics, the students typically emphasized the importance of its function of providing a supportive social network. What was also helpful for some students was their exposure to students who were at higher levels of school than they were. Cesar, for example, was able to get guidance and support from community college students through MEChA while he was still in high school.

The greatest limitation of MEChA as an educational support system is that the guidance students received came from others who were still struggling to make sense of the world of school and to carve a path for themselves and others to follow. Although MEChA faced limits as an educational support system, its role in the development of positive identities for Chicana/o youth was unmatched by any other form of support students had. This finding speaks to the need to create comfortable spaces for Chicana/o youth to discuss the issues that they confront as racialized subjects in the schools and in their communities. Of course, MEChA cannot serve this function for all students. Some students do not find it helpful, and others find the identity politics that often prevail in MEChA to be problematic. Other forms of support networks will be valuable to other Chicana/o youth. The concluding sections of this chapter integrate this type of support into innovative models that may be used to help Chicana/o youth empower themselves.

ALTERNATIVE EDUCATIONAL ENVIRONMENTS

As Mari explained at the beginning of the chapter, in an ideal world Chicana/o students would get the type of support MEChA provides (to some of them) from the schools themselves. Because of the power of racial hegemony, however, this is usually unrealistic. A few students, however, found environments that came close—in alternative schools. These nontraditional schools were small, less rigid, and much more student-centered. Two of the students who attended alternative schools received a great deal of support from both teachers and peers. They found strength in the mentorship they received from their teachers and also from the ability to develop friendships with them. They also appreciated the opportunity to express their individuality in unique settings. In one student's school, students met in small groups to discuss what they were struggling with and needed to share with others.

What is most compelling about these examples is that alternative schools are typically seen as last chances for troubled students who would not otherwise graduate. They are seen as less intellectually challenging and as an easy way to get a diploma. The students in the study who attended alternative schools, however, were very successful in those schools and were admitted to universities afterward.

Although alternative schools are not a focus of this chapter or the book, the experiences of these two students suggests that innovative approaches to organizing schooling are one means of addressing the needs of Chicana/o students. Charter schools, for example, might be a powerful means of confronting the issues raised by students through the culture, policies, and curriculum created in new schools. The following two sections provide models that can be integrated into these facets of alternative and charter schools. Having these models is particularly important because many charter schools have difficulty with approaching education in truly innovative forms.

A FRAMEWORK FOR CHICANA/O YOUTH EMPOWERMENT BASED ON EDUCATIONAL AND IDENTITY NEEDS

This book has considered two critical aspects of the lives of Chicana/o youth: schooling and identity development. In Chapter 7 we saw how these two arenas of students' lives meld through the forces that shape students' experiences and outcomes. That analysis, along with the student insights from Chapters 3 and 6, are used here as the foundation for describing interventions that can be transformative for Chicana/o youth.

As discussed above, school is something that most Chicana/o youth want to succeed in, for they are both excited about learning early in their lives and motivated by their parents to do well in school. In fact, all of the students in the study explained that they had been excited about learning in elementary school. It was not until junior high that many of the students began to lose interest, when problems in their schools became more apparent to them.

The students exposed how power defined both their identity development and their schooling. Power constructed their identities when the students were confronted with their low status in a given realm of their social lives. Most often, this process took place after they realized that Chicanas/os were devalued in their schools, because they were then confronted with the need to make sense of this situation, given their interest in doing well in school and the reality that they were Chicana/o. Because these confrontations most often occurred in the school itself, students simultaneously needed to make sense of the role of power in school. Doing that was particularly difficult because the students' families and communities were typically outsiders, and the efforts of the students to understand their own role in school were heavily influenced by those who had power within the school.

Power was not wielded against Chicanas/os simply on the basis of race, however. In addition, some Chicana/o students did not experience or understand the school as a racialized site. Nevertheless, power typically defined both identity and school for these students. Students who did not experience racialized disempowerment usually defined their identities in another arena of their lives in which they were disempowered, such as gender, class, or sexuality. Other students who lived in a highly racialized world often surrendered to familial contexts for their identity development as a means of survival. Again, for all of these students, identity was intricately tied to schooling because their disempowerment was understood or clarified through life in school. Furthermore, who they were was deeply connected to their lives in school.

Helping Chicana/o youth empower themselves therefore demands interventions that address their identities and their educational needs, because both are shaped by the power dynamics they face. Students need the opportunity to discuss, analyze, and understand how they can achieve educational success within the contexts in which they live, as well as to integrate their sense of identity into these efforts. These interventions have to be grounded in mentorship. The students in the study frequently discussed their need for active guidance in their lives. Furthermore, the students who were most successful were always those who had had a mentor who helped them negotiate their educational and identity development simultaneously.

A MODEL FOR A CHICANA/O EMPOWERMENT INTERVENTION PROGRAM

As this book has shown, context is critical to understanding the world of Chicana/o youth. No model can be developed that will "work" for every Chicana/o everywhere. Nevertheless, there are key strategies that can help most students develop their own processes for empowering themselves through their schooling.

Voice

Many Chicana/o students are socialized by the schools into a voicelessness that is often difficult for them to acknowledge. Because they do not know anything else, they rarely even realize how the school silences them and their stories. Educational empowerment for Chicanas/os begins with helping these students claim their voices and recognize their own insights on their lives and schooling. For example, students can begin by talking about what needs to change in schools. Usually students are trained to believe that if anything needs to change in schooling, it is the students. Thus, when students are given the chance to analyze and critique schooling, it opens the floodgates through which their own voices pour. The specific way this analysis is conducted must be grounded in the experiences of the students and their communities. Not only do students appreciate the chance to share their insights, but, as they have told me, they also find it empowering.

Power

The process of students claiming their voice requires an analysis of power. This analysis is critical to the empowerment of Chicana/o youth. They need to see beyond the immediate incidents and problems they identify in schools (tracking, low expectations, and so on) and to understand the larger forces that support these practices. Students need the chance to carefully unpack the way in which power shapes daily life in schools, as they begin to think about how they themselves can lay claim to power in their own lives. As they start to stake out a space for their own voices, they will recognize how power has been used to keep them silenced. An in-depth analysis of power will help them think critically about the forces at work in their lives.

Identity

As students begin to understand how power is manifested in their lives, they can then carefully analyze their own identities. They can critically look at who they are in their world and the role of power in shaping that, so that they can understand the specific external forces (e.g., the local social power structure, patriarchy within the family, and so on) that have shaped their identities and experiences.

This process is necessary so that the students can then begin to envision who they want to be in terms of their identities and also in their educational and professional lives. Mentors can help students realize that—despite the forces that may have worked against them in establishing their own voices and identities—they can use their evolving understandings to create identities that are grounded in the pursuit of school success and that rely on their insights and critical-thinking skills to help them achieve those goals. Mentors can also share their own strategies with students.

Helping students understand their own identities is essential in their educational empowerment. The students need to understand how their school lives are shaped by their identities and how these identities are shaped by a power structure that attaches messages of intellectual ability and potential to specific identities based on little more than appearance. They will see how power itself hides the inequities involved in this process and constructs these inequities as if they were natural, silencing the voices of the students who become victims of this reality. As the students come to understand these things, they will then also recognize their ability to reconstruct their identities, with mentors providing them with models for doing that. The students highlighted in Chapters 3 and 6 made this point powerfully, despite their lack of formalized mentorship. Mentors can tap into the creativity of students and help them, for example, develop affirming *rasquache* identities that allow them to empower themselves in the face of these conflicts and contradictions.

Holistic Identity Work

The process of students beginning to take control over their own identities and over the role of school and power in their lives is demanding work. It requires a great deal of care and responsiveness to the needs of each student. These requirements become even more important as students are then guided through a more detailed analysis of their identities. In looking at their lives, the students will identify the facets of their identities that are most central to them at that given moment in their lives. However, there are other facets of their identities of which they may not be as aware. For example, young Chicano males almost never see the role of gender in shaping their identities, and yet gender is an essential factor in defining who they are and shaping their experiences.

The next phase of this empowerment process, therefore, allows the students to hunt for the unseen forces that shape their lives and identities. This process involves not only looking at aspects of identity that may be unconscious but also considering those facets of identity that students have chosen to suppress. For some females, for example, the gender dynamics they confront are so powerful and so deeply woven into their daily lives that they choose, sometimes consciously and sometimes unconsciously, to push them out of their voiced understanding of their identities. Mixed-race youth, as another example, are often better able to suppress their racial identities—because of their physical appearance, for instance—but this very suppression can be both psychologically demanding and painful.[1] Similarly, as Chela noted in Chapter 6, many

Chicana/o youth and even their families try to suppress their ethnicity in order to facilitate their own efforts to succeed in school. Chicana/o youth need help dealing with the identities that they consider central and those that they have chosen to suppress or of which they are just not conscious. To help the students gain a more complete self-awareness, mentors can work closely with them to help them identify aspects of their lives that they have chosen to ignore or conceal. These unconscious and suppressed identities may be related to gender, class, sexuality, physical appearance, or other areas in which power influences their lives.

Students need the opportunity to more clearly understand who they are, how that shapes their lives in and out of school, and how this knowledge can assist them in achieving their goals. Chicanas, for example, can learn ways of connecting with other young women to develop strategies for succeeding in school, as well as strategies for helping their parents understand the importance of their pursuing a college education. Chicanos can serve as a support system for their sisters, partners, and mothers who are striving to achieve educational goals, and they can also develop strategies for dealing with the stress that accompanies their own gender roles and expectations as they begin to develop new roles with the women in their lives.

If students are to truly understand themselves, they must be encouraged to look at these issues and their effects on their lives. They will then be able to construct holistic identities that confront any of the psychological trauma they may be covering up in unconscious and suppressed identities as part of survival strategies.

Linking Identity to School Trajectories

The final aspect of this model is allowing students the opportunity to develop plans for achieving school success that are grounded in their own identities and realities. Mentors can help students recognize their strengths and the skills they need to develop and map out plans for achieving specific educational goals. The key to this final step is to help students understand their own power, which they will have demonstrated by going through this whole process. This understanding then becomes the foundation for helping them confidently envision the future they seek. A key component of this last step is to help students develop plans for making successful transitions from one phase of schooling to the next (e.g., high school to college) and for gaining access to continued mentorship as they make those transitions. As the students in the study made clear, all this work needs to be grounded in the realities the students live in the hallways and classrooms of their schools.

Responding to Students' Specific Needs

Clearly, the foregoing is only an outline of a process that can help Chicana/o students address the issues that were raised by those students who contributed to this book. The process has to be shaped by the students themselves and by their experiences, families, communities, and histories. The issues these students face vary among communities, schools, and individuals, and they shift every year, but this book and Chicana/o educational history tell us that all of these issues can be addressed within this model. During the process, students and mentors need to decide which issues they want to tackle and the best ways to do this. The students in this book, for example, frequently discussed the need to learn their own history and the link between their lives and this history. This might be work that the students and mentors could do one-on-one or in larger groups. As students in the study suggest, this historical analysis is particularly important because without this knowledge, Chicanas/os do not know the strength and perseverance of their ancestors and they are less able to challenge the mainstream explanation of Chicanas/os as intellectually and culturally deficient. However, this historical analysis may take many different forms. Every student and every group will have a different set of factors and forces that influence them and that they need to address in their own empowerment process.

Furthermore, this is not a process that has a clear ending. Not only will this process need to be repeated throughout the students' lives, but it also might not take place in clear steps. At times, students may be taking on several of these tasks at once.

Finally, it is important to note that anyone can engage in this process. It could be an approach taken on by a school or a given teacher. It could also be facilitated at a community center or by a student group. Most important, it is something that parents can do with their children. Although this process may be developed into organized programs, it can just as easily be undertaken informally in regular conversations within a family or group of friends. The mentors can be professionals, college students, peers, parents, other family members, or teachers. As the students in the study suggested, this work should begin as early as possible (by junior high school at the latest) and continue throughout students' schooling. Some people may be concerned that going through this process can open students up to painful realizations, but our work has to help students recognize the benefits of their awareness and has to show them all the positive things that can be attained through this process. Furthermore, we must recognize that most students are already dealing with a great deal of psychological turmoil that they often are not addressing at all.

The students who contributed to this book actually demonstrated how this process can work. They used the discussions in which we engaged as an opportunity to make sense of their world as they fought to change it for the better. They showed the power and intellectual depth of Chicana/o students and served as visionaries as they sought to map out strategies for addressing the issues they faced. It will clearly take visionaries to overcome the long-standing problems that Chicanas/os have faced in the educational system. This book has been an effort to direct the work of visionaries and to push them to think in revolutionary ways about the educational work we must do.

PUSHING BOUNDARIES: INNOVATIVE APPROACHES TO EDUCATIONAL WORK WITH *RAZA* YOUTH

The previous section outlined a process for helping Chicana/o youth to educationally empower themselves. Although it was necessarily sketchy in order to allow for the context-specific needs of any given group of students, it did not describe the basic principles of this work. Although those of us in Chicana/o Studies have done little research on such principles, my own recent involvement with *MAESTR@S* has allowed me to develop a preliminary framework.

MAESTR@S is an institute designed to work toward the educational self-determination and liberation of *raza*. Our work is grounded in the notion that we need radical teaching methods that fundamentally challenge the way teaching has been traditionally done in schools. Our work responds to the need—identified by Mari at the beginning of this chapter—for a complete rethinking of schools. It also strives to confront the fundamental educational contradictions that Angel exposed in Chapter 6, whereby schooling and student success often have nothing to do with intellectual exploration and instead focus on simplistic regurgitation of information. Furthermore, since the empowerment of the disenfranchised is antithetical to the goals of universities, *MAESTR@S* recognizes that efforts at empowerment must emerge from the community itself, as they always have. For this reason, our work is rooted in community networks and not in formal educational, institutional processes such as those at a university. What follows is a brief analysis of the key ideas behind the *MAESTR@S* project.

The central component of the work *MAESTR@S* does is to view the students as resource-rich. This component dictates that students must be at the center of the learning process. Putting them at the center by emphasizing their own resources in turn requires a constant challenge to conventional educational processes.

Chicanas/os rely on a system of knowledge and learning that is thousands of years old. Although it has not been formally passed on in U.S. schools, Chicana/o families teach this knowledge system to their children as they have for generations. This system is based on the central constructs of living in the Chicana/o community, including such ideas as the importance of *educación*,[2] *familia, respeto, comúnidad, historia,* and elders. In Chapter 3, Ernesto helped us understand the need to look within Chicana/o communities for the power to make change. This is the approach that *MAESTR@S* fosters. The goal of this analysis is not to describe a static system of knowledge, for that knowledge is constantly evolving and adapting to its context. The critical idea that *MAESTR@S* attempts to demonstrate through our work is that students bring this wealth of knowledge with them into the classroom and that it does not necessarily fit into the conventional educational model of schools, which sees students as empty vessels that need to be filled with knowledge from schoolteachers. Our work attempts to foster *raza* literacy—a literacy grounded in a Chicana/o system of knowledge—and to use that literacy as a means toward educational empowerment in the schools.

MAESTR@S' work asks that we begin with the students and allow them to shape their learning in terms of both process and content. According to conventional schooling, teachers and schools have to make all the decisions about learning. In the end, this is the very idea that denies students their voice. The *MAESTR@S* model suggests that students can make almost any decision that is needed with regard to learning. As we have seen in specific instances in our work, students can decide what we study, how we do that work, and what we do with the knowledge we acquire.

MAESTR@S' work is also centered in process. Content is often irrelevant, simply because strong content can easily become useless with poor teaching, while strong teaching can attack poor content in ways that are empowering to students. We have found that true educational work focuses on processes for developing skills that allow participants to understand and transform themselves and their world. By continually emphasizing education as process, we show that transformative education *is* social justice rather than being *about* social justice. *MAESTR@S* engages in consciousness-raising that emerges from a shared revolutionary ethic that is grounded in the realities of *raza* youth, like those who shared their stories in this book. Our work simply requires that we continually push people to challenge the way in which educational conventions live within us and to examine and critique the educational processes in which we engage.

Finally, we have learned in *MAESTR@S* that our work cannot be written into rigid directives that readers can simply pick up and implement.[3] It has to be learned in the way that knowledge in Chicana/o communities is learned. It must be learned by engaging in it as members of a community of learners.

These ideas are vital to the educational empowerment process discussed earlier in this chapter. Readers who are interested in engaging in such a process have to recognize that they must do it *with* Chicana/o communities, parents, and teachers and not *for* them. We must be willing to engage in a learning process together through which we struggle to understand what has happened in our lives so that we can work to change it if need be. This is revolutionary work that demands as its foundation, as Che Guevara expressed it, our commitment to love—of ourselves and of Chicana/o youth.

EPILOGUE

Through my work with *raza* youth, I have learned the power of Che Guevara's emphasis on the importance of love in social change (mentioned at the end of Chapter 8). This love is not the love of cheap novels and trashy TV shows. It is a deeper, spiritual love that is bonded to the realities of twenty-first-century oppression and that demands our work with others for justice. I elaborate on these ideas through the examples of a movie and an alternative school.

Follow Me Home is an innovative independent film that analyzes the meaning and role of race in the United States. I have recently seen two showings of this film, and both times stayed to hear its writer and director, Peter Bratt, discuss his work. In talking about the impact of racism on people of color, he spoke of his work with Native American elders. They told him of a concept that they call the soul wound. This wound first emerged as a result of the dehumanization that occurred during the conquest and colonization of North America. The dehumanization of the indigenous peoples of this continent left not only physical scars but also spiritual ones. Bratt explained that this wound has been reborn in each generation since the conquest.

When he said this, emotions flowed to the surface of my consciousness that are still hard to describe. I realized that much of what I felt deep inside of me came from places I had lost touch with. I knew that, in my own world, the concept of the soul wound had been very real. I had seen it in friends, my family members, and those who I had worked with in Chicana/o communities across the West. I saw how the memory of our ancestors lives deep within our consciousness.

That night I understood this work with Chicana/o youth much more clearly. Although the realizations I am describing have no basis in science or fact as those terms are typically defined in this society, these realizations have become critical to my understanding of the lives of the Chicana/o youth with whom I worked. These youth continue to reel from soul wounds of which most of them are unaware. Most of them are struggling to find comfort with the meaning of their race and ethnicity in their lives. Some are quite comfortable with their racial identity and yet are still struggling to find a way to be comfortable in a society that challenges their worth. Others are struggling to find a way to acknowledge their race and ethnicity after trying to ignore or overcome its importance by blending in, but they have paid a heavy emotional, psychological, and spiritual price along the way. Of course, there is a wide spectrum of students, each with a unique understanding of identity. Still, the concept of the soul wound seems to capture the struggles I heard them describe and those that I saw in their eyes, heard in the tone of their voices, or simply felt hanging in the air as we spoke.

The elders Bratt spoke of told him that the reborn victims of these wounds have to find new ways both to understand and to transcend the legacy of the conquest. In some ways, that is the message of this book. Chicana/o youth and their families and communities have to seek ways to understand their immediate experiences through the history that is embedded, but often hidden, in their consciousness. They have to find ways to reconcile the contradictions that often define their very existence. This effort involves mentorship and guidance in terms of education and identity, but it also involves working to heal soul wounds. Through this process, Chicana/o communities and all of us connected to them may understand how history and race and other facets of our social lives define our psychological and spiritual beings and how we can honor and transcend this. As Bratt explained, "The heart of the race issue is a spiritual issue."

Recently, I witnessed how these ideas can and must be placed into schooling contexts. The Foundry is an alternative high school in San José, California, that serves youth who are at extreme risk for failing and many of whom who have histories of substance abuse. The staff base much of what they do on teachings and "informal" educational practices in Native American communities. Their approach is truly holistic. In their educational work, they connect the spiritual, emotional, psychological, and physical facets of their students' lives by spending a significant amount of time doing work that most schools would consider nonacademic. The result is that the students become stronger and better people, with skills for overcoming their substance abuse and for being good people in all aspects of their lives. Although this is the most important product of their approach, the other powerful effect is that the students do phenomenal schoolwork. Their thinking, writing, and speaking abilities exceed those of most students in high schools and even in the college where I work.

The connection between the Foundry and this book is deep, although perhaps not overt. The Chicana/o students who participated in these projects were dealing with the complexities and contradictions of their lives on many different levels: psychologically, emotionally, spiritually, and even physically. The ways in which race, gender, sexuality, class, and other facets of their identities had shaped them often left them struggling to find affirming ways of dealing with their realities. The book focuses on the possibility of contextualized mentoring to help them through this process. The point of this final idea is to recognize that this contextualized mentoring must also move into the realms of emotions and spirit, for example, to help these youth do the necessary work for healing and then transforming their lives and communities.

The impact and manifestation of twenty-first-century racial hegemony is exhibited in deep and complex ways, and the concept of the soul wound helps us consider the full weight of the challenge before us. I share this idea now to urge readers to look into these areas as they embark on efforts to help Chicana/o youth educationally empower themselves.

Clearly, this is not a conventional intellectual argument. The strength of the research conducted for this book stands on its own. The central ideas that underlie this work have a validity grounded in Chicana/o realities that cannot be adequately understood or questioned with mainstream academic approaches. This final spiritual message emerged from those realities, although only long after the projects were over and in a way that the students and I were not able to fully absorb at the time. My hope is that this insight resonates with the reader and moves us all toward a more holistic means of pursuing the goals that the students urged us to take on as our own.

NOTES

INTRODUCTION

1. The percentage of Latina/o youth in poverty, 34.4 percent, is more than double that of white youth (15.1 percent). The number of Latina/o youths who live in economic and social jeopardy, however, far exceeds these formal poverty figures.

2. Acuña (1998) provides a compelling analysis of the lack of objectivity in academic work and even in the calls for objectivity themselves.

3. The analysis of past research discussed in the next two sections is by no means exhaustive. Key works are discussed to reveal trends in the research.

4. See Pizarro and Vera (2001) for a more in-depth analysis of this research. Unfortunately, the 1990s boom in this field has ended, and in recent years much less work has been done in this area.

5. During this same period, the dropout rate for whites decreased from 12.3 percent to 7.7 percent, and that for blacks dropped from 21.3 percent to 13.8 percent (National Center for Education Statistics 1999). Unfortunately, these data do not provide information specific to the "Hispanic" subgroup of Chicanas/os.

6. As some of these sources explain, official figures often misrepresent the severity of this situation by undercounting dropouts on technicalities that ignore the simple fact that they are not in school.

7. In California, Hispanics constituted 27.5 percent of public school students in 1986 and 37.9 percent in 1994 (National Center for Education Statistics 1996). The vast majority of those students were of Mexican descent.

8. The work of Matute-Bianchi (1986) is perhaps the most widely cited of this research. While she provided an important application of Chicana/o (and Japanese) youth to Ogbu's cultural-ecological model, her analyses focused on static Chicana/o identities without considering the external forces that shaped them. Although she did mention the importance of such forces, she focused

more on student choices in placing themselves in different identity categories, and in so doing, she betrayed the complexity of the Chicana/o experience. In short, Matute-Bianchi explained that Chicanas/os exploited their ethnicity (usually leading to failure) or subdued it (usually leading to their success) in response to their situational context, but she did not describe the continuous interactions that occurred between the context and the choices students are often compelled to make. In contrast, researchers who have engaged in qualitative analyses have questioned the idea that academic and ethnic identities are mutually exclusive (Anderson and Herr 1992; Mehan, Hubbard, and Villanueva 1994).

9. Readers interested in these ideas should see earlier work in which I discuss Social Justice Research in detail (Pizarro 1998).

10. I have used a pseudonym because the small size of the area makes it easy to know the schools discussed.

11. To maintain the anonymity of the students, their real names are never used. In some places, names are simply cut and in others pseudonyms are used. This is also the case for the places and names of others that students discussed. Similarly, the names of their schools and towns have also been changed (although East Los Angeles is big enough that it was not necessary to conceal this name).

12. Descriptions given by students of their parents' jobs and their families' economic conditions were used to determine class.

13. A few students did not provide information about their birthplace, so these numbers might be slightly larger.

CHAPTER 1

1. Throughout this chapter, students' analyses are discussed as a whole rather than at each site because the general patterns that emerged held constant at the high school, community college, and university levels. Any differences in the findings at the sites are mentioned throughout.

2. It is essential to note that this analysis focused on students' conscious understandings of their identities. Many facets of identity have effects on students of which they may not be aware (unconscious identities). This issue is discussed in depth in Part 3.

3. Other identity researchers have noted these potential distinctions both in theoretical discussions and in analyses of quantitative data (Gutiérrez 1989; J. Rodriguez and Gurin 1990).

4. This example also illustrates the intricacies involved in the formation of gang identities, for this student was involved in gangs during his high school years. Although such identities are fairly uncommon for the vast majority of Chicana/o youth, those who form identities around location and gangs are responding to unique experiences with, and manifestations of, power in their daily lives.

CHAPTER 2

1. The translation for "Chino" is "Chinese," as in "Chinese person," but the term is commonly used among Chicanas/os to signify Asians in general.

2. Richard Rodriguez (1982) and others have pointed out that the discomfort of Mexicana/o parents in this society often leads them to make their homes sanctuaries from the United States and/or to withdraw from any unnecessary contact with the non-Mexican world. This approach often creates distance between parents and their Chicana/o children, leading to more individuality in the children.

3. This is a Spanglish term that is a derogatory reference to someone who is Irish.

4. *Cholas* and *cholos* are Chicana/o gang members.

5. Other researchers have described this process in other areas. Valdés provides a perfect example as she describes a student who was struggling with her negative classification as a marginal ESL student: "Her sense of identity and her presentation of self to her peers required that she not accept the judgment of her teachers about who she was and what she could do. Becoming even more rebellious and outspoken, she joined a gang, started fights, and angrily moved about the school" (1998, 9–10).

6. For Chicanas, gender is a particularly significant identity arena that should not be ignored just because it was not significant in some students' conversations. Gender is of great importance to many Chicanas in the project, and yet they often incorporate it into their racial identity or give it less priority because of the gender problems they see within their own communities. As Chicanas age, however, gender often takes on an even greater significance than race.

CHAPTER 3

1. *"Veteranos"* refers to older gang members, who are considered the ultimate authority by young Chicana/o gang members and wannabes.

2. The "truck" refers to food trucks that are often present in areas where Chicanas/os work and live. They are similar to food trucks that supply construction sites and other working-class job sites, but their menus cater to their Chicana/o clientele. "Dickies" are work pants that were integrated into the cholo attire in the 1970s. Gangbangers and wannabes often wear them oversized, with sharp creases.

3. Marcos is one of the leaders of the Zapatista revolt in Chiapas, Mexico, in which a unified indigenous front is renewing the cry of revolutionary leader Emiliano Zapata for land redistribution. "Todos somos Marcos" is a slogan used among the people that means, "We are all Marcos."

4. *"Mojado"* is a Spanish word used to describe an illegal alien, and although it means "wet," the most direct translation is the term "wetback."

CHAPTER 4

1. Several of the interviews in Part 2 were conducted in Spanish. For space reasons, they appear only in English. The translations are mine.

2. The two students who were struggling with their identities (and in a state of identity confusion) discussed the importance of school to them, although not in the context of helping their families, and another student did not focus on schooling in her discussion.

3. These three students seemed to differ from the other two mixed-race Chicanas/os. Perhaps the reason is that, of the two mixed-race students who had developed strong racial identities, one was clearly identifiable as Chicana because of her dark complexion and had been raised in an almost all-white context, and the other had been raised by a Chicana who always pushed him to care about and address Chicana/o issues.

CHAPTER 5

1. It is critical to note that most of the questions that led to the student responses covered in this chapter were general open-ended questions about important influences and experiences. The students themselves chose to focus on racial issues and other conflicts.

CHAPTER 6

1. Of course, we should acknowledge that MEChA itself is not a cure-all. This specific MEChA chapter was helpful to these women, but in other contexts MEChA may not provide the types of support that students need.

2. I have entered this excerpt exactly as it appeared in the journal entry.

CHAPTER 7

1. We should also consider the recent shift in the political climate, as Democrats and Republicans both make moves to sway the Latina/o vote in their favor. This is a political move to make a down payment on the future of these parties, because in the post–2000 census flurry of numbers revealing the rapid browning of the United States, the parties realized that Latinas/os will soon reshape the voting populace. What is often lost in the political analysis of this new trend is the simple fact that this increased attention has not translated into shifts in the popular portrayals or understandings of Chicanas/os, nor has it affected the issues described in this book that face so many Chicanas/os today.

CHAPTER 8

1. As the number of mixed-race Chicanas/os continues to increase, this issue will become even more important.

2. Valenzuela (1999) provides a helpful definition of *"educación"* in Chicana/o and Mexicana/o communities as "the family's role of inculcating in children a sense of moral, social, and personal responsibility [that] serves as the foundation for all other learning" (23) and "a foundational cultural construct that provides instructions on how one should live in the world" (21).

3. We have published key ideas to help people begin this work (Pizarro and Montoya 2002).

BIBLIOGRAPHY

Acuña, R. 1998. *Sometimes there is no other side: Chicanos and the myth of equality*. Notre Dame, IN: University of Notre Dame Press.

Almaguer, T. 1994. *Racial fault lines: The historical origins of white supremacy in California*. Berkeley and Los Angeles: University of California Press.

Alva, S. A., and A. M. Padilla. 1995. Academic invulnerability among Mexican-American students: A conceptual framework. *Journal of Educational Issues of Language Minority Students* 15:27–48.

Anderson, G., and K. Herr. 1992. The micro-politics of student voices: Moving from diversity of bodies to diversity of voices in schools. In *The new politics of race and gender: The 1992 yearbook of the politics of educational association*, ed. C. Marshall, 58–68. London: Falmer Press.

Anzaldúa, G. 1987. *Borderlands/La Frontera: The new mestiza*. San Francisco: Spinsters/Aunt Lute.

Apple, M. 1993. Constructing the "other": Rightist reconstructions of common sense. In *Race, identity, and representation in education*, ed. C. McCarthy and W. Critchlow, 24–39. New York: Routledge.

Applebome, P. 1997. Schools see re-emergence of "separate but equal." *New York Times*, April 8, A-10.

Arce, C. 1981. A reconsideration of Chicano culture and identity. *Daedalus* 110:171–191.

Arellano, A. R., and A. M. Padilla. 1996. Academic invulnerability among a select group of Latino university students. *Hispanic Journal of Behavioral Sciences* 18:485–507.

Atkinson, D. R., G. Morten, and D. W. Sue. 1998. *Counseling American minorities: A cross-cultural perspective*. 5th ed. Madison, WI: Brown and Benchmark.

Bennett, W. [Secretary of Education]. 1988. *American education, making it work: A report to the president and the American people*. April. Washington, DC: U.S. Government Printing Office.

Bernal, M., D. Saenz, and G. Knight. 1991. Ethnic identity and adaptation of Mexican American youths in school settings. *Hispanic Journal of Behavioral Sciences* 13:135–154.

Brice, A. E. 2002. *The Hispanic child: Speech, language, culture, and education.* Boston: Allyn and Bacon.

California Postsecondary Education Commission. 1994. *The state of the state's educational enterprise: An overview of California's diverse student population.* Sacramento, CA: California Postsecondary Education Commission.

Carter, T., and R. Segura. 1979. *Mexican Americans in school: A decade of change.* New York: College Entrance Examination Board.

Casas, J. M., and S. D. Pytluk. 1995. Hispanic identity development: Implications for research and practice. In *Handbook of multicultural counseling,* ed. J. G. Ponterotto, J. M. Casas, L. A. Suzuki, and C. M. Alexander, 155–180. Thousand Oaks, CA: Sage Publications.

Castillo, A. 1994. *Massacre of the dreamers: Essays on Xicanisma.* Albuquerque: University of New Mexico Press.

Chapa, J., and R. Valencia. 1993. Latino population growth, demographic characteristics, and educational stagnation: An examination of recent trends. *Hispanic Journal of Behavioral Sciences* 15:165–187.

Cervantes, L. D. 1994. Poem for the young white man who asked me how I, an intelligent, well-read person, could believe in the war between races. In *Unsettling America: An anthology of contemporary multicultural poetry,* ed. M. M. Gillan and J. Gillan, 248–249. New York: Penguin Books.

Cuéllar, I., L. C. Harris, and R. Jasso. 1980. An acculturation scale for Mexican American normal and clinical populations. *Hispanic Journal of Behavioral Sciences* 2:199–217.

Cuéllar, I., B. Nyberg, R. E. Maldonado, and R. E. Roberts. 1997. Ethnic identity and acculturation in a young adult Mexican-origin population. *Journal of Community Psychology* 25:535–549.

Deaux, K. 1993. Reconstructing Social Identity. *Personality and Social Psychology Bulletin, 19,* 4–12.

De León, A. 1983. *They called them greasers: Anglo attitudes toward Mexicans in Texas, 1821–1900.* Austin: University of Texas Press.

Duran, R. 1983. *Hispanics' education and background: Predictors of college achievement.* New York: College Entrance Examination Board.

Ethier, K., and K. Deaux. 1994. Negotiating social identity when contexts change: Maintaining identification and responding to threat. *Journal of Personality and Social Psychology* 67:243–251.

Franquiz, M. E. 2001. It's about YOUth! Chicano high school students revisioning their academic identity. In *The best for our children: Critical perspectives on literacy for Latino students,* ed. M. L. Reyes and J. J. Halcon, 213–228. New York: Teachers College Press.

Flores-Gonzalez, N. 2002. *School kids/street kids: Identity development in Latino students.* New York: Teachers College Press.

Gándara, P. 1995. *Over the ivy walls: The educational mobility of low-income Chicanos.* New York: State University of New York Press.

Garcia, E. E. 2001. *Hispanic education in the United States: Raíces y alas.* New York: Rowman and Littlefield Publishers.

García, I. M. 1997. *Chicanismo: The forging of a militant ethos among Mexican Americans.* Tucson: University of Arizona Press.

Gey, F. C., J. E. Oliver, B. Highton, D. Tu, and R. E. Wolfinger. 1992. *California Latina/Latino demographic handbook.* California Policy Seminar. Berkeley, CA: Regents of the University of California.

Gitlin, A. 1990. Educative research, voice, and school change. *Harvard Educational Review* 60:443–466.

———, ed. 1994. *Power and method: Political activism and educational research.* New York: Routledge.

Gitlin, A., M. Siegel, and K. Boru. 1989. The politics of method: From leftist ethnography to educative research. *Qualitative Studies in Education* 2:237–253.

Gonzalez, G. G. 1990. *Chicano education in the era of segregation.* Philadelphia: Balch Institute Press.

Gonzalez, M. L., A. Huerta-Macias, and J. V. Tinajero. 1998. *Educating Latino students: A guide to successful practice.* Lancaster, PA: Technomic Publishing Co.

Gutiérrez, L. 1989. Critical consciousness and Chicano identity: An exploratory analysis. In *Estudios Chicanos and the politics of community: Selected proceedings of the National Association of Chicano Studies,* 35–53. Ann Arbor, MI: McNaughton and Gunn Lithographers.

Hurtado, A., R. Gonzalez, and L. Vega. 1994. Social identification and the academic achievement of Chicano students. In *The educational achievement of Latinos: Barriers and successes,* ed. A. Hurtado and E. Garcia, 57–74. Santa Cruz, CA: Regents of the University of California.

Hurtado, S. 1994. Latino consciousness and academic success. In *The educational achievement of Latinos: Barriers and successes,* ed. A. Hurtado and E. Garcia, 17–56. Santa Cruz, CA: Regents of the University of California.

Knight, G., M. Bernal, M. Cota, C. Garza, and K. Ocampo. 1993. Family socialization and Mexican American identity and behavior. In *Ethnic identity: Formation and transmission among Hispanics and other minorities,* ed. M. Bernal and G. Knight, 105–130. Albany: State University of New York Press.

Koss-Chioino, J. D., and L. A. Vargas. 1999. *Working with Latino youth: Culture, development, and context.* San Francisco: Jossey-Bass Publishers.

Ladwig, J., and J. Gore, 1994. Extending power and specifying method within the discourse of activist research. In *Power and method: Political activism and educational research,* ed. A. Gitlin, 227–238. New York: Routledge.

Lai, E. W. M., and G. R. Sodowsky. 1996a. Acculturation effects on client reactions. In *Multicultural assessment in counseling and clinical psychology,* ed. G. R. Sodowsky and J. C. Impara, 355–359. Lincoln, NE: Buros Institute of Mental Measurements.

———. 1996b. Acculturation instrumentation. In *Multicultural assessment in counseling and clinical psychology,* ed. G. R. Sodowsky and J. C. Impara, 347–354. Lincoln, NE: Buros Institute of Mental Measurements.

LAUSD (Los Angeles Unified School District). 1985. *A study of student dropout in the Los Angeles Unified School District.* Report presented to Dr. Harry Handler, Superintendent, and Board of Education, Los Angeles.

Lechuga, F. S. 1997. Anti-Mexican hate group stirring in California. *Salt Lake Tribune,* July 16.

Lopez, E., E. Ramirez, and R. Rochin. 1999. *Latinos and economic development in California.* Sacramento, CA: California Research Bureau.

Matute-Bianchi, M. 1986. Ethnic identities and patterns of school success and failure among Mexican-descent and Japanese-descent students in a California high school: An ethnographic analysis. *American Journal of Education* 95:233–255.

Mehan, H., L. Hubbard, and I. Villanueva. 1994. Forming academic identities: Accommodation without assimilation among involuntary minorities. *Anthropology and Education Quarterly* 25:91–117.

Menchaca, M., and R. R. Valencia. 1990. Anglo-Saxon ideologies and their impact on the segregation of Mexican students in California, the 1920s–1930s. *Anthropology and Education Quarterly* 21:222–249.

Moraga, C. 1983. *Loving in the war years: Lo que nunca pasó por sus labios.* Boston: South End Press.

National Center for Education Statistics. 1989. *Digest of education statistics, 25th edition.* Washington, DC: U.S. Government Printing Office.

———. 1996. *Digest of education statistics.* Washington, DC. http://nces.ed .gov/pubsearch/pubsinfo.asp?pubid=96133.

———. 1999. *Digest of education statistics.* Washington, DC. http://nces.ed .gov/pubsearch/pubsinfo.asp?pubid=2000031.

———. 2001. *Digest of education statistics.* Washington, DC. http://nces.ed .gov/pubsearch/majorpub.asp.

National Commission on Secondary Education for Hispanics. 1984. *Make something happen.* Vol. 1 of *Hispanics and urban high school reform.* Washington, DC: Hispanic Policy Development Project.

Okagaki, L., P. A. Frensch, and N. E. Dodson. 1996. Mexican American children's perceptions of self and school achievement. *Hispanic Journal of Behavioral Sciences* 18:469–484.

Olsen, L. 1997. *Made in America: Immigrant students in our public schools.* New York: New Press.

Omi, M., and H. Winant. 1994. *Racial formation in the United States: From the 1960s to the 1990s.* 2nd ed. New York: Routledge.

Pardo, M. S. 1998. *Mexican American women activists: Identity and resistance in two Los Angeles communities.* Philadelphia: Temple University Press.

Perez, L. 1993. Opposition and the education of Chicana/os. In *Race, identity, and representation in education,* ed. C. McCarthy and W. Critchlow, 268–279. New York: Routledge.

Phinney, J. 1989. Stages of ethnic identity development in minority group adolescents. *Journal of Early Adolescence* 9:34–49.

———. 1992. The Multigroup Ethnic Identity Measure: A new scale for use with adolescents and young adults from diverse groups. *Journal of Adolescent Research* 7:156–176.

———. 1993. A three-stage model of ethnic identity development in adolescence. In *Ethnic identity: Formation and transmission among Hispanics and other minorities,* ed. M. Bernal and G. Knight, 61–80. Albany: State University of New York Press.

Pizarro, M. 1997. Power, borders, and identity formation: Understanding the world of Chicana/o students. *Perspectives in Mexican American Studies* 6:142–167.

———. 1998. "Chicana/o power!" Epistemology and methodology for social justice and empowerment in Chicana/o communities. *Qualitative Studies in Education* 11:57–80.

———. 1999. Racial formation and Chicana/o identity in the twenty-first century: Lessons from the rasquache. In *Race, ethnicity, and nationality in the United States: Toward the twenty-first century,* ed. P. Wong, 191–214. Boulder, CO: Westview Press.

Pizarro, M., and M. Montoya. 2002. Seeking educational self-determination: *Raza* studies for revolution. *Equity and Excellence in Education* 35:276–292.

Pizarro, M., and E. Vera. 2001. Chicana/o ethnic identity research: Lessons for researchers and counselors. *Counseling Psychologist* 29:91–117.

Reddy, M. 1995. *Statistical record of Hispanic Americans.* 2nd ed. Detroit: Gale Research.

Reyes, M. L., and J. J. Halcon. 2001. *The best for our children: Critical perspectives on literacy for Latino students.* New York: Teachers College Press.

Reyes, P., J. D. Scribner, and A. P. Scribner. 1999. *Lessons from high-performing Hispanic schools: Creating learning communities.* New York: Teachers College Press.

Rodriguez, J., and P. Gurin. 1990. The relationship of intergroup contact to social identity and political consciousness. *Hispanic Journal of Behavioral Sciences* 12:235–255.

Rodriguez, R. 1982. *Hunger of memory: The education of Richard Rodriguez.* New York: Bantam Books.

Romo, H. D., and T. Falbo. 1996. *Latino high school graduation: Defying the odds.* Austin: University of Texas Press.

Rumberger, R. W., and G. M. Rodríguez. 2002. Chicano dropouts: An update of research and policy issues. In *Chicano school failure and success: Past, present, and future,* ed. R. Valencia, 114–146. New York: Routledge/ Falmer.

Rymes, B. 2001. *Conversational borderlands: Language and identity in an alternative urban high school.* New York: Teachers College Press.

Sanchez-Jankowski, M. 1999. Where have all the nationalists gone? Change and persistence in radical political attitudes among Chicanos, 1976–1986. In *Chicano politics and society in the late twentieth century,* ed. D. Montejano, 201–233. Austin: University of Texas Press.

Sandoval, C., and C. Tambini, producers and directors. 2004. *Farmingville.* Documentary film. *P.O.V.* series, Public Broadcasting Service.

San Miguel, G., Jr. 1987. *"Let all of them take heed": Mexican Americans and the campaign for educational equality in Texas, 1910–1981.* Austin: University of Texas Press.

Schick, F., and R. Schick. 1991. *Statistical handbook on U.S. Hispanics.* Phoenix: Oryx Press.

Slavin, R. E., and M. Calderon. 2001. *Effective programs for Latino students.* Mahwah, NJ: Lawrence Erlbaum Associates.

Solórzano, D. G., and R. W. Solórzano. 1995. The Chicano educational experience: A framework for effective schools in Chicano communities. *Educational Policy* 9:293–314.

Stanton-Salazar, R. D. 1997. A social capital framework for understanding the socialization of racial minority children and youths. *Harvard Educational Review* 67:1–40.

———. 2001. *Manufacturing hope and despair: The school and kin support networks of U.S.-Mexican youth.* New York: Teachers College Press.

Trench, T., and L. A. Simón, producers. 1997. *Fear and learning at Hoover Elementary.* Documentary film. P.O.V. series, Public Broadcasting Service.

U.S. Census Bureau. 1998. *Poverty 1998.* Washington, DC. http://www.census .gov/hhes/poverty/poverty98/table5.html.

———. 2000. *Educational attainment in the United States (update).* Washington, DC. http://www.census.gov/population/socdemo/education/p20-536/ p20-536.pdf.

U.S. Commission on Civil Rights. 1971. *The unfinished education: Outcomes for minorities in the five Southwestern states.* Mexican American Education Study, report 2. Washington, DC: U.S. Government Printing Office.

Usher, R. 1996. A critique of the neglected epistemological assumptions of educational research. In *Understanding educational research,* ed. D. Scott and R. Usher, 9–32. New York: Routledge.

Valdés, G. 1998. The world outside and inside schools: Language and immigrant children.

———. 2001. *Learning and not learning English: Latino students in American schools.* New York: Teachers College Press. *Educational Researcher* 27(6): 4–18.

Valencia, R., ed. 1991. *Chicano school failure and success: Research and policy agendas for the 1990's.* London: Falmer Press.

Valenzuela, A. 1999. *Subtractive schooling: U.S.-Mexican youth and the politics of caring.* Albany: State University of New York Press.

Velez, W., T. Longoria, and J. B. Torres. 1997. Academic performance and ethnic consciousness: Latino students at a mid-western university. *Latino Studies Journal* 8:82–96.

Vigil, J. D. 1997. *Personas mexicanas: Chicano high schoolers in a changing Los Angeles.* Fort Worth, TX: Harcourt Brace College Publishers.

Ybarra-Frausto, T. 1991. Rasquachismo: A Chicano sensibility. In *Chicano art: Resistance and affirmation, 1965–1985,* ed. R. Griswold del Castillo, T. McKenna, and Y. Yarbro-Bejarano, 155–162. Los Angeles: Wight Art Gallery.

INDEX

Acculturation Rating Scale for Mexican Americans, 10–11

Bratt, Peter, 267–268

Chicana/o education history, 15–16
  Americanization, 15
  deficit models, 15
Chicana/o epistemology, 13, 25, 265, 275
Chicana/o identity
  border identities, 55–56
  class identity, 46
  community identity, 44–45
  empowerment, 107–111
  ethnic-cultural identity, 51
  ethnic identity: acculturation, 8; development, 9; enculturation, 8; family and social ecology, 8; socialization model, 8
  as fighters, 156, 225, 249
  gender identity, 45–46
  labels and definitions, 2–4; Chicana, 4; Chicana/o, 3–4, 8; Chicano, 4, 8; gender influences on, 4
  qualitative research on, 12
  racial/ethnic identity, 47
  racial identity, 11–12
  racial-political identity, 51, 107

religious/spiritual identity, 44
research on, 7–13
sexuality-based identity, 45
suppressed identities, 30, 154, 247, 261–262
unconscious identities, 30, 147, 154, 246–247, 261–262, 272
Chicana/o school performance, influences on
all-girls school, 73, 75
Chicana/o studies, 179–180
contextualized educational mentoring, 63–64
curriculum, 69
desegregation, 76
employment, 81
English as a Second Language (ESL), 66–67
ethnic support centers, 194–195
family, 92, 160–163, 171–174, 185–187, 198; financial situation, 174–175, 187; observational influences, 78, 171–174
financial need, 82–83
friends, 166–168
goals, 195
identity, 62, 221–222
intersecting influences, 64–65

MEChA, 168–169, 180–181,
203, 212–213, 220–224, 274
mentorship, 90, 99, 199–200;
contextualized mentoring, 100,
197; lack of, 166, 181–182
police, 71
power, 65, 98–100
racial conflict, 61–62, 193–194
racialization, 77, 196, 205–208,
211–213
racial-political climate, 60–61,
198–199
role models, lack of, 191, 204
school bias, 169–170
student racial tension, 192
teacher bias, 68, 70, 92, 165–166,
177–179, 188–191, 203
teacher conflict, 214–217
teacher disinterest, 81, 177, 202
teachers, of Mexican descent,
208
teacher support, 78, 89–90, 164–
165, 175–177, 188, 217
tracking, 158
Chicana/o social justice research, 25,
272
Chicana/o student empowerment,
strategies for:
alternative educational environments, 257–258
MEChA, 256–257
parents and family, 252–254
peers, 256–257
teachers and school staff, 254–
255
Chicana/o student empowerment
framework, 258–259
Chicana/o student empowerment intervention proposal:
role of holistic identity work,
261–262
role of identity, 260–261; and link
to school, 262–263
role of love, 266–267
role of power, 260

role of responding to students'
needs, 263–264
role of voice, 259–260
Chicana/o student silencing, 117–
118, 255
Chicano/a studies, influences of
Chicana/o identity on, 211
class, 147–148
cultural, 51
English as a Second Language
(ESL), 105
family, 52, 74, 120–126, 134–
136, 138–139, 149–151
family values, 153
gangs, 45, 231–232, 272
gender, 129, 136–137, 146–147,
273
generational status, 3–4
immigration, 139–140, 228
interracial interaction, 52
language, 229
MEChA, 133–134, 209,
232–233
media, 87–88
mentorship: contextualized, 249,
269; lack of, 130–132
mixed-race ancestry, 145–149,
274
police, 53–54, 85–86
political, 51
power, 52–57, 156, 226
power conflicts, 245
racial conflict, 53, 105–106, 125–
126, 151–152
racial isolation, 143–144
racialization, 150
segregation, 133
sexism, 129, 136–137, 146–147
sociopolitical context, 247–249
soul wound, 268–269
teacher bias, 58–59, 127–128,
133, 140
teacher conflict, 210
teacher support, 88
Zapatistas, 109, 273

Chicana/o studies, radical, 5–6

dropout rates, 1, 13–14
ethnicity (definition), 4–5

Foundry School, 268–269

Guevara, Che, 266–267

MAESTR@S, 264–266
Multigroup Ethnic Identity Measure
(MEIM), 9, 11

National Chicano Survey, 7–8

Proposition 187, 5, 42, 101, 125,
241–244
Proposition 209, 241–244
Proposition 227, 241–244

race (definition), 4–5
racial formation theory, 102
historical context, 102
racial hegemony, 244–245
racialization, 5, 48–51, 102–103, 134
racialized minority, 5
racial profiling, 36, 116, 239–244,
246, 248–249
state legislation, 241–243
teachers, 240
rasquachismo, 104–111
research limitations, 34–36
research validity, 6
objectivity, 24

subtractive schooling, 21

teacher expectations, 16–17
self-fulfilling prophecy, 16–17